# ADVENTURES IN GRACE

# GOLDEN MEASURE BOOKS

The measure of the things of the spirit transcends the classification of any school. It has to do with genuine achievement in true liberty of spirit. The books which are to appear in the *Golden Measure* series will fall under very varied headings: history, works of the imagination, memoirs, essays on politics and esthetics, spiritual writings, philosophical and religious research; their authors may come from various countries and be of different spiritual families. The unity of the series will be due to its spirit — to a common respect for the image of God in man and in a common feeling for liberty. Such was the idea behind the collections published in France — the *Roseau d'Or* and *Les Iles*. It is our hope that the *Golden Measure Books* will form a part of the library of all those who love truth and beauty, who are anxious to understand the world and the problems of the present day, and who are solicitous of all that is bound up with the destiny of the human person.

*Adventures in Grace* is the fifth volume in the series to be edited for Longmans, Green and Co. by Jacques Maritain and Julie Kernan.

# ADVENTURES IN GRACE

*Sequel to*
## WE HAVE BEEN FRIENDS TOGETHER

BY
RAÏSSA MARITAIN

*Translated by*
JULIE KERNAN

LONGMANS, GREEN AND CO., INC.
NEW YORK · TORONTO
1945

LONGMANS, GREEN AND CO.
55 FIFTH AVENUE, NEW YORK 3

LONGMANS, GREEN AND CO. Ltd.
OF PATERNOSTER ROW
43 ALBERT DRIVE, LONDON, S.W. 19
17 CHITTARANJAN AVENUE, CALCUTTA
NICOL ROAD, BOMBAY
36A MOUNT ROAD, MADRAS

LONGMANS, GREEN AND CO.
215 VICTORIA STREET, TORONTO 1

MARITAIN

ADVENTURES IN GRACE

FIRST EDITION

*This complete copyright edition
is produced in full compliance with
the Government's regulations for
conserving paper and other
essential materials.*

PRINTED IN THE UNITED STATES OF AMERICA

TO VERA

La Vie Donnée, poems (Raphael Labergerie). Paris.

Lettre de Nuit, La Vie Donnée, poems (Desclée de Brouwer). Paris.

Le Prince de ce Monde (Desclée de Brouwer). English translation by
G. B. Phelan, The Prince of This World (St. Dominic's Press, Ditchling,
Hassocks, Sussex).

L'Ange de l'École, Vie de Saint Thomas d'Aquin racontée aux enfants;
illustrated by Gino Severini (Desclée de Brouwer). English translation
by Julie Kernan, The Angel of the Schools (Longmans, Green and Co.).
New York.

Les Grandes Amitiés, tome I (Editions de la Maison Française). New York.
English translation by Julie Kernan, We Have Been Friends Together
(Longmans, Green and Co.). New York.

La Conscience Morale et l'état de nature (Editions de la Maison Française).
New York.

Marc Chagall (Editions de la Maison Française). New York.

IN COLLABORATION WITH JACQUES MARITAIN

De la Vie d'Oraison (Louis Rouart). Paris. English translation by
A. Thorold, Prayer and Intelligence (Sheed and Ward). New York.

Situation de la Poésie (Desclée de Brouwer).

TRANSLATIONS

Des Mœurs Divines, opuscle attribué à Saint Thomas d'Aquin (Louis Rouart).
Paris.

Les Dons du Saint-Esprit, traité de Jean de Saint-Thomas (Editions du Cerf).
Paris.

# TABLE OF CONTENTS

# LIST OF ILLUSTRATIONS

# NEW YORK 1944

When exactly four years ago I undertook to write *We Have Been Friends Together* it was in an effort to escape from the despair which gripped us in that summer made memorable by the disaster into which Europe and France — the whole world perhaps — very nearly sank. In beginning this task I was following friendly advice, but with a certain reluctance ; in fact, the idea of writing my memoirs had never before entered my mind, and I did not know how to slant my account. It was the title which came to me first, it gave me the direction I would follow, and reconciled me to the whole undertaking.

The first volume of these memoirs was received with a sympathy I was far from expecting, and has brought me many precious friendships. Many beautiful and moving letters have come to me from American and French correspondents, and it is no small sorrow to me not to have been able to reply to them all, as sometimes I lacked the time and at others the health. . .

Thus encouraged I decided, after rather lengthy hesitation, to follow through with the intention expressed at the end of *We Have Been Friends Together* to continue my account.

But this time I no longer write to struggle against despair ; on the contrary I am sustained, despite the anguish and sorrow which do not cease to assail my heart, by the certainty of Allied victory, and of the liberation of France and of Europe.

All of us who in exile have had the privilege of the large hospitality of this free country, who have known and loved its spirit, who have been present at the miracle of its rapid and gigantic preparation for war, — we are overwhelmed with enthusiasm and gratitude for the American people, and for the generous forces which on this continent and in the entire world, in France, in Great Britain, in Russia, in Poland and in

the whole of oppressed but not enslaved Europe, have risen up
to deliver and purify the world of the infernal powers of pride,
covetousness and cruelty. All that has been suffered, all that
remains to be suffered, visibly and invisibly, has henceforth
no more power over hope.

*

*   *

In this book, *Adventures in Grace*, I have tried to say what I
have been privileged to know of the extraordinary spiritual
flowering which in France preceded and followed the first
world war. Nothing is richer in human interest nor better
reveals the hidden treasures of our country than these adventures at once in and beyond time, in which so many powerful
personalities took part at that time. Of some of them I have
spoken in the first volume of *We Have Been Friends Together* ;
their names will be found here, in company with new names,
some known to all, and others unknown to the world and dear
only to our heart.

*New York, July 31, 1944.*

# CHAPTER ONE

## THE ANGELIC DOCTOR

### Rue des Feuillantines

The second year of our sojourn in Germany (1907–1908) was a year of blessed solitude and one of profound inner activity. Since my unhoped-for cure of the preceding winter we were relieved of the cruel cares of illness. Vera was with us. Every day we attended the first mass, in all kinds of weather, even through the thickest snows of Heidelberg. In the peace which had been given us, the liturgy of each day impregnated our souls and enlightened us with the spiritual significance of its symbols, revealing to us, little by little, the beauty of the Scripture and accustoming us to its light and its mysteries.

With the exception of Hans Driesch and a small number of kind people who took up very little of our time, we did not know or wish to know anyone, and were free all day to read and meditate at leisure, to keep silent, to pray, or to talk endlessly between ourselves of the eternal questions of philosophy and of life, some of which were a part of our own personal problems. We learned to concentrate in silence, we aspired toward the contemplation of divine truths, and in this way each of our own individual tendencies grew and developed without constraint.

Jacques was busy making a critical survey of the knowledge he had acquired, and he had ample leisure to allow it to distill from its bookish and didactic forms, and to become a living substance.

He confronted ceaselessly the certainties of faith with the propositions of reason, making both more clear and definite

3

by means of each other.   The lines in his Preface to the second edition of the *Philosophie Bergsonienne* which I have already quoted in the first volume of *We Have Been Friends Together* express the essential.   He writes : "My philosophical reflection leaned upon the indestructible truth of objects presented by faith in order to restore the natural order of the intelligence to being, and to recognize the ontological bearing of the work of the reason.   Thenceforth, in affirming to myself, without chicanery or diminution, the authentic value of reality of our human instruments of knowledge, I was already a Thomist without knowing it.   When, several months later, I was to come to the *Summa Theologica,* I would erect no obstacle to its luminous flood."

This happy year of solitude just missed ending in a catastrophe.   In the spring of 1908 I was suffering from a sore throat of an undetermined nature and was obliged to remain in bed for a whole month, while on the other side of the partition in my room lay Jacques, a victim of diphtheria.   Vera, with the aid of a nursing sister, took care of one and then the other, and had the charity not to fall ill herself although the doctor, each day, was expecting it.   This amiable doctor cured us solely by means of large doses of Apollinaris water which he made us drink daily in unbelievable quantities.   This unique remedy proved efficacious and Jacques recovered within a normal period.

On returning to France, after spending two months in Paris at our parents', and a month in a small village on the Normandy coast where I was constantly ill, we settled at last in our own place on Rue des Feuillantines, in the heart of the Latin quarter, very near the Church of Saint-Jacques-du-Haut-Pas, Rue Gay Lussac and Rue d'Ulm, and not far from the Sorbonne and Péguy's shop.

It was there that Jacques, with the help of my sister, wrote the *Lexique Orthographique* which Hachette had requested from him on the recommendation of Péguy, and which was destined to appear in a rather odd volume entitled *Tout-en-Un* (All-in-One). Then came the *Dictionnaire de la Vie Pratique*. In order to retain his independence as a philosopher, after a few months' hesitation Jacques had given up a university career and, to earn his living, accepted work which allowed him to retain his freedom of spirit.

While he was working and meditating on his own problems I made the acquaintance of the Angelic Doctor. This privilege was due to two causes : the return of illness in my life, and the entry in our lives of Father Humbert Clérissac.

The illness we resolved to conquer by negative means which meant withdrawing all pretext from it, so to speak ; that is, no doctor. I had had too many unfortunate experiences with doctors, never having encountered any good ones (though several years later it was altogether different). No doctors then, and an alimentary diet which was reduced to rice, water and indefinable vegetarian products ; an absurd diet indeed, and in which vitamins played little part, but which, for a long time, seemed wonderful to me because it reduced my suffering to a minimum, made me as light of body as it did of spirit, and permitted me to read and pray as I wished.

This fine régime ended one day when Léon Bloy, tired of seeing his god-daughter grow weaker and paler, became exasperated and wrote Jacques a furious letter accusing him of letting me die of hunger, and straightway procured for me the advice not of a doctor but a sculptor who was none other than his friend Frédéric Brou who lived at Montmartre and who was an expert in various arts and helpful recipes. He was a connoisseur in *bonne cuisine* and perhaps also in alimentary hygiene ; and even if he did not actually cure me, he helped me to regain some strength by prescribing a better balanced diet.

So, in spite of my health, and in spite of this slight agony

so well known to invalids which eats into hearts yearning for
life, I enjoyed my leisure hours. The solitude which had been
our privilege in Germany was hardly encroached upon in Paris,
where, that year, we saw scarcely anyone save our relatives and
Ernest Psichari, the Bloys and Péguy, until the day when we
made our first visit to Father Clérissac at Versailles.

### Father Humbert Clérissac

Jacques, at the time of his first visit to the Benedictines of
Solesmes, in exile on the Isle of Wight, where Péguy had sent
him to take the good news of his return to the Catholic faith,*
had had long interviews with the Father Abbot, Dom Delatte,
on religious and spiritual questions. Perfection then seemed
to us easy to attain providing there was someone to show us
the way ; — a Socratic error, as we were to learn later. The
spiritual beauty of the saints, radiating in them that integrity,
brilliance, and harmony peculiar to all beauty, appeared so
desirable to us that we could not conceive of any other goal
worthy of man. In fact all the beauty that we loved most in
the world could be found in them at the highest degree of in-
tensity and savour. Even to contemplate it from afar, like
a star in an immaterial heaven, was already a beatitude. In
our eyes time has effaced nothing of this beauty and its attraction, and has not turned our hearts from it, but has shown
us a little more each day the mysterious perseverance with
which, as we pursue it, it withdraws farther beyond our reach,
and how exceedingly rare are those who ever attain it. One
blessing had at least been accorded us : that of meeting among
so many of our fellow-sinners some genuine saints who have
been our comfort and our consolation in the difficult ways
which at times have been ours.

* See *We Have Been Friends Together*, volume I, page 192 *et seq.*

In these days of our youth, in this rejuvenation of our lives through baptism, starting from which it was as if I had lost all notion of time (the years gone by merge into one another, and a single instant, at times, grows in depth at the confines of Eternity), it seemed to us that all those were saints who should be saints — priests, religious. . . The warnings of our godfather, the severe judgement which he brought in all his books upon certain among them, and the conduct which could hardly be called saintly of certain members of the Church in the past as well as the present, all that was forgotten, effaced from our minds, and our confidence was boundless in all those who had chosen to consecrate themselves to the service of God. I should add, that if we had any disappointments in this regard, they came many years later as our glimpse upon the world became more extended. From priests and religious whom God placed in our path in those first years of our Christian life, and from those who have been intimately associated with us by friendship, we received such precious spiritual help that the suffering sometimes caused by a few was in comparison very small.

But I must now come back to Jacques' first visit to Appuldurcomb. We knew that a Benedictine monastery was a school of perfection and that the head of the school was the Abbot who, elected for life, represented the irremovable divine paternity. It was therefore in a spirit of enthusiastic docility — and one of our strokes of luck at that time — that Jacques took the advice of the Father Abbot who was at that time the magnificent and genial Dom Delatte, a veritable high priest, impressive for his authority and prestige — as also for his haughtiness and his intransigence. But it was only many years afterwards that we became aware of these defects which cast a shadow upon this great personality.

One of Jacques' questions and one of the Father Abbot's replies which played a great rôle in our lives concerned the matter of spiritual direction. The saints whom we loved, whose biographies or works we had read — Saint Teresa of Avila for instance — attributed extreme importance to the spiritual director. We did not wish to neglect their advice. Dom Delatte joked at first about it, made a few paradoxical remarks, and while conversing of other things, told his young interlocutor, whose novice-like, somewhat strait-laced fervour he liked to jolt, that a director was necessary only in three cases : if one were uncertain of his vocation, or if one were morbidly overscrupulous, or if one were led by the extraordinary ways of visions and revelations. Now it happened that two members of our trio were settled in the married state, Dom Delatte felt our consciences to be at peace, and we were not in the least visionary. He recommended us, however, to pray to God for a year in order to obtain a guide of whom, in spite of the theories he had pronounced, we might have need. And right then and there he named one of his greatest friends : Father Clérissac, whose character and intelligence he admired without reserve. It was thus that, when the time had come — a year later — he sent us to him.

*
*　　*

On our way for the first time to Father Clérissac's in Versailles, we recalled with much emotion those first steps we had taken towards the Church when, three years earlier, we had mounted the steps to Montmartre, in answer to the call of him who was to become our godfather. We were now accomplishing our first important advance, not indeed towards the Church but into the very bosom of that Church where for two years we had been like lonely children and like beggars ; beggars for Heaven, for truth, and for peace, receiving our comfort, not from the hands of men, but from the divine life of the Sacraments.

Now, we felt, our period of solitude and loneliness was nearly ended, and it was time to begin learning to live in the world without yet conforming to the world — on account of the Gospel, which we wished to follow. We were aware that we would have to learn to hold fast to our Faith in difficult circumstances, and that we would have to pray to God more than ever to keep and to allow to grow within us that life of grace received in baptism, without at the same time refusing to ourselves a fair increase of the life of human experience.

We quite naïvely entertained these great desires, seeing in them the natural aspiration of every Christian living in this world. And it seemed very simple to go and say to a man of God : "Direct us towards their accomplishment."

Jacques and I received a flashing and penetrating gaze from two deep-set eyes full of secrets and knowledge, and before those eyes we felt completely young and ignorant.

As Father Clérissac spoke, telling us of the difficulties in what we were seeking, I admired his noble and ardent face with its strong, clear-cut features, the brow furrowed by wrinkles and crowned by a brush of gray hair, and the perfect folds his white Dominican robe made around him, making him resemble a personage in one of Fra Angelico's paintings. The program he proposed was severe. The face of the Father was also severe, in spite of his painful sensitivity which showed through the formal rigidity of his bearing. Willingly he took our souls in his care, and for the five years which followed until his premature death at the age of fifty, he was our friend and our guide. Not once did he betray the magnificent impression he made upon us at that first interview.

Jacques has written a short biography of him as a Preface to Le Mystère de l'Eglise * — a small, incomplete work which Father Clérissac never finished, but such as it is, one of the finest works that has ever been devoted to this great mystery,

* Humbert Clérissac, Le Mystère de l'Eglise, Téqui, Paris.

and which in France has become a classic.  The moral and intellectual stature of Father Clérissac stands out in high relief in this book, exactly as we had the privilege of knowing him, and it is easy to see how he could not fail to attract and captivate us.  He loved truth, he loved intelligence.  How often we heard him say : "Christian life is based on intelligence. . . Before everything else, God is truth.  Go to Him and love Him under this aspect."  He thought like Saint Augustine that eternal bliss consisted in the joy of Truth — *gaudium de veritate.*  He loved the Church and delved ceaselessly and profoundly into her mystical character of participation in Jesus Christ, her leader, and the Holy Ghost, her animator.  He said : "Let us embrace the Church for eternal and divine reasons," and not because she is "a cause defensible before reason and history."

He loved everything that had life, that was beautiful and sincere.  At the age of sixteen, having read the life of Saint Dominic by Lacordaire, he became a Dominican.  He was a friar preacher in the fullness of his vocation, a preacher in the grand style, carrying his ardent message to France, Italy, and England.  He lived in England quite some time.  He liked the English, their minds and their culture.  He was a friend of Robert Hugh Benson ; and the character of the Pope in *The Lord of the World* resembles him very closely.  He prayed ardently "that intelligence and beauty be rendered to their Lord," and he had the consolation of being a witness to the Christian death of Oscar Wilde.*

From Léon Bloy to Father Clérissac we had been led from one man of the Absolute to another man of the Absolute; both

---

* Father Clérissac never spoke to us about Wilde.  But he told one of our friends, who repeated it to us, that he was sure Wilde died a Catholic, for he was there at his death.  In the *Revue Hebdomadaire* of November 28, 1925, Mr. Robert Ross names Father Cuthbert Dunn of the Passionists as having given Wilde baptism and extreme unction.  In this case Father Clérissac would doubtless have assisted Father Dunn.

had an heroic faith, an unshakable fidelity, and both were intransigent concerning our obligations in regard to Truth, hating mediocrity.

We were not submitted to the trial of a lowering of standards or any conflicting ideas between these two people who were our guides as well as our models between the ages of twenty and thirty. At the same time, one could hardly imagine men more dissimilar in their background and education. Their identity was only in their outlook. Father Clérissac, from the age of sixteen until his death, lived within the strict discipline of the Dominican Order where his mind had been formed according to the highly intellectualized traditions of the theology of Saint Thomas. Léon Bloy, on the contrary, misanthropic and solitary, never depended on any other man in the world, and had no other discipline than that of faith and the Church. So, aware of their differences — for one is always aware of any difference in education — they were surprised to discover themselves so simply united in our hearts, where their influence caused not the slightest contradiction. From both of them we received the fundamental teaching of a proved doctrine and a holy tradition. Both had a mystical love and understanding of the Church in her divine mystery, which is beyond all human contingencies. Both freely admitted the errors and faults of the members of the Church, whatever might be their rank in the hierarchy. And scarcely was there any difference in the way in which in these matters they expressed their grief, disdain, or saintly anger. Léon Bloy as a matter of fact used expressions that were considered "vulgar," while Father Clérissac's language was always chastened. But their high requirements and severity were the same in both cases. They both gave us an example of a rather hard attitude in regard to people, and an imperviousness concerning renewals in temporal matters — whether social, psychological, or esthetic — and from this we suffered, not knowing at first how to distinguish between these traits of their characters and the essential and excellent principles of their guidance.

For several months while we were at Versailles, Jacques went every morning to see Father Clérissac (Boulevard de la Reine) where he served his mass; and afterwards there followed treasured and memorable conversations about the things of God. Father Clérissac seemed in haste to give an avid mind the treasure of the lofty thoughts he nurtured during his solitude. The exigencies of a Christian life dedicated to absolute truth, the doctrine of the saints, the mystical life of the Church and its heritage of sacred wisdom — these are the subjects on which they constantly dwelled.

Father Clérissac's discipline was an austere, interior discipline which demanded an inflexible and pure objectivity and required from the soul that it lose itself in the Light. He was merciless to what he called the "reflex mind" — the mind that turns back on itself and is egocentric. He went so far in this direction that he sometimes misunderstood certain aspirations and certain secret sufferings in which the soul, goaded on by God, struggles with itself, no longer seeking itself but seeking a union with God deeper than that which can be procured by theological knowledge. For if faith can become experimental and, to a certain degree, grasp its object — *fides oculata* — the "eyes" which it receives are given by divine love ; and because in love the entire subjective element is involved, Father Clérissac sought to keep himself free from its ways. The gifts of the Holy Spirit are present in all saintly souls but every one of them manifests one gift more than another. One could say that Father Clérissac had the gift of intelligence more than the gift of wisdom.

"If," wrote Jacques, "one had to formulate one of the great themes — but presented as an hypothesis rather than as an affirmation, and with many undefinable nuances — to which his mind was constantly returning, I would say that in his eyes the history of Christian perfection such as one can read it in the life of the saints as well as in the history of the Church's institutions, is a history which pertains, on the one hand, to a sort of providential accommodation to the needs of the world, and on the other hand, to the laws of growth and organic progress of the Mystical Body of Christ. In fact he could not help giving his greatest admiration to the grandeur, the simplicity, the divine spontaneity of the early saints — who were nearer to Good Friday and Pentecost, and the undivided fullness of the great effusion from which the Church was born. . . He who so loved Saint Thomas, who discovered his happiness in enshrining within the *Summa* the reading of the Gospel, liked to repeat that the wisdom of Saint Paul, like a springing forth of sheer inspiration, was more purely divine than the scientifically elaborated wisdom of the *Summa Theologica*.*

When we became oblates of Saint Benedict, Father Clérissac rejoiced to see us thus attached to the spirituality of the sixth century, to an age when Christians did not worry about knowing in what inner dwelling of the interior castle they were.

"Saint Teresa has captivated you," he wrote in a letter to me, "and that is quite natural, for it is good to be reminded sometimes of the notion of acquired virtue and of positive effort through the example of these saints of the reflex age, whom God has doubtless brought forth in order to show us that all that is good and true in individualism does not escape his grace but derives from it, and also because of his condescending pity for Man when the simple life of the Church no longer suffices him — and finally as an effect of vindictive judgement with regard to the infidelity of the older orders who, alas, permitted the torch within their hands to grow dim.

"But don't forget that you are Merovingians, feodal people — what am I saying? You are primitives. Don't forget that we must eventually come to let divine grace operate within us,

* Preface to the *Mystère de l'Eglise*.

and consider the products of your activity as of hardly any
account. . ." In truth we were not at all sure of being Merovingians. And our love for Saint Benedict did not hinder
us from seeing in Saint Teresa and Saint John of the Cross the
doctors *par excellence* of the spiritual life.

## My First Reading of the "Summa Theologica"

"Una est vera philosophia." (Saint Augustine, "Con-
tra Julianum pelagianum," 4, 14, 72.)

"Et il n'y a pourtant qu'une vérité." (Henri Bergson.)

The first and admirable advice which Father Clérissac gave
me, advice which was truly inspired, was to read Saint Thomas.
While Jacques was busy at his work for Hachette and with his
first articles, I — a recluse because of illness and therefore dispensed from any obligation to see people or to go about —
could devote the best part of my time to reading and meditating on the *Summa Theologica.*

For two years, ever since our baptism, the starting point of
all our thinking, whether about philosophy or life — and for
us the one has always been inseparable from the other — the
starting point had been the faith by which we now lived, whose
praises we sang incessantly in our heart and whose power to
give order to all things we ceaselessly admired. We left the
philosophers for the time being to argue among themselves ;
we were at rest in a temporary neutrality in their respect ; we
set aside all their philosophies until further notice. It was a
delight to live far from their quarrels and little by little to let
our human reason grow strong again, to let it repair itself in the
sunlight of the eternal truths.

The future inspired in us no fear, since we had the good
fortune to know through faith truths of a certainty so penetrat-

ing that it is inferior only to the intellectual intuition in the beatific vision, and to which the strength of no natural intuition can be compared ; truths radiating such a pure and universal light that they seemed to us to draw to them all truth, the fragments of truths scattered in the most diverse minds, the fruit of all intuitive knowledge.

We felt that to implant reason in faith, to graft reason upon the tree of Jesse, does not weaken reason but strengthens it, does not enslave it but frees it, does not denature it but restores it to the purity of its true nature — just as to light the way for a man stumbling forward uncertainly in the darkness does not divert him from his true path but shows him the road he chooses to travel.

Meanwhile this frame of mind remained more philosophical than theological. The theologian possesses the principles of his science in divinely revealed truths, and starting from these he proceeds to fathom mysteries by rational paths, themselves tributary to some philosophy. Whereas the philosopher finds his very principles in the order of intelligence and reason. And in this purely natural order his reason talks sense or nonsense as he may please. In the period which here concerns us, nonsense it was that generally had the upper hand, because through the idealistic denial of the ontological ties between intelligence and being and existence, philosophy extolled to the skies a human knowledge the nature and validity of which had in reality been ruined. Bergson provided a partial remedy to the situation by assigning to intuition the prerogatives which had been torn from intelligence. Thus, provisionally, he had helped us, but with the advent of faith in our souls, and of those certainties peculiar to it, we found ourselves faced with a new problem : that of the certainties which reason can itself attain. Our frame of mind remained therefore philosophical and not theological ; we were not seeking, then — we were too ignorant for that — to fathom rationally the mysteries of faith, nor to deduce, starting from revealed truths, other, congruous and less universal truths, yet we felt an urgent desire to seek out what truths of a philosophical and universal order were implied in the tranquil assurance of the propositions of faith. And it is these philosophical truths which first in the *Summa Theologica* shone forth to us. They were stated or implied ; everywhere they were present. The other truths, more precious and belonging to a higher order, were to become apparent to us later. Aristotle was now rising in his grandeur, taking on his true face through the grace of an inspired theologian.

It was not without trembling with curiosity and foreboding that I opened for the first time the *Summa Theologica* on the "Treatise on God." Was not scholasticism, according to the reputation which had been given it, a tomb of subtleties fallen to dust ? And would not even the Prince of the schoolmen himself throw a little of this dust on the flames of our young faith ?

From the very first pages I understood the emptiness, the childishness of my fears. Everything, here, was freedom of spirit, purity of faith, integrity of the intellect enlightened by knowledge and genius.

The serene calm of the style, in appearance so impersonal, the peaceful bearing of the reasoning which gives to each word the meaning closest to the intellectual intuition from which it was born and, for this very reason, giving it the fullness of its savour ; the spiritual power, almost angelic, which allows Saint Thomas to enfold within the briefest of his propositions innumerable truths each linked the one to the other according to the very hierarchy of real beings — everything was luminous for me in what I read, and it was with incessant thanksgiving that I pursued my reading.

Writing these pages I find myself again in the happy emotion of that first contact with the thought of Saint Thomas.

So great a light kept flowing into both my heart and mind that I was carried away as if by a joy of Paradise. To pray, to understand, was for me one and the same thing; the one made me thirst for the other, and that thirst in me I felt to be constantly, and yet never, quenched. At that time, also, I read Saint Gertrude, a German Benedictine of the thirteenth century; often I repeated one of the prayers that she most loved to say: "Glory be Thine, O most gentle and benign, O most noble and most excellent, O most joyful and most glorious, O resplendent and ever tranquil Trinity . . ." and the work of Saint Thomas was wedded marvelously to those praises.

This first reading of the *Summa Theologica* was as if I had been given a very pure gift. From it I received once and for all the certainty of the essential truths concerning the intelligence and the joy of seeing that this last was strong enough to lead the principles of reason into the very heart of the starred night of faith. I received what I could receive according to my feeble capacity, but with fullness. All problems had disappeared — as they are wont to vanish in times of happiness — only to reappear later. But later on it was not I who would be called upon to face them, but Jacques, a philosopher by vocation.

That time was not to come immediately. We spoke together a great deal about what I was reading; but busy then preparing the *Lexique Orthographique* which Hachette had ordered, and — engaging his interest to a far greater extent — with writing his first articles, a year was to pass before Jacques undertook the direct study of Aristotle and Saint Thomas. In what manner he understood their principles, and how he carried out his own philosophical work, appears in all his writing, from his first book which was a critical analysis of Bergsonism. But *La Philosophie Bergsonienne* was published in 1913; and so I will speak of it a little later.

My great privilege will have been to receive, undeserving

and without effort, to receive from so dear a hand, the spiritual
fruits of his labours, fruits which I could not have attained without his help, and yet to which I aspired with a deep and living
desire.

Thus I have been favoured beyond all measure ; I have lived
in an atmosphere of intellectual strictness and of spiritual rectitude, thanks to Saint Thomas, thanks to Jacques, and I cannot
write of these things without tears of humility and love.

## Short Eulogy of Saint Thomas Aquinas

I must interrupt these memoirs to bring to Saint Thomas the
modest tribute of my praise, for it is just to praise what one
loves.   Before knowing him I had wondered how "particular
devotions" started.   They seemed strange to me, like a diminution of the love involved in the immensity of the unique devotion that was owed God alone.   I was to learn through experience that these particular devotions come into being in the
same way as do admiration and friendship.   And in no case
can friendship, which is a very gentle virtue, diminish the love
which one bears for God.

We therefore became attached to Saint Thomas as to a real
friend, by sympathy, by admiration and by gratitude.   It is
very certain that no one could know him without loving him,
and it is greatly to be deplored that he is known even less for
his life as a saint than he is for his monumental work.

After six centuries of dazzling light radiating from his intelligence and his doctrine, people have come to forget the
grandeur of his charity, the gentleness and humility of his heart
— and the collection of his *fioretti* has been neglected.

Today no one knows that the greatest and most gracious
divine favours constantly marked his life (neither roses nor
stars were wanting on his path) ; that countless miracles fol-

lowed his death and endeared to all Christian people him who was not yet known except to the Scholastics. How blessed were the people of the thirteenth century who could receive the doctrine of Christ from such columns of light as Saint Dominic and Saint Francis of Assisi, Saint Thomas Aquinas and Saint Bonaventure!

Is it known that Saint Thomas prayed without cease, that he possessed the grace of the gift of tears so dear to the Christian of the Middle Ages, that he preached with a gentleness which touched the hearts of the humble people, but also with a severity which made the learned professors and students of theology tremble when he reminded them of their great responsibility to those souls who expected to receive the Truth from them?

A theologian *par excellence*, it is nevertheless as the metaphysician of the intellect and of reason, in which he defends the value of the authentic faculties of real knowledge, that Saint Thomas first impressed us. Because of these things he is also dear to the Church, which is the guardian of human integrity as well as of revealed Truth.

Indeed, following the theories of Aristotle, he teaches that our intelligence naturally knows Being, first in the things perceived by the senses and then, due to the abstractive intuitions of metaphysics, in its transcendental intelligibility ; and in him this calm apperception is so vast, so pure and so penetrating that the principles of his metaphysics are capable of integrating all the truths of the philosophical and natural order ; somewhat as — and keeping all proportions — the revealed principles of faith integrate those truths of the supernatural order which will come to be defined in time. And in everything regarding the ontology of the faculties of desire and the moral science of human acts, his doctrine observes in such a saintly manner both speculative truth and all the rights of charity and justice that one can say it is an evangelical theology.

And so great is its purity that even its best commentators can hardly abide by it with complete fullness.

The more one knows of his teaching, the more one admires the knowledge, intelligence and wisdom so marvelously united in the saintliness of the Angelic Doctor. This is the reason it has been said of him that "his holiness is that of the intelligence." * It is in the very intelligence of Saint Thomas that the miracles of his saintliness are accomplished : all his intelligence is turned towards God ; it is entirely consecrated to the Truth — known or to be discovered. It was through Truth that the Saint was raised from the earth ; it was to the works of the philosopher and the theologian that God gave his approval : "Thou hast spoken well of me, Thomas."

\*

\*         \*

In a world like ours where discrimination and discord reign, where all personal experience tends to oppose instead of uniting with other experiences ; where to distinguish essences or circumstances is to cut with an axe and not to render justice to every being in its originality and peculiarities, and in the truth of its existence ; where no union of science and faith is conceived, nor that of science and wisdom (even an intellectual like Husserl, who exalts philosophy as a science, abhors wisdom — "It awoke in him all the indignation of which he was capable," writes Chestov) — Saint Thomas by his life, his spirit and his teaching offers us an example of the most harmonious and efficacious union of the light of reason, of faith and of mystical experience. The three wisdoms are in him : that of one of the greatest geniuses of the intelligence, that of one of the humblest children of the Church, and that of one of the saints most miraculous and most mercifully given to mankind in order that it might be cured of its ignorance. And he himself, when

* Jacques Maritain, *The Angelic Doctor.*

his immense erudition did not suffice, assaulted the heavens. He would lean his head against the tabernacle and remain there, praying with many tears. Heaven then took the trouble to come to the rescue of this harassed theologian and philosopher. Then, as his companion Brother Reginald tells us, he would come out of his prayers and return to his cell delivered from his doubts, and taking up his work again, he would continue to write or dictate to his numerous secretaries.

And yet this peaceful soul, this pure light, whose genius and saintliness the Church was not to delay in proclaiming, was obliged to submit to the trial, doubtless inevitable, of being misunderstood by those about him. At the end of his life he was obliged to defend himself from violent attacks against his teaching from a large number of masters in theology, of whom some belonged to his Order. And three years after his death several of his theses were condemned by bishops (Etienne Tempier, bishop of Paris; Robert Kilwardby, archbishop of Canterbury) who believed they were protecting the supernatural character of Catholicism against a theologian whom they accused of subscribing to the principles of the pagan Aristotle.*

---

* It is known that Saint Thomas met the strongest opposition from the supporters of the old Augustinian school, who did not understand the clear-cut distinction he had established between philosophy and theology. They did not see that his particular work was to extricate Aristotle from the false interpretations of the Arabs, above all of Averroes; and they sought to include in their condemnation of Averroism the great destroyer of its errors.

The bishop of Paris, Etienne Tempier, attended the debate in which certain theses of the Angelic Doctor, above all his thesis on the unity of substantial form, according to which the spiritual soul of man is also the principle of his physical life, were attacked as contrary to Faith.

Charged by Pope John XXI to proceed with an inquiry into the teaching of the University of Paris, Etienne Tempier promulgated on March 7, 1277, a condemnation of the 219 theses of Averroes; a condemnation which had considerable historic importance and in which he included nine theses taught by Saint Thomas. (It is also on the 7th of March that the whole Church celebrates the feast of Saint Thomas Aquinas.) On the 18th of March, 1277, the Dominican archbishop Robert Kilwardby had the professors of Oxford condemn a series of theses which were specifically Thomist (passivity of matter, unity of substantial form in the human compound, etc.).

But these ill-considered judgements have long since sunk into oblivion, whereas the theses of the hóly Doctor live on with the life and vigour of truth.

This great disciple and friend of Christ was not deprived of the joy of singing His praises "in hymns and canticles." And while the world lasts men will rejoice in the divine sweetness of the poetry and music of Saint Thomas in the Office of the Blessed Sacrament which he composed at the request of Pope Urban IV, when the feast of Corpus Christi was inaugurated. For the Angel of the Schools — the Angelic Doctor — is also the Doctor of the Eucharist.  His devotion to the Sacraments which he called "the relics of the Incarnation" reveals all the faith and gentleness of his soul.  In his last words, in his last tears as, dying, he received his last communion his love for the Eucharist burst forth :

"I receive Thee, the price of my redemption.  I receive Thee, Companion of my life on this earth, for whose love I have watched, studied, laboured.  Thee whom I have preached and taught."

*

*        *

How could the Saint capable of such a "confession" cease to remain forever the very pure model of every Christian philosopher, of every lover of the Truth ?

# CHAPTER TWO

## SOME CONQUESTS OF THE UNGRATEFUL BEGGAR

### Georges Rouault

We remained only one year on the Rue des Feuillantines. In order to be nearer Father Clérissac, and also to safeguard our solitude, we settled in Versailles, Rue de l'Orangerie, in October 1909. There we soon had as our neighbours two families who were friends of the Bloys — the Martineaus and the Rouaults.

René Martineau, Anne his wife, and later his son André, his sister-in-law, Elizabeth Joly, as well as Madeleine, his sister, were extremely helpful friends of the Bloys and unstinting admirers. René Martineau rendered a fine tribute to Léon Bloy in *Un vivant et deux morts*. It was precisely on the 31st of March, 1901, that Léon Bloy received the first letter from him. It seemed to be a reply to an injunction to the invisible sent forth by Léon Bloy, overcome by destitution. And this is the way it is told in his diary :

"March 29th. — Devoted especially to the Mother of God, I beg her with fervour to bring forth a Christian who will deliver us. Then, by the Faith that God has given me and by the promises of the Gospel, I command this unknown person to reveal himself and to act. . .

"March 31st. — Palm Sunday. Letter from a native of Touraine by the name of René Martineau. Could this be the unknown friend to whom I was calling the day before yester-day? This thought flashes through my mind. . ."

\*

\*   \*

23

During our stay and theirs in Versailles we were on friendly terms with the Martineaus, without being intimate; and I do not know why, when they later left Versailles, they decided to bear a grudge against us.

As for Rouault whom we had met in Paris at the Bloys' four years earlier, it was only at Versailles that we learned to know him. He also had preceded us in the circle of the Bloys. I believe his name appears for the first time in Léon Bloy's diary in March 1904. The 16th of March, Bloy wrote in *Quatre Ans de Captivité*:

"I have just learned that the painter Georges Rouault, pupil of Gustave Moreau, is very enthusiastic about me. Having discovered at his teacher's house *La Femme Pauvre* sent there some time ago with these words inscribed: 'To Gustave Moreau, to avenge him for M. Folantin,' this book ate into his heart and wounded him incurably. . ."

On March 24th Bloy adds:

"Georges Rouault has embarked, not for Cythère, but for my sombre desert isle — his friend and comrade, Georges Desvallières, another pupil of Gustave Moreau. . . For these two hearts I am indebted to Auguste Marguillier, that amiable secretary of the Gazette des Beaux Arts, who has always been so loyal in spite of the inconveniences of my ingratitude. . ."

During his early visits Georges Rouault showed a circumspection and hesitation which did not hide his assurance of being right, yet which revealed his extreme self-consciousness in respect to his art and his uncertainty regarding our reaction. He started showing us his albums of satirical designs, which, in their way, are an "Exegesis of Stock Phrases" * permeated with the same formidable irony that one finds in Bloy. He was grateful to us for never laughing at these gigantic onslaughts, and for understanding by what depths of moral necessity and by what painful sensitivity these so-called caricatures had been

* *Exégèse des Lieux Communs.*

inspired. In one, for instance, could be seen one of those fearful "good women" comfortably ensconced in her armchair, with the title reading : "I'll go straight to heaven." These words Rouault had actually heard, probably during one of those big family dinners, where he had had the experience of fainting with indignation. Rouault, feeling the deep sincerity of our enthusiasm and our emotion, put his confidence in us, and thus we had the privilege of admiring many of his drawings and paintings before they were shown at the exhibitions.

Convinced of his value as an artist and respectful of his secrets, we never dared ask him to show us "what he was working on." This tended to make him even more communicative. We learned afterwards the extent of his distaste for people who were indiscreet. One day we were coming back together from Bourg-la-Reine where Léon Bloy had lived since leaving Montmartre and Rue de la Barre ; Ricardo Viñes was with us. Through real interest or perhaps only through what is considered as being a politeness when speaking to a painter, Viñes asked Rouault if he might visit his studio. Rouault gave a grunt that was supposed to be a vague reply, froze up, and from that day on he cordially detested the poor musician, to whom naturally he never showed his studio.

I am not very fond of anecdotes, but I would like to mention another example of Rouault's untamed spirit. Quite unbelievably he had succeeded, with a few rare exceptions, in hiding his address from his acquaintances for ten years at a time. He always gave as his address the Museum Gustave Moreau. But as to where he lived with his family — whether it was in Paris or in Versailles — I wonder whether two or three more people, besides André Suarès and we, ever knew. As for ourselves, we had to swear never to divulge the secret, and we piously kept our oath. And even Ambroise Vollard, in whose house Rouault later had a studio, for a long time was ignorant of the painter's personal address.

When he came to live in Versailles towards 1909 or 1910, Rouault was about forty years old, since he was born in Paris in 1871 "in a cellar," he claimed, during the Prussian bombardment of the capital.

He was living through the most painful period of his life — on the path of artistic discovery in which he entered a few years after the death of his master, Gustave Moreau, and in which he persevered heroically.  His sombre and direful paintings astounded and disconcerted his first friends, his comrades of the Ecole.  Léon Bloy reproached him with these as an error.  Still unknown to the picture dealers, esteemed only by a few rare amateurs and a small number of far-sighted critics who yet were frightened by the direction he had taken, and in which he became confirmed from 1903 on, when we knew him he painted judges, trollops, shrews, clowns in dark and sumptuous paintings, landscapes of misery in transparent colours, and figures of Christ with the face and body prodigiously deformed to express the paroxysm of the divine Passion and human cruelty.

Thus it was that he expressed his horror of moral ugliness, his hatred for bourgeois mediocrity, his vehement need of justice, his pity for the poor, — finally his lively and profound Faith as well as his need of absolute truth in art.

This tremendous human load seeking ways of expression would have bent under a less firmly rooted "artistic virtue." In Rouault it gave but greater stature to the artist in him.  Far from causing him to deviate, this spiritual mass weighed upon him as a most absolute necessity which called for expression in a work, that is to say, according also to the most absolute requirements of art.  And it is thus that Rouault, faithful to his soul, to his God, to his art, became the greatest religious painter of our time, one of the greatest painters of all time.  "In the spontaneous search for a synthetic form in unison with

JACQUES MARITAIN
Portrait by Otto van Rees

GEORGES ROUAULT
Self-Portrait (Collection of John U. Nef)

religious conscience," says Lionello Venturi, in the magnificent study that he devoted to the glory of Rouault,* "Rouault has taken us back through the centuries to that moment when every image on earth reflected the function of God."   The moment of which he speaks is that of Romanesque art to which Rouault's art conformed, not consciously or imitatively, but through the very identity of inspiration.

This conformity became evident in his works of the last ten or twelve years.   In the earlier years when we knew him at Versailles, Rouault was but groping his way toward it.   At that time he had scarcely emerged from that sombre phase which reached its climax in 1906.  He started to treat in a freer, more universal and serene manner, the same motifs which between 1903 and 1910 had provoked his vengeful pity.   And even feminine grace began to spring forth from under his fingers, in elegant lines — a grave and noble elegance without any insipid prettiness, needless to say.

From that time on Rouault stood for us as the revelation of contemporary art ; it was from him we passed on to Cézanne with whom, in spite of his absolute originality, Rouault had a very real affiliation.   From him also we went to the "Fauves," to whom he can be related only by certain very broad principles, for his art has a different inspiration, a different form, a different kind of colouring, from that of Matisse or Derain.

But Rouault was for us above all the first revelation of the true and great artist.   It was in the concrete example he fur-

---

* Lionello Venturi, *Georges Rouault*, New York, E. Weyhe. — Why is it that in this fine book, so understanding of the art and character of Rouault, Léon Bloy, the great friend of the painter, is the object of a judgement which does not succeed in being altogether correct ?  Mr. Venturi recognizes the sincerity and depth of his religious sentiment, but he commits the error, so often committed, of seeing in him only the polemist, and of underestimating his greatness as a writer.

nished that we first perceived the nature of art, its imperious necessities, its antinomies and that very real and sometimes tragic conflict between opposed duties for which the mind of the artist can be the battleground.

In this respect Léon Bloy — whose meeting with Rouault had for the latter a considerable spiritual significance, although Bloy never did really understand the artistic evolution of his friend * — Léon Bloy represents but an exception. First, because while he lived in a period when a rebirth of art was taking place in every field, he remained, writer of genius though he was, connected by every fibre of his being to the art of a period that was over. Then, for his own part having satisfied the requirements of his art he had, so to speak, exorcized it, having always been able to find in the mode of his contemplative life a transcendent harmony which settled all contradictions ; an outlet from on high, outside the tragic mode, in the religious and mystical field to which he had the grace of having access without losing anything of his virtues and privileges as an artist. He had escaped the curse with which art is threatened, and his problems presented themselves otherwise.

With Rouault it was different. He possessed the makings and the destiny of one of the great reformers of art. In consequence he willy-nilly had to live out within himself the separation from accepted forms of beauty, to abandon the heritage of the past, to renounce easy success and to leave the beaten track in order to establish his own rules and to trace his own path toward a goal which he felt was there but which was still

---

* Léon Bloy dedicated to him the first chapter of *Belluaires et Porchers*, devoted to the "Songs of Maldoror," which he had previously mentioned in *Le Désespéré* in 1887. He was one of the first to understand the importance of Lautréamont. In a sombre style of unparalleled richness, reminding one of the complex and shining red colour of Rouault's best canvases, Léon Bloy expresses his terrified admiration for those "songs" which he calls "the Good News of Damnation." Does not the dedication of this chapter to Rouault signify that Bloy saw a striking resemblance between the inspiration of the painter and that of the songs of Maldoror ?

shrouded in the obscurity of the future. He never skipped any stages. His patience regarding his art (the only patience of which he was capable) is one of his great virtues.

Up to a certain point we were witnesses of this struggle, of this effort toward a new form and toward "an inner order" (these words were always on Rouault's lips) — a deliberate effort, an irrepressible tendency towards a personal form of art, adequate to express his deepest necessities, and for him, the only one that was real and truly authentic.

Rouault thus half consciously followed his sure instinct; and without realizing it, placed before the young philosopher, his ardent admirer and the chosen witness of this most rare manifestation of a renewal in art, — placed before him without realizing it, and in his own person, all the great problems concerning art and its demands. From there on they seemed to us analogous to those of the perfection of the heart, analogous and yet not identical, opposed, and in conflict to them; for the artistic habitus, having as its sole aim and care, its sole moving force the inner vision and the outer bringing into form of the object, is therefore inhuman, whereas the whole Man is interested in purity of heart. But in Rouault the artist himself was impregnated with the demands of the absolute and the postulations of his faith, simple and profound as that possessed by the builders of cathedrals.

That did not make the conflict any less serious, on the contrary, for Rouault could not treat it lightly. Often in our conversations he came back to it. Although he did not experience it in the same way as those poets who were called "cursed" — Lautréamont, Rimbaud, Nerval, Baudelaire, Oscar Wilde — he nevertheless really suffered from it, torn as he was, among other things, between his imperious vocation which led him through the paths of solitude and poverty ("Go forth! Go forth, poor artist! Go forth!") and his duty toward his family : his elderly parents, his wife and four children. A blundering and narrow-minded priest having urged him to paint pictures "which sold," his conscience was profoundly offended by such advice and his wounded spirit suffered from it for years. But the God of art and goodness at last took pity on this heroically honest man and sent him success, at first in the guise of an enormous art dealer — a genius in his profession — by the name of Ambroise Vollard. Prosperity came with success, and Rouault no longer had to know other antinomies than those inherent in art itself; but those he solved without thinking of them; in painting and in weighing down with the whole load of his gifts and his demands onto the possibilities of the pictorial matter.

*

* *

It was with Rouault in mind that Jacques wrote *Art and Scholasticism* (an austere work the first edition of which appeared in 1919) and where, in analyzing the great problems of esthetics in the philosophical perspectives of Aristotle and Saint Thomas, he shows what justification — if art were seeking it — modern art as well as all the greatest things art has produced in the past centuries — can be found in the most certain and lofty principles of metaphysics.

I trust I will not be accused of partiality if I pause a moment — since it happens these pages also contain personal reminiscences — to speak about works the author of which is so near to me, and the preparation of which amounted in our lives to a decisive adventure of the spirit.

In *Frontières de la Poésie* which completes *Art and Scholasticism* and which appeared much later, Jacques Maritain speaking of Rouault in an essay devoted to him (which first appeared in 1924 in a magazine) remarks that "a philosopher could study in him the virtue of art in its purest states." Glancing back over the immense territory the painter had covered since his years at Versailles, he recalls that in all his work it was his own inner harmony that he sought in the universe of form and colour. "He found himself, but that is a road one must travel alone.

"Fervent as he was about his art, Rouault never hurried to gain public recognition . . . or to bring out into the open all the potentialities that needed to be brought to their point of unity. He never did violence to his gifts. He let the sap rise, the fruit ripen. . . He always felt himself called to a certain spiritual order" — his "inner order" — "bound to an exquisite sense of proportion and fleeting nuances which had to be discovered within himself. He seized from reality and made spring before our eyes a certain refulgence which no one before him had discovered ; these trollops and clowns, these monstrous and repulsive masses of flesh, caught in the precious transparency of the most complex matter — all this is the wound of Sin, the sadness of fallen human nature — penetrated by a look without connivance and an art that does not yield. The pathos in such art has a profoundly religious significance. For the quality of a work does not depend on its subject but on its spirit. So from 1892 on Rouault painted religious subjects. He has always continued in this direction. His passage through the world of human pitfalls should not cause us to forget the essential orientation of his heart" — (on the contrary it explains his personal vision of these tragic realities) — and should not cause us to forget "that profound movement toward serenity and clarity. Like his admirable landscapes, his religious works — and all his great output of thirty years of uninterrupted labour . . . has many surprises in store even for those who have long been acquainted with his works."

\*

\* \*

For years Rouault came to dine with us at Versailles nearly every week. We entertained him alone in order to allow him that freedom to talk spontaneously which he found so necessary. As soon as he came whatever was on his mind would burst forth in talk that was as rich as it was disordered. He never bothered with preambles or explanations, and it was quite useless to ask him for any ; this never helped. It was better to listen until the end ; then it was possible, on mentally going back, to get in order all those facts he had related with his far-away gaze, so clear and cold, and which was gifted with such infallible precision.

His great preoccupation for a long time was the Gustave Moreau Museum of which he had been the curator since 1898 — his duties regarding the sacred legacy of his master. Rouault's interest in all those who were in any way associated with the life and interests of the museum never flagged — from the administrator Monsieur Rupp, down to the *concierge* ; his fits of impatience and his claims were endless, and he had the gift of couching everything he said in the most picturesque language. To try to pass them on would be futile. These innumerable anecdotes were a most rich commodity, but perishable, alas.

After days spent in feverish, secret work which no one was ever allowed to see, and in thrashing out the difficult problems of his art and of his material life, he would arrive exasperated, and would begin to pour out all the troubles that had weighed on him or merely annoyed him. Little by little he would grow calm, pass into a lighter vein, and recover his irony and laughter ; he would start to tell funny stories, which were never vulgar — he detested vulgarity, and possessed to an extreme degree that delicacy and reserve so characteristic of the real man of the people and of the real craftsman, which he always remained.

Often he would take from his pocket papers so illegible that only he could decipher the last poem he had written, or an earlier one he wanted to show us according to his humour of the day. It is perhaps known that this great painter also wrote an incalculable amount of verse. His imagination always at work, his keen feelings of compassion and antagonism, and his satirical wit needed this mode of expression. Of course he never wrote sonnets ; he never limited himself to any set form of versification. The rhymes and assonance came to him haphazardly. He took liberal advantage of the freedom of modern or any other kind of poetry that he needed. He eliminated for instance nearly every article. The style of his poems with which we were familiar resembled that of the popular ballad, that of a milder Villon.

Rouault always hesitated to publish them. He was diffident about doing so, not feeling himself to be a master of poetic technique as he was a master of painting technique. Once, however, he had a collection of songs printed at his own expense. He showed us this collection ; but soon afterwards he changed his mind and ordered the complete edition destroyed. At least that is what he declared he would do. It is certain that it never appeared in the bookstores. Only a few rare poems were published at different times.

## Pierre and Christine

At that time we received from the hands of God and through our godfather an infinitely precious gift : two beings wonderfully worthy of love were given us as brother and sister, following the deepest aspirations of our heart.

Several years older than ourselves, Pierre van der Meer de Walcheren and his wife Christine — he Dutch of Protestant family ; she Belgian of Catholic family ; he a writer, she a painter — after an evolution singularly like our own, and having found no satisfaction elsewhere, had knocked on the door of the "Ungrateful Beggar." Like ourselves they had been helped, and their hope had been rewarded, and like us they had come to the Church, the depositary of divine peace. Our godfather was also theirs, and on February 24, 1911, the feast of the Apostle Saint Matthew, Pierre and his seven-year-old son were baptized in the Church of Saint-Médard ; Christine joined them in the refound faith of her childhood.

Pierre has described in his *Journal d'un Converti* * which covers about four years of his life — from November 1907 to June 1911 — his spiritual evolution from the start of his anguished search to the first days of his life as a Christian.

"While for several years," he says in the Introduction written in 1913, "I had been noting down all that had come to me in the way of joy or sorrow, all the yearnings of my spirit filled with anguish and hope, or tortured by a frightful despair, and overwhelmed by the tragic spectacle of humanity and my own soul, I was writing without realizing it the story of my unrelenting search for the Truth. . . I looked at life eagerly, I wanted to embrace it in its entirety with all its contrasts ; I thought I could rise above it and thus dominate it like a king, forging for myself, by means of my will, a system of ironical resignation. . . But I could not smother that painful longing for the Truth. . ."

Jacques met the Van der Meers for the first time at Léon Bloy's on February 22, 1911, just two days before the baptism of Pierre and his son, which he attended, coming back very much moved, and impressed above all by the joyous, conscious and determined attitude of the child, young Pierre-Léon, who was destined to a life of exceptional perfection.

The Van der Meers came to see us at Versailles a little later. We did not then know what a beautiful future was reserved for

* Translated into French from the Dutch by the author. Introduction by Léon Bloy.

our budding friendship. Yet from that time forward there began between us that perfect understanding that nothing could ever trouble or belie.

I liked them immediately because of their beauty. They seemed like a legendary couple, slightly romantic, slightly Wagnerian — they were to become Christians of the Golden Legend.

Both were tall and slender, blond with blue eyes. Christine had very thick hair with reddish tints and the clear glowing complexion so characteristic of the Flemish. Pierre had a quiet and noble face with that half ironical, half phlegmatic expression typical of the Dutch.

In 1911 Pierre was thirty-one. He and his wife had been living through four years of feverish anxiety in search of a truth they divined and desired before knowing it, — which they had sought, to use Pierre's own words, "with every beat of the heart."

Although they were much enamoured with each other, their love and happiness did not make them deaf to the urgent problems of knowledge, did not blind them as to their ignorance of the essential truths ; neither did it stifle the aspirations of their souls toward the plenitude of an order which transcends the fragility of human life, nor fill their solitude. "A man without a God is bitterly alone," thought Pierre, and he was astonished not to hear among those he met "the dull cry uttered by despair when it is seeking."

Pursuing their quest through the experience of life and through the works of man, Pierre and Christine had had quite a long sojourn in Italy. There they had discovered the power of religious inspiration in the art of the Primitives ; and their joy as artists had certainly been impregnated from then on with a presentiment of Faith. But nothing decisive had yet been accomplished in them, and after many days of vibrant enthusiasm they had come back somewhat disappointed to

their Nordic dwelling.    According to their own words, all that
was not what they were expecting.

But it seemed that another influence, deeper and more mysterious than that of art, had for a long time been working in
them, and was increasing in them that certain fruitful anxiety
which generally leads in the end to a peace that is stable and
without illusions.    For already several years they had been
reading Léon Bloy with great admiration for his works.    So
great was this admiration that it is difficult to believe that it
was inspired simply by the style of the author.    In fact Pierre,
when he found himself with writers who were in the habit of
treating Bloy as a fanatic or a madman, in the same breath as
he affirmed that he saw in him "only a great artist who has
something to say and who says it magnificently," would add :
"Sometimes he seems to me more than a great poet when he
displays before our eyes, in lightning flashes, the strange beauty
of the spiritual world. . . He sheds by his words, sometimes
even for me, a strange light on the mysteries of life and
death. . . He has Faith. . ."

I could also see the influence of Léon Bloy in the fact that the
Van der Meers were among the very rare people who then
read Anne Catherine Emmerich, Saint Angela of Foligno,
Saint Teresa of Avila, the Vulgate and even "The Liturgical
Year" of Dom Guéranger ; a reading reserved, so it seemed,
to Catholics exclusively.

Pierre made his first visit to Bloy in December 1909.    Bloy
did not note it in his journal, but Pierre wrote : "It was a great
joy for me, as I already knew him so well through his books. . .
As I had foreseen, I did not feel in him any acrimony, any bitterness.    His humble mind reflects infinite tenderness, infinite
love. . ."    Pierre and Christine then started to go often to the
Benedictine chapel on the Rue Monsieur.    And through the
liturgy they learned to know the attitude of the Church in regard to the Mysteries it is its mission to celebrate, to illumine

and to safeguard. Then they returned to Uccle, in Belgium, where they had lived for seven years. But Paris attracted them again, more than it ever had before ; they made plans to settle there. They moved to Paris in November 1910, and this time for a long period. . .

Pierre did not long delay in writing Bloy, and under the date of December 5, 1910, Bloy notes in *Le Pèlerin de l'Absolu*, one of his diaries:

"Got a letter from Pierre van der Meer de Walcheren, that kind Dutchman, a celebrated writer in his own country, who came to see me last year. He asks permission to call on me, which is granted spontaneously and with joy."

Then, on December 11th : "A gigantic event. Pierre van der Meer asks me to recommend a priest who will instruct him. He is a Catholic by desire and wishes to become one completely. . ."

Pierre went through hours of doubt and darkness still, but soon he reached a state of certainty, and his baptism was decided upon. It was only due to the illness of their son that the Van der Meers were obliged to postpone the day. The baptism finally took place, and Bloy wrote in *Le Pèlerin de l'Absolu* :

"Saint Matthias. — Baptism of the Van der Meers at the Church of Saint-Médard, the present parish of my godchildren. . . The father was given the name of Pierre-Matthias and the son that of Pierre-Léon, which are the patron saints I suggested ; and here they are now, luminous Christians. I feel as though I were becoming blind with joy. I hardly know what the weather is. It 's as if it were raining gold and perfumes. Am I someone from Heaven to have been able to give these souls to God, these dear souls who will speak on my behalf against all the hounds of hell when I'm in my death throes ?"

The last six years of Léon Bloy's life were filled with precious

friendships rich as these.  The number of those whom his
books led to God constantly grew — and since his death has
not ceased to grow — and his own sorrowful heart derived from
this an increase in peace.

He had greatly desired a brotherly friendship to grow up
between the Van der Meers and ourselves, and this took place
without difficulties.  At this period of our lives we saw no one
so frequently as we did them, and all that affected them, either
joy or sorrow, touched us just as deeply.

After their souls were at peace their rich and beautiful characters remained just as sensitive as when they had lived in so
much anxiety ; more than ever they were capable of enthusiasm
and love.  Pierre was happy in his work, and his influence in
his own country was growing, especially among the younger
artists.  They continued to live in Paris.  In the summer they
took over a house we had discovered several years before in a
charming village called Bures (in Seine-et-Oise, near Orsay).
Sometimes we spent our vacations there together.  It was at
Bures that Jean-François was born on September 17, 1915.  It
was there that one morning, coming back from mass with
Jacques, little Pierre-Léon announced that he had heard an
inner voice telling him he would become a Benedictine monk.
And he asked Jacques to tell his parents of this message.  Pierre-
Léon was then nine but his self-assurance was far from being
childish.  Reassured by the answer of his father who left him
entirely free, the child lived happily, studied and played wholeheartedly but never ceased to think of his vocation.  From the
age of fifteen he wanted to enter the monastery of the Benedictines at Oosterhout in Holland, which had as its head a French
monk from the Abbey of Solesmes.  The Father Abbot, Dom
Jean de Puniet, considered Pierre-Léon too young and wished
to try him ; he asked him to spend two or three years in a college in Luxembourg where he would finish his secondary studies.

Pierre-Léon accepted and came through the test victoriously. We wondered how this child who could not bear to be separated from his mother for even a day, could live so far away from her. But from the first he was absolutely at peace ; and feeling that his religious life was at hand, he became so happy and cheerful that children in the college who needed to be consoled and encouraged were sent to him. From college he went to the monastery, where he was to die in the odour of sanctity at the age of thirty, carried away in three days by an infectious grippe.

The grief of Pierre and Christine was tragic, though borne with complete resignation. Too perfect, too wonderfully swift was this resignation : it shattered them.

They had had three children, and yet they remained alone. Their little Jean-François, a three-year-old baby whom we all adored, was taken from them in only a few days after a terrifyingly rapid illness. And this wound in their heart was not curable. But then after Pierre-Léon's departure for the monastery there had remained their daughter, Anne-Marie. She had grown into an exquisite young girl with many talents, gifted in painting and in music, instinctively going to their modern forms as though she had absorbed their spirit as she breathed. But in her also surged up the irresistible vocation, and at the death of her brother Léon she had already been for two years a nun in the convent of the Benedictines of Oosterhout.

Pierre and Christine had generously accepted this sacrifice. Their two children who had given themselves to Saint Benedict were happy ; their souls, which had never known any kind of disturbance, blossomed pure and strong in the atmosphere of contemplation and discipline, and quite naturally bore fruits of grace and wisdom.

Two or three times each year Pierre and Christine went to spend a few days, and at rare intervals a few weeks, in the neigh-

bourhood of the two convents at Oosterhout. Each time after
their return we felt that they were stronger and more courageous, as if reflecting the humble and gentle glory of their
children. Although they bore the inevitable wounds of such
a separation, they lived in the peace of a sacrifice generously
accepted, and with the feeling that they had given all and that
God could not ask anything more of them. But the love of
God is insatiable — yes ! indeed : "It was not for a joke that
God loved us." And now He had altogether removed from the
world the young monk who had so quickly attained perfection.

When our friends received blow after blow, the news of the
illness, the approaching death and the actual death of their
son, Jacques was not there to help them carry their heavy cross
— Jacques was then in America. How they missed him on
that day ! Vera and I were stricken as we received the tele-
phone messages from Issy-les-Moulineaux where the Van der
Meers were then living. We rushed to their house to find
them as two great Paupers, this time shorn of everything.
Where they drew the strength to be up and about was more
than we could fathom. They embraced the law of sorrow with
their whole hearts. These two noble and proud beings never
argued with God. A fearful resolution took birth within them
from that time on, inspiring them to conquer Him by generosity, to take Him at His word when He said : "And to him
that would . . . take thy tunic, give up thy cloak also."

\*

\* \*

When they returned from the funeral of their son they had
decided to give to God not only their tunics but their skins and
the heart of their lives, they were going to break up — if not
their truly indissoluble love — at least their life in common,
their blessed life of perfect fulfillment and beauty. They had
conceived this folly : each should go to a monastery and endure

until death the martyrdom of their separation.   It was a challenge to God.   God accepted it.

The Abbot of Oosterhout, to whom they first confided their
intention, made them wait one year.   Once the year had gone
by their resolution was still as firm.   So they separated.   Pierre
took his wife to the convent of Sainte-Cécile in Solesmes ; then
he went to Oosterhout.

No act of heroism on their part could surprise us, but this
time their resolution did not seem really wise.   We thought
that if the Abbot had known as we did the holiness and beauty
of their union, he would never have authorized their separation.
Also he could not realize all the good they did round about
them, or the value of their calm and radiant presence in the
troubled shadows of the world ; and then too, their happiness,
which was of such a rare quality, seemed to be something sacred
on which a hand should not be laid.

But God had accepted their challenge and for a year and a
half they lived separated, their tortured souls never asking for
mercy.   It was only when the date for the taking of their vows
approached that the Father Abbot, before giving his definite
consent, wanted once more to assure himself of the reality of
their vocation.   Christine let him read the letters she had
received from Pierre during this time, which had been written
with the consent of their respective superiors.   Having read
them the Father Abbot realized what their love was, and he
told them to return to the world in peace.

They met at our house in Meudon.   Pierre came from Holland and Christine from Solesmes.   She arrived shorn of her
magnificent hair, looking much older and thinner, but so
humble and touching in her frailness that one could not
look at her without weeping.   Physically Pierre had stood
the terrible test much better, but at the expense of a certain
nervous tension.

They came back to their old life with the greatest simplicity.

In a few weeks Christine had regained her youth, and Pierre his Dutch calmness. They settled in our neighbourhood, at Bellevue. Christine again had her garden to work in, and embroideries to design and sew on. Pierre took up once again, in Paris, the management of the publishing house, Desclée de Brouwer, where Stanislas Fumet had replaced him. Of our dear Stanislas and Aniouta Fumet I hope to be able to speak later, to tell of the friendship which unites us, their part in the Catholic renaissance in France, the work carried out in common by Stanislas and Jacques, to recall the work accomplished by Stanislas Fumet with the weekly *Temps Présent*, and especially since the dark days of 1940. We know with what firmness and greatness of soul he has suffered and struggled for the sacred cause — French and Christian — of the resistance. But all that is very far away from the time we are dealing with in this book. . .

All the old collaborators of Pierre greeted his return with joy. Jacques gave him several of his books to publish and continued to edit with him the series *Les Iles*, which had superseded that of *Le Roseau d'Or*. We were again in harmony on all things, and together we saw with one same anguish the approach of the new war which, in 1939, separated us from one another, as the Van der Meers had to return to Holland. Pierre has recently published the second and third volumes of the diary of his life.

# CHAPTER THREE

## Péguy's Religious Difficulties

### *"I have found the Faith again, I am a Catholic"*

From our final return to France date those conversations with Péguy which centred almost exclusively around his return to the faith, the stringent requirements of the Church, and Péguy's own difficulties and resistance. A little later Jeanne — Jacques' sister — was also to take part in these conversations, as well as Dom Baillet — through his letters — and Ernest Psichari. None of us succeeded in justifying Péguy's position of reserve. He had accustomed us to clear-cut acts which left no room for equivocation, and now we no longer could recognize him in this. However convinced we were of the sincerity and depth of his faith, we went from disappointment to disappointment. Neither Péguy's actions nor, it sometimes seemed to us, his intellectual attitude revealed the simplicity of a commitment without reservations, whereas we expected of them clearly to manifest his allegiance to the Church of which he was a member, and to the religion which he professed. Péguy, on the other hand, went from reservation to reservation, from irritation to irritation, until finally conversation between us became entirely impossible, up to the time of a tardy reconciliation, founded upon a friendship which everything had wounded but which nothing could destroy.

Péguy would say : "When one loves one can not unlove." Jacques' mother quotes these words in her *Souvenirs sur Péguy*,* and adds : "During interminable months 'the friendly soul' had been disconsolate, wounded; suddenly from the trial it emerged triumphant. Under the sun of that magnificent

* Geneviève Favre, *Europe*, February 15–April 15, 1938.

43

spring of 1914 the way of reconciliation opened before him (Péguy) ; my son and he found each other in it ; and this happiness spread itself to all of us." Jacques' mother says further : "Through all differences, all silences, all separations, Péguy remained closely bound to his friend, bound by an invincible fidelity."

And we who through all these things had not ceased to love him, perhaps with a little too much anxiety and too much impatience, had never lost the assurance that Péguy's faith was real and living despite all the incompleteness his conversion showed up to the day of his departure for the war.

This discord between infused faith and the acts, and the thoughts even, of a man who has received this gift from God, we were seeing it for the first time ; since then we have met with it often. A long time is needed in these cases for the supernatural faith received by baptism in infancy and later driven back into the depths of the subconscious, to break away and little by little to take possession of all the faculties ; or, when this gift is received in adulthood, for it to succeed in correcting the deep-rooted habits of the mind and in changing the whole conceptual apparatus and the speculative language which has already become well constituted. Sometimes there is not time for this transformation to be accomplished. Often it has hardly begun when life comes to its end. And nevertheless faith is manifested in acts which emanate from the depths of the soul, such as fervent prayer and the desire for the sacraments. It is more difficult, for example, for a great philosopher to allow his philosophy to be changed than his soul, and sometimes God does not consider this necessary. It is more difficult for someone who all his life has thought in the language of mathematical and physical sciences to express his faith in exact theological formulas ; and this too doubtless is not necessary. Thus it has been with Bergson ; the same too with our friend Catherine Pozzi.

Thus it was with Péguy. When he returned to the faith of his childhood, the gift of God entered into an intellectual and psychic organism which was strongly constituted and solidified in all its parts. At that time — 1907 — he had reached his thirty-third year. He had worked out his own interior discipline with an upright heart, and with the fervour of genius — and the discipline of the Church had had no part in this. Had he not written as late as 1905 : "The thirteen or fourteen centuries of Christianity in my ancestors, the eleven or twelve years of Catholic instruction and even education sincerely and faithfully received passed over me without leaving a trace." * He had learned all that from then on he could learn — poverty, destitution, the history of our country — Corneille — Victor Hugo — Bergson's philosophy. He could no longer penetrate the deeper meaning of theology, nor, in consequence, its necessity ; he only came up against its boundaries, its defenses, as he was to do with the doctrine of Saint Thomas which, without having any real knowledge of it, he imprudently called a compilation ; he never reached its living soul — with its power of unifying and quickening knowledge. A compilation ! It is as if one blasphemously described the Chartres Cathedral as a "patchwork" of stone and styles. . . But in the midst of all this his faith lived, and his influence, which has grown all the greater after his death, is a Christian and Catholic influence ; less speculatively than morally Christian and Catholic. People may cavil at his conversion, put it in doubt — these facts remain. Péguy, who knew the value of words, has said it himself : "I have found the Faith again, I am a Catholic." In his last pages written two days before the mobilization (*Note conjointe sur M. Descartes*), he described himself in regard to the Church as "a big son, half rebellious, entirely docile and of a staunchness above every trial."

It was his deep and living Christianity, even when he had not

* Charles Péguy, *Toujours de la grippe*. Complete Works, vol. I, p. 165. Gallimard.

yet become aware of it, which gave him so exact and ardent an
understanding of France, so great a love of his earthly fatherland, and which at the same time preserved him from the
pagan nationalism of Maurras and the political cynicism of
Machiavelli.

It was the delicacy of his Christian understanding, of his
Christian intuition of history and his Christian passion for
justice which made him examine the mystery of Israel with so
much intelligent attention and inspired his struggle against
anti-Semitism and all the iniquities it contains. To Daniel
Halévy, one of the pro-Dreyfus companions of Péguy, and one
of the first contributors to the *Cahiers de la Quinzaine,* but who
in 1907 published an "Apology for our Past Life" in which he
said : "Let us not sing we have been conquerors, for the battle
has been confused . . ." Péguy replied in *Notre Jeunesse* :
"And what were we saying ? We were saying that a single
injustice, a single crime, a single unlawful act, above all if it
is officially registered and confirmed, a single affront to justice
and law, above all if it is universally, legally, nationally, con-
veniently accepted, a single crime breaks and suffices to break
the whole social pact, a single forfeiture, a single dishonour suffices to lose honour, to dishonour a whole people." Shortly
afterward the collaboration of Péguy and Halévy came to an
end.

From the years in which we knew Péguy and of which I am
writing here, I am violently thrust back to the present. Several of the actors in a great drama, united by friendship, separated by death, are now reunited in the life that knows no end.
The first to leave us was Father Baillet, whose precocious vocation to the Benedictine order early took him away from Péguy
and the group of their friends in the Collège Sainte-Barbe.
Then the First World War came to take Ernest Psichari,

killed on August 22, 1914 ; two weeks later, on September 5th,
Péguy himself fell at the battle of the Marne.   Father Clérissac,
who played so great a rôle in Psichari's conversion, also died
in 1914 — on November 16th.   Finally Geneviève Favre,
Jacques' mother, Péguy's great and ever faithful friend, has just
joined him in the bosom of God at the age of eighty-seven.
Now all is clear for them concerning their inspiration, and
doubtless concerning ours too ; but in the sorrowful days on
earth, in the twilight of this life, how much groping we had
to do to know and understand one another !

Our grave misunderstandings with Péguy began the very day
when all should have been clear between us — the day of January 1907, when Jacques having told him of our conversion,
Péguy cried : "I too have come to that !"   Jacques had then
understood that all was settled with Péguy as it was with us,
and in the simplest manner (for us it was the only one possible), by the acceptance of both the doctrine and discipline
of the Church.   But all was not settled for Péguy.   Jacques
had come back to Heidelberg with his marvelous secret which
Péguy had asked him to keep for a certain time, time for him
to prepare the *Cahier* subscribers to understand him.   Then
Jacques took the good news to Father Baillet — in exile with
the entire community of Solesmes on the Isle of Wight — a
friend whom Péguy had always held in high veneration since
the years at the Collège Sainte-Barbe.   There, in those far-
off days, had been grouped about the already dominating personality of Péguy the Tharaud brothers, Porché, Baudouin
(whose sister Péguy was to marry), and Lotte, later a professor
at the lycée of Coutances, killed also in the First World War.
Lotte had always been the confidant closest to Péguy's heart,
and yet Péguy did not reveal to him his conversion until 1908.
Here is Lotte's account of this confidence.   Having no other

documents at my disposal, I am quoting it from *Péguy* by
Daniel Halévy : *

"Each year in September," wrote Lotte, "I went to see him.
In 1908 I found him in bed, exhausted and ill. All the enormous fatigue he had borne for twelve years without flinching
had finally crushed him. I too had suffered immense misfortunes. He spoke to me of his distress, his lassitude, his
yearning for rest. . . At one moment, he lifted himself upon
his elbow, his eyes filled with tears : 'I did not tell you everything. . . I have found the Faith again. . . I am a Catholic.'
This was as sudden as a great emotion of love ; my heart melted,
and the hot tears falling, head in hands, I said to him almost
despite myself : 'Ah, poor old fellow, that's what we've all
come to.'

" 'That's what we've all come to !' Where did these words
come from, when only an instant before I was still an unbeliever ? The action of what working, of what slow, dark and
deep working did it reveal ? At that moment I felt I was a
Christian."

"That is all that is known and doubtless there is no more
to know," added Daniel Halévy. The essential is there certainly ; "I have found the Faith again, I am a Catholic," is
the testimony of Péguy himself. There are nevertheless many
more things to be known ; and since, in the *Addenda* to his
book on Péguy, Daniel Halévy regrets the absence of the testimony of Jacques Maritain, and calls upon him for it, I will say
here on behalf of my husband and myself, what more we know.

## Indecisions and Torments

"Ah, my poor old fellow, that's what we've all come to !"
Lotte's cry is like a retort to almost the same words which

* Daniel Halévy, *Péguy*, p. 159.

escaped Péguy when Jacques, twenty months earlier, had told
him of our conversion. — "But I too have come to that !"    I
am inclined to believe that this exclamation, revealing a deeply
hidden reality, this statement drawn forth by emotion and surprise, was a kind of premature fruit in Péguy's inner life.    Faith
would live, would grow in his soul, but a longer interior ripen-
ing in secret would doubtless have saved Péguy some painful
discussions.    A shock coming from without brought forth too
soon to the light of a consciousness slower than the subconscious, that faith that was living anew but still all entangled
with human cares.    Péguy did not want any one to speak of
conversion in connection with himself.    It was because he had
not known the break that is produced by a sudden illumination ; it was necessary in his case that the work of grace be developed by a continuous process.    Time was needed for it to
assimilate all that substance already humanly elaborated, and
the value of which Péguy realized.    But on the contrary, grace
was immediately to encounter the thorny way of inevitable
conflicts and tragic difficulties.

After his confidence to Jacques, Péguy's secret had been
strictly kept by us and by Dom Baillet, and by Péguy himself,
since friends like Lotte and Daniel Halévy knew nothing of it
until September 1908.    Péguy was always waiting until his
"subscribers" were ready to understand him, ready to approve
of his faith for him, if not just to accept it for themselves.    But
henceforth his Catholic faith, more or less explicitly, was present in all his writings.

From Heidelberg Jacques wrote Péguy letters which savoured
of anxiety and criticism.    Péguy was hurt, and misunderstandings began to thicken.    But when Jacques went to see him, at
the "Shop," it was enough for them to look at one another "in
order for those shadows, at least as far as our affection for one
another was concerned, to disappear," wrote Jacques in his
diary.    Yes, "so far as their affection was concerned."    At that

time we still had much to learn regarding Péguy's obstacles. On June 12, 1908, Jacques noted with surprise : "Péguy did not go to mass last Sunday, and appears not to wish to go on Ascension Day. What is the matter with him ?" he added naïvely. Our naïveté was indeed extreme. We thought that if one was a Catholic one believed in the Incarnation of the Word, in the presence of the Word made flesh on the altar where mass is celebrated ; in the infinite spiritual value of this Presence, in its invitation to us, in the sweetness of the duty which calls us, in the ease with which we could, in general, answer this call of God and the Church, and in the gravity in this case of an absence which wounded Christ's love for us.

Now Péguy did not disavow his words ; as he said to Jacques more than a year before and as in several months he was to again affirm to Lotte, he was a Catholic. He believed in the Incarnation, in the Eucharistic presence of Christ and nothing, absolutely nothing exterior prevented him from attending mass. Might there have been an interior obstacle ? We could neither conceive of its nature nor admit its validity. Péguy said, and sometimes we believed him, that he did not go to mass because his sorrow was so great at not being able to go to communion with the rest of the faithful. That is distressing, and if it was a weakness it was a holy weakness. Still we had the impression that this was not the whole reason for his keeping away from mass ; that doubtless he did feel this pain and distress, but that he was resigned to it because of considerations he never clearly expressed, and which were doubtless compelling to his conscience. We wondered whether the expectation of the day when his public presence in the midst of the faithful would crown as a victory, as an honour after hardships, the return with him of his own flock, the whole band of his subscribers and friends — and perhaps also a feeling of human justice towards his wife * — were not the reasons that made him consider it legitimate to defer the accomplishment of what he owed God. If he had only been thinking of this last obligation he would have acted in a manner to make Eucharistic communion possible. He would have had his children baptized — they were then very young ; he would have asked the Church to bless his marriage. Well ! all this he did not want. As I mentioned in the first volume of these memoirs, Péguy wished neither to impose his will on his family nor to risk a break with it, nor to seek a secret regularization of his marriage. He waited, he wanted to wait, and he wanted others to accept that he wait.

Péguy, since his return to the Catholic faith, felt himself more and more estranged from his family : "those closest to him did not follow him," writes Geneviève Favre, "the entire house was dominated by the authority of Madame Baudouin and the influence of her son Albert. . ." Albert with untiring devotion gave himself up to the children of Péguy — who "was absolutely unable to do this," being always absent from home, at the Shop or Printing Press, weighed down as he was by the material difficulties involved in the work of the *Cahiers*, occupied by his own writings whose importance he could feel ; and, it would seem, also having an intuition of the brief time which would be left to him.

* To quote the generous explanation of a theologian : "One sometimes wonders why, after finding his faith again, he did not practise it and did not have his children baptized ? The reason, however paradoxical it may seem, was a reason of justice. Let me explain. Péguy had married when he was a socialist and revolutionary and no longer had the faith ; his wife shared his ideas, and their marriage was only a civil one. Therefore, having engaged himself in this manner, Péguy had made a sort of contract always to respect the convictions of his wife, who came from old revolutionary stock and was indifferent to Catholicism ; and his wife never wished to regularize their marriage or baptize their children. And Péguy waited for grace to do its work, living in hope." L. M. Regis, O.P., *Revue Dominicaine*, Montreal, May 1944, pp. 275-6.

In July 1908, after lunching with Péguy, Jacques noted rapidly in his diary : "At table Péguy showed his extreme affliction. He spoke of it to Raïssa and myself, and we are distressed by his excessive suffering." He was exhausted by worry, fatigue, was ill ; and his own family did not follow him in his spiritual evolution (that is, they did not yet ; it was necessary for him to die and for his greatness to appear). His wife and her mother refused to consent to the children's baptism. They, too young to realize the drama which was being played between their parents, suffered nevertheless from the troubles of a divided family and from the absence of tranquillity and joy, and they instinctively took refuge at their mother's side. Péguy came to feel himself a stranger to his family, a stranger in his own house. Where would he find consolation equal to his sorrow ? And now a "youthful and precious friendship" was springing up at his side, harmonious in every way and burning with admiration . . . a perfect communion." In this trial Péguy's loyalty did not flinch. "Péguy wished to bear alone the suffering which no one around him suspected ; his young friend founded a home of peace and affection ; Péguy wished to be alone before the disturbing mystery of sorrow." He wrote to his great confidante Geneviève Favre : "Work and the aid of God have helped me get over the great sorrow I confided to you." And again, "I work full steam to bring myself back to reason. It made me a little ill, but I would rather be a little ill from overwork than to miss my vocation because of a disorder in my heart." Yet Péguy told his secret in the following moving poem :

### Prière de Confidence

*Quand il fallut s'asseoir à la croix des deux routes*
*Et choisir le regret d'avecque le remords,*
*Quand il fallut s'asseoir au coin des doubles sorts*
*Et fixer le regard sur la clef des deux voûtes,*

*Vous seule vous savez, maîtresse du secret,*
*Que l'un des deux chemins allait en contre-bas,*
*Vous connaissez celui que choisirent nos pas,*
*Comme on choisit un cèdre et le bois d'un coffret.*

*Et non point par vertu car nous n'en avons guère,*
*Et non point par devoir car nous ne l'aimons pas,*
*Mais comme un charpentier s'arme de son compas,*
*Par besoin de nous mettre au centre de misère,*

*Et pour bien nous placer dans l'axe de détresse,*
*Et par ce besoin sourd d'être plus malheureux,*
*Et d'aller au plus dur et de souffrir plus creux,*
*Et de prendre le mal dans sa pleine justesse.*

*Par ce vieux tour de main, par cette même adresse,*
*Qui ne servira plus à courir le bonheur.*
*Puissions-nous, ô régente, au moins tenir l'honneur,*
*Et lui garder lui seul notre pauvre tendresse.**

\* Prayer of Trust

When we had to sit at the crossroads
And choose between regret and remorse,
When we had to sit at the corner of the two fates
And fix our gaze upon the crown of the two arches,

You alone, mistress of the secret, know
That one of the two roads led downwards,
You know the one our steps chose,
As one chooses a cedar or wood for a chest.

And not through virtue, for of that we have hardly any,
And not through duty, for we do not much care for it,
But as a carpenter arms himself with his compass,
Through a need to place ourselves at the centre of misery,

And to place ourselves squarely at the core of distress,
And by that secret need of being more unhappy,
And of going to what's most painful and of suffering in greater despair,
And of accepting misfortune in its full measure.

By that old sleight-of-hand, by that same skill,
Which will no longer serve to pursue happiness.
May we, O Queen, at least retain our honour,
And keep for it alone our poor love.

We did not know this secret at that time ; we learned of
it a little later.  We lived from day to day in anxiety, doubt,
pity, and pain to see Péguy so disturbed, so reticent and unhappy.  From a distance his friend Dom Baillet suffered as we
did, and gave Péguy the same advice as ourselves.  There was
nothing else to say — divine truth is no respecter of persons ;
particular cases have to do with a mercy and a justice whose
decrees are unknown to us.

*

*          *

One day Péguy spoke to us of one of his friends, gravely ill,
of a vow to be made for his cure, of a pilgrimage to Chartres —
the great spiritual weapon of Péguy.  The question of communion again arose.  "We felt the soul of our dear Péguy tormented and unhappy," Jacques noted, "filled with goodness
and love for the Blessed Sacrament."  Jacques told him that
he should absolutely separate in his mind the question of communion, at that time impossible for him, and the consideration of those acts which he could perform in order to bear
witness to his faith — such as attending mass and confession.
That day again we had hoped for his consent.  He had not
said no ; he had not wished to bind himself by replying in the
affirmative.  And up to the time of the War he never did go
to mass, that is before August 15, 1914.  On that day there
doubtless were no difficulties for him, in him.  On the 16th,
in fact, he wrote to Jeanne Garnier-Maritain : "Perhaps some
day I shall tell you in what parish I heard mass on the feast of
the Assumption.  If I do not return, kindly go to Chartres
once a year for me."
At this mass of the Assumption he perhaps received communion.  It is possible he went to confession to a young Capu-
chin, one of the soldiers in his company, of whom he speaks
praisingly in his letter of August 17, 1914, adding : "I name

him the chaplain of my company and my private chaplain." *

But all this we were not to know until after the death of our friend ; all this was to ripen only in the utter abandonment of his last days, in the enthusiasm of his acceptance of the total sacrifice.

The five or six years which preceded these days of light and blood were years of hesitation and trouble in which divine faith and human friendship seemed at times to undo themselves. But the ship weathered the storm ; God supported everything with His hands, and saved all in the end. But of this period I should say what I know, even though such memories are painful to recall.

We are in 1909. Jacques, having been to lunch with the Péguys, saw that Madame Péguy did not hide her bitterness. She said that her husband was "suffering a violent attack of Catholicism." Péguy let things go on and the bitterness increased on both sides. At certain times Péguy seemed beaten and spent ; he admitted that a terrible combat was taking place within him, and that he felt physically exhausted.

Jeanne, Jacques' sister, sometimes had very lively discussions with him. She was not in the habit of mincing words, and one day she reproached him "with wanting to serve two masters and with being an ignoble coward !" She told us that Péguy was sitting in a chair, crushed. In the end he exclaimed : "It would be better for you to go and say all those things in Lozère !" — "Do you want me to ?" asked Jeanne. — "Yes," replied Péguy. — "Let this be our last word on the subject."

What a difficult errand ! Jacques wrote to Dom Baillet to ask his advice. The latter replied that some one should certainly go and speak to Péguy's family.

* Quoted by Victor Boudon in *Avec Charles Péguy de la Lorraine à la Marne, Août–Septembre, 1914.*

So the visit to Lozère was decided upon ; but it was not Jeanne who was commissioned with it ; in the end it was Jacques. That was a pity. A woman would have known better how to handle things ; she would have screamed with the women, and of all those screams nothing would have remained ; doubtless no result would have been obtained either, but at least nothing hurtful would have weighed upon the memory of any of them.

In place of this, a visit, which could not but seem indiscreet, from a young man who said things they could not forget, engaged in a theological discussion and set forth absolute truths. Poor generous ambassador ! That was not the last time that he accepted an ungrateful rôle in a cause lost in advance, in overtures which should have been made (I am thinking of a certain visit to André Gide) by others who did not have to resign themselves to it from lack of courage ; and Jacques took upon himself the humiliation of an anticipated defeat and the risk of seeing his words and intentions misinterpreted in order not to miss what might have been a chance of bringing souls together. At least in those days we had the excuse of our youth and inexperience. . .

It was Péguy's duty to settle with his wife the question of the baptism of their children. And Madame Péguy could only be hurt and irritated by the presence of a stranger in this grievous discussion.

Therefore, as was really to be expected, the conversation was painful, tempestuous, and without result. Jacques did not write of it in his diary ; under date of July 22nd he set down merely : "Visit to Madame Baudouin and Madame Péguy." But Jacques' mother speaks of it in her *Souvenirs sur Péguy*.

"One morning Péguy appeared . . . in the tiny room where I was working. . . Without seating himself, he said in a curt tone : 'I would appreciate it if you would go to Lozère today.' 'Is anyone ill ?' I asked him. 'No, but do not fail to go today.' "

The ravages of Jacques' visit were considerable !

"A disaster seemed to have fallen upon the poor house.

"In what state did I find Madame Baudouin and Madame Péguy ?  In what state of vexation and exasperation . . . and against whom ?  Against my son . . . I first tried, and in vain, to calm them, but soon I was in consternation at their revelations.

"Jacques had, in fact, as he explained to me later, gone at the request of Péguy to see the Baudouin family ; he wished, a little naïvely perhaps, but without any idea of hostility, to say to Madame Péguy and her mother that as the baptism of the children was in their eyes a meaningless gesture they could without difficulty make this concession to Péguy.

"The conversation thus begun became a heated religious discussion ; Madame Baudouin and her daughter retained the bitterest memory of it, which did not in any way correspond with my son's intention."

Péguy blamed Jacques for the aggravation of his family situation.  "A coldness grew between Péguy and my son ; they drifted apart."

\*

\*    \*

Little by little Péguy persuaded himself that the requirements of the Church were just in themselves but not in regard to him.  He built up a justification of his attitude : he was one of those poor sinners of which the Middle Ages knew the place in Christianity ; he was filling a function ; he wanted to be left in peace ; all he asked — as in his admirable "Presentation of Beauce to Notre Dame of Chartres" — was the last place in Purgatory. . . An arch humility !  Who does not desire that last place which assures salvation ?  And who even would dare claim it by his own merits ?  Divine logic — we neither have the right to believe ourselves worthy of it, nor that of not desiring more ; are we not explicitly commanded to be perfect "even as your heavenly Father is perfect" ?

Péguy therefore considered himself misunderstood by Jacques and Father Baillet. . . As the latter, who was now at the Abbey of Oosterhout, in Holland, asked him to come to see him, Péguy confided to Jacques that his friend's letter had "pained him, pained him greatly." That was because he no longer hoped to bring Father Baillet to his way of thinking.

His religious attitude was by then no longer a secret ; it was publicly discussed. In a very laudatory article which delighted Péguy, Marcel Drouin (who signed himself Arnauld) wrote in the *Nouvelle Revue française* of November 1, 1909 : "Péguy is not ready for a second conversion and draws his strength from sentiments which are all the more sure as they are purely human." Of course we were happy at any praise bestowed on Péguy. But for Péguy to rejoice without measure in such ambiguous compliments broke our hearts. Was Péguy himself going to deny the divine source behind the best of his thought and strength ?

For a long time Péguy had showed a deeply touching gentleness and humility in his sufferings and hesitations. Now he was becoming hardened in his feeling that his was an exceptional case. Sometimes it seemed to us that he was veering toward Protestantism. But this was only in appearance ; if he was defending himself against the Church in which he believed, but whose face he did not see clearly, at least he always kept up his private devotions ; first to Our Lady, whom he constantly invoked, and to whom in grave circumstances he would go to pray in her Chartres Cathedral, "the Cathedral unique in the world" ; to Saint Genevieve, the miraculous patron of Paris ; to Saint Louis, king of France ; finally to Jeanne d'Arc, under whose emblem his whole militant life had been placed, since the time he had consecrated to her, in his first book on Jeanne, the early fruits of his genius. He puts down as a special grace his having been "designated during military manoeuvres to parade at the head of his platoon before the statue of Jeanne d'Arc and to salute her with his sword." And does he not tirelessly extol the three theological virtues in his greatest works ? And was it not always with the mystery of grace that he was preoccupied ? "The working of grace," he would say to Jacques, "that is the reply one must make to the imbeciles who demand reasons for faith." "But I know," he wrote in *Clio*, "that grace is insidious, that it is shrewd and unexpected. And that it is stubborn. . . When one throws it out the door, it comes in again by the window. . . When it's not coming straight, it's coming sideways." "How great must be my prudence," he makes God say. "This free will must be created : it must be taught to men. Without endangering their salvation. Because if I hold them up too much, they will never learn how to swim. But if I don't hold them up just at the right moment they will take a nosedive and swallow more water than is healthy for them ; they will sink. And they must not be allowed to drown in that ocean of turpitude." * God could not have spoken in a more Catholic manner in the language of the people of France. The Catholic faith was till the end the very sap of Péguy's thought.

In 1909, with the idea of regularizing his marriage, Péguy approached Mgr. Batiffol whom he had known since he was chaplain at the Collège Sainte-Barbe and to whom he had always remained attached. He told Jacques that Mgr. Batiffol was going to study the latest regulations of canon law on marriage. But Mgr. Batiffol was no more able than Dom Baillet to give Péguy a reply which would satisfy him : the Church required that the Christian education of children be actually carried out and not merely promised. Péguy's perplexity continued.

* *Le Mystère des Saints Innocents.*

### *"The Mystery of the Charity of Jeanne d'Arc"*

New complications between Péguy and Jacques. *Le Mys-tère de la Charité de Jeanne d'Arc* appeared in December 1909. "*Cahier* for Christmas Day — and for the Feast of the Kings — eleventh series," wrote Péguy. The writing was magnifi-cent, literarily ; yet we were disappointed. What had we ex-pected ? It disappointed us and it wounded us. And Jacques wrote this to Péguy, and Péguy was irritated. That day we were unjust toward him ; and he was right to be irritated with us. Our impression was caused by reasons so lacking in objec-tivity that I cannot even recall them. I have just reread the entire book and ask myself how it could have possibly failed to have touched us at that time. The only explanation — which is not a "reason" — was our underlying sorrow : the grief, the wound that was represented for us by Péguy's general attitude — of which I have spoken and of which I will again speak here. And thus we were less apt than others who loved Péguy much less than Jacques did, to receive a correct impression of this *Mystère de la Charité*. Perhaps, in addition, we expected a drama on the life of Jeanne herself and her interior martyrdom before those judges and accusers who represented themselves as the Church ; this was for us the most sublime secret and the heroic test of her sanctity ; it was not the subject Péguy had treated.

Now I find nothing in it which does not move me. And I see, even more than Jeanne d'Arc in "the mystery" of her charity, Péguy himself in the mystery of his renewed or re-found faith. This faith so new, so fresh, so simple in its piety — Péguy was happy to allow it to speak for itself, to tell its story, to describe itself. The substance of his faith and the love that animated it. He also found this means to instruct without seeming to do so the potential disciples and believers who, in his eyes, made up the readers of the *Cahiers*. He thus found a way of relating first through Jeanne, then through Madame Gervaise the whole story of Christ, from His birth to His death. The Passion of Jesus. And the compassion of Mary. The Apostles' vocation, their greatness. The inexhaustible source of grace and sanctity that is in Christ. The Communion of Saints and prayer.

This simple, unadorned, unified account, yet filled with love, adoration and anguish, flows almost without interruption of the dialogue from one end of the book to the other. For there are but three who speak : Jeanne and Madame Gervaise ; and Hauviette, only at the beginning.

Jeanne begins. She meditates on the Kingdom of God which after twenty centuries of prophets and fourteen of Christianity, has not yet come. "O God, if one could only see the beginning of Your kingdom. . . Everywhere one sees war and perdition. . ." She loses herself in the vision of Jesus. "Blessed are they who have seen Him pass in their country." She contemplates Bethlehem. "Thou shalt shine eternally above all the cities of the earth . . . eternally, infinitely." She contemplates and envies and rejoices with the saints who surrounded Jesus — Madeleine and Veronica ; Lazarus ; Simon of Cyrene and Saint Simeon, "that righteous and God-fearing man, awaiting the consolation of Israel. . ."

Here Jeanne resumes her sorrowful meditation :

"Awaiting the consolation of Israel ; and the consolation came ; and the consolation was not enough. . . The consolation did not console Israel ; and it did not console your Christianity either, O God. . . How long, O God, shall we await the consolation of the kingdom of France ; the consolation of the great pity which is in the kingdom of France. . .

"But he, this old man . . . happy in that he no longer knew

any other history.   Happy, the happiest of all, in that he no longer knew any other history of the earth. . .

"He had held in his hands the greatest royalty of the royalty of the earth.

"And he no longer knew any other history of the earth."

"And so everyone could approach you."   She meditates on the happiness of all those, even the executioners, who could approach Him. . .   "Blessed are those who could drink the glance of Your eyes ; blessed are those who ate the bread from Your table . . .   blessed are those who ate one day, one single day — on that Holy Thursday — blessed are those who ate the bread of Your Body ; Yourself consecrated by Yourself . . . when You Yourself said the first mass. . .   What had they done, O God, those people, to be honoured with that honour, favoured, fortunate, blessed, graced by that grace. . ."   "Those people," were the Jews.   And Jeanne meditates on their singular election.   "And you, Jews, people of the Jews, my God, my God, what did this people do for You — that You preferred it thus to all other peoples . . .   what did it do for You that it might be Your chosen people . . . ?   So that from century to century . . .   You took from it, among it, the lines of prophets, the race of prophets.   What people, O God, would not have considered itself blessed . . . to be Your people . . . what race would not have desired to be the chosen race ; Your race . . . Your people ; chosen, and by such an election ; at no matter what price, O God, at no matter what temporal price, even if at the price of this dispersion.   You have chosen . . . You have taken from among it, from generation to generation You have taken from among it the long line, the high, the mounting line of prophets ; and like a summit the last of all, the last of the prophets ; the first of the saints ; Jesus who was Jewish, a Jew, a Jew among you . . . chosen race ; what has not been given to the greatest saints, to the greatest saints of the Christian people, that you have had . . . for the rest of you, Christian saints, great saints of Christianity, in your eternity you do not contemplate Jesus except in His glory ; and you Jews, singular Jews, singular people, unique people, first among peoples, you beheld Him in His misery . . . And His misery was your misery. . . We are brothers of Jesus in our humanity. But you, Jews, you were His brothers in His own family. Brothers of His race and of the same line. Upon you He shed tears unlike others. . . Of the same line for eternity." And the long and admirable meditation finally ends with the cry, to which all else was but the prelude : "Jesus, Jesus, will You ever be present to us in this way. If You were here, God, everything really would not happen as it does. All this would never have happened as it did."

Madame Gervaise appears and carries on the discourse :

"He is here,
He is here as on the first day.
He is here among us as on the day of His death.
Eternally He is here among us, as He was on the first day.
Eternally every day. . ."

Almost all that follows (three quarters of the book) belongs to the monologue of Madame Gervaise. Jeanne interrupts her, but seldom, with brief and obstinate phrases concerning two or three themes which have to do with her particular vocation. But for the wide and universal Christian vocation the true speaker is the humble Gervaise. Sometimes one reads her discourse a little quickly — which one does not do for the discourse of Jeanne — one skims through it. But more often the reader pronounces every word from his heart. The discourse expresses a deep and assured faith, in popular language, in a French that is ample, pure and honest, with several grammatical errors that are common and intentional.

In the whole book one assertion appears to me out of place; and one word, a single word, sounds a false note. This word, spoken by Hauviette, is nothing but a fault of taste. The assertion is this — a surprising one from humble Madame Gervaise. She insists upon it, she keeps repeating : "This is what the doctors of the earth did not understand." What could Madame Gervaise know of the doctors of the earth ? that is, doubtless, of Saint Thomas and the theologians ? The assertion occurs, out of place, in the very last pages of the book. You have the impression that Péguy had long had it in mind, and had not been able to find a place for it. And that in the end he decided to put it in regardless anywhere — at the end as in any other place — because of his absolute need to exhibit his anti-theological bias. Had we ever made such a remark ? I cannot remember that we did. In any case the doctors meant less to us than the doctrine, but we knew that it was the doctrine, in so far as it was not restricted to the simple formulas of the catechism, which Péguy distrusted.

What I recall is a minor matter ; I remember that we took it ill that Péguy had Madame Gervaise say that the mother of Christ had become "ugly, frightful to see" as she was climbing up Calvary following her Son. And I still believe we were right.

It is certain that we always expected marvels from Péguy, but not always of the kind he gave us. Youth has reactions which are harsh to the point of injustice, unreasonable demands and hopes ; and in its intact freshness the imagination builds up images which easily eclipse what little reality it has experienced. Doubtless it was thus that we reacted when Jacques was twenty-five. And thus it was that further misunderstandings sprang up between Jacques and Péguy, and were added to their differences — founded in objective reality — of judgement.

However this may be, Jacques' letter to Péguy regarding the

*Mystère de la Charité de Jeanne d'Arc* not only hurt and annoyed Péguy, but also made Jacques' mother terribly angry ;
and all the more so because she had just read Léon Bloy's *L'Invendable* in which our own story was told. . . A deluge of
bitter words rained down upon us, of resentment against the
Church, anger against Bloy, against us.   We were at the heart
of the storm which our adherence to Catholicism had provoked ; a resentment aggravated, it is certain, by the evolution
of Péguy himself, the conversion of Jacques' sister, and the
first symptoms of the conversion of Ernest Psichari — the prelude to several others among Geneviève Favre's intimates, a
phenomenon extremely disconcerting to her and similar to
what happened a little later in the circle about André Gide.

The anxiety which our spiritual evolution caused Jacques'
mother is set forth in her *Souvenirs sur Péguy* :

"This year 1908 went on for me full of surprises and struggles,
of distress which Péguy shared with me without reservation.

"A source of anxiety tortured me ever since my son became
so enthusiastic over the writings of Léon Bloy.

"From Germany where my son and his wife had settled for
two years, what distressing letters I received. . .

"However much two very trustworthy persons . . . could
tell me of Jacques' conversion and that of my daughter-in-law,
I shrank from believing it, I was indignant, convinced that it
could not be."

Jacques had tried in his letters to prepare his mother to understand us, to consent to our adherence to Catholicism ; he
had no success whatever.   He therefore did not mention our
baptism to her when he came to France for several days in
1907.   His mother wrote :

"In 1907 my son spent a few days in France, giving me to
understand that he was interested in spiritual questions, noth-

ing more. The evening of his departure, when I went with him to the Gare de l'Est, I was stupefied to see a priest appear and be very warmly greeted by our dear traveller.

"I returned home extremely upset.

"In the way that a doctor watches the effect of a fever in a sick person, Péguy and Maurice Reclus watched over me, tormented by the consequences of my distress.

"It was then that Péguy would repeat to me : 'O, my children can become priests, ministers, rabbis ; I would not lose any sleep over them. . .' "

Doubtless these are soothing words such as one addresses to ill people or children. Geneviève Favre deserved better. Péguy, perhaps only the very day before, had replied to Jacques' confidence concerning our baptism by the exclamation : "I have come to that too !" Why did he not even try to make Geneviève Favre understand that he shared her son's faith, and that she was not faced with a catastrophe but with a blessing ? Perhaps, however, she felt some hesitation in him, for she adds :

"Was he not hiding his own torment from me ?" But she at once interpreted it thus : "Jacques Maritain on whom he had counted so much to take an exceptional place with the *Cahiers*, perhaps to assume . . . some day, their management . . . was escaping from him. . ."

### Péguy is Wary of Clerics

We therefore had much to suffer on our return from Germany from those who were so dear to us. But this hatred of Bloy, which Péguy also allowed himself to share, caused us more indignation than pain.

Péguy had never read a page written by our godfather ; his injustice toward him therefore was absolutely gratuitous. And

in this way he helped to embitter our relations with Jacques'
mother.  He tried sincerely to improve them, but went about
it in the wrong way, because of his own hesitations.

When after reading *Jean Coste*, Bloy wrote to Péguy expressing his unreserved admiration, Péguy spoke of this to Madame
Favre.

"One evening when I was dining at Orsay ? . . . at Lozère ?
. . . I no longer exactly remember which, Péguy, as he usually
did, accompanied me to the station very early ; we walked up
and down the dark and deserted platform chatting ; suddenly
he spoke of a letter he had recently received from Léon Bloy ;
all my antipathy, all my fears poured out in hurried words. . .
'If you go near that fanatical man, he will strangle your freedom, the integrity of your thoughts ; your whole work will fall
to pieces, and the suffering which tears apart my motherly love
will tear apart our friendship. . .' The train stopped ; Péguy
helped me up into a compartment and standing on the running
board before closing the door, he exclaimed : 'Don't worry ;
I'm not going to see him ; I won't even answer him.' "


A little later Péguy gave us to think that indeed he considered
the unreserved acceptance of the Church by one of his friends
as a loss for himself.   I am alluding to an event of which I will
speak later — the conversion of Ernest Psichari, Renan's grand-
son.   Here again I shall quote Jacques' mother :

"A few days went by (after his return from Mauretania in
December 1912) and there took place the great event of Ernest's conversion.

"An impressive silence on Péguy's part until the morning
when he appeared at my home, his face drawn. . .

" 'We must go into mourning for Ernest ; he is lost to us ;
he is in the clutches of the priests.   All the letters you 've received from me must be bequeathed to Reclus alone, as of
today.   Will you promise me to do this right away ?'

"There was nothing to do but comply.

"Then with infinite sadness he continued : 'How could he, who has always been so marvelously inspired, have come to that ? How could he let his grandfather's enemies triumph in this way ?' "

And, we say in turn, how could Péguy, always so careful to distinguish between politics and mysticism, put on the same plane and compare the triumph — which was in any case quite hypothetical — of Renan's enemies and the accession of a soul to the fullness of faith ? And how could Péguy fail to think that if he himself, in a domestic situation that was exceptionally difficult and delicate, had reasons which sufficed his conscience not totally to accept the discipline of the Church — Ernest Psichari, who was entirely free to dispose of his life, would have had no excuse to refuse the infinite grace of the sacraments. This showed that there was in Péguy's attitude still another cause than the one, entirely exterior after all, of his difficulties with his family. He was so accustomed to look upon everything in the light of temporal debate and in a human and "carnal" perspective, that what he now saw in the conversion of a soul was not a victory of grace, in which he nevertheless believed with all his heart, but a victory on the clerics' side. There he fell into the trap of that old Catholic anti-clericalism which he cherished as a popular French tradition. The shell hid the substance from him, "the clerics" kept him from seeing the Church in its profundity and supernatural reality. To sum up, it was concerning the mystery of the Church that between Péguy, on one side, and Father Clérissac and ourselves on the other, the opposition was fundamental.

Péguy's feeling about Ernest's conversion, which I recalled above, these entirely worldly — and almost academic — considerations in the face of a purely religious event, marked the gravest moment in that spiritual confusion in which Péguy

sought to justify his reserve, now by dwelling upon how exceptional his case was, now by a singular theory regarding "clerics"
and the sacraments. He would say, for example, to Lotte :
"The nuisance is that we must be wary of priests. They do
not have the faith, or else they have it so little. It 's among
laymen that faith is still to be found. Besides, priests are very
smart — the rascals. As they have the administration of the
sacraments, they make believe that sacraments are all there
is. They forget to say that there 's prayer, and that prayer
comes in for at least half ! The sacraments, prayer, those are
two different things. Priests hold the one but we always have
the other." Thus Péguy consoled himself. What did he
know about "clerics" ? He never listened to them, he never
read them ; had he done so, he would have known that they
speak at least as often of the necessity of prayer as of that of
the sacraments. His friend Dom Baillet in his monastery
chanted the praises of God seven times a day. But he too
was a priest, and that by the grace of a sacrament : no doubt
Péguy thought that was a nuisance.*

Dom Baillet was going to die ; it distressed Péguy ; nevertheless he would not go to see him.

"He is in a most serious condition ; he is asking for me," he
said to Jacques' mother ; and she answered :

"If you don't go to your friend, I fear you will regret it terribly."

"Perhaps I would regret it more terribly if I saw him
again. . ."

He never did.

Perhaps he thought Dom Baillet would ask him to act in a
way that he did not wish to. No doubt he was wrong ; he

* He had nevertheless written, several years previously : "Today I can say
without offending anyone that the metaphysics of our teachers no longer has
for us or for anyone else the slightest reality, and the metaphysics of the clerics
has taken possession of our being to such an extent that the priests themselves
should not be allowed to suspect it." (L'Argent.)

did not yet know that saints pray much more than they speak, and much more than they demand.

Dom Baillet died in the last months of 1913. I must go back a little once more. *Le Mystère de la Charité de Jeanne d'Arc* appeared in December 1909, only several months after the beatification of Jeanne d'Arc on April 17th of the same year — a singular synchronism between the Church's devotion and that of Péguy. In January 1910, Jacques told him of his disappointment and Péguy was more sensitive to the criticism of his writing than of himself. Nevertheless when Jacques met him two months later, Péguy received him as his friend and with an open countenance, and spoke to him at length of his difficulties. Here I will go back to Jacques' diary :

". . . The whole Sorbonne is against him, never yet has he waged such battles. . . On the other hand, he has the whole Catholic world standing up for him. Goyau will write an article about him ; Tavernier in the *Univers* ; the Jesuit fathers of the *Etudes* will do a study on him ; Trogan spoke of him in the *Correspondant*, etc. So Péguy suffers because I am not with him in this combat. I told him that I indeed do stand up for him, but from the outside, that my viewpoint was not concerned with this literary battle — it was his soul, his faith that interested me." Péguy then said to Jacques that his position was that of a monk, that he had no understanding of public action. — "Yes, I do," replied Jacques, "but in Jeanne d'Arc's way" — that is to say, with full commitment of himself, a full confession of faith. And I think of Jacques' twenty-six years, of the disgrace of being in the right against a man of more sorrowful experience. Péguy reproached Jacques "of holding more against his friends than against his enemies." "But," replied Jacques, "isn't that the sign of a greater love ?"

In what way was Péguy wrong, in our eyes ? What was this painful and tiring discussion all about ? We thought that a believer owes always to God and to men a clear and forth-

right confession of his faith.   And that the real difficulties
which Péguy encountered in his home did not excuse him
from this.   We thought that the Church is covered from without, as if by a cloak of contradiction, by the defects of its members, engaged and sometimes quite ill engaged, in the affairs
of the world, but that she herself is holy and immaculate, without wrinkle or blemish in her essence, and that the doctrine
she dispenses is the food for which every Christian should
hunger ; and that reformers are unfortunate.   And we reproached Péguy with too easily dispensing himself from religious acts which were lawful for him to perform ; of taking
too many precautions against the Church ; of distrusting in
the name of faith the theological wisdom of which he gloried
in being ignorant.

## Péguy's Vocation

Péguy did have a very deep intuition of one thing : that he
should bear witness to the temporal vocation of a Christian.
This conviction in itself implies the living reality of his faith.
Despite his demonstrations of anti-clericalism he was not a
theorist of secularism ; he was conscious of the mission and the
dignity which belonged to lay persons in the Church and in
Christendom.   It is this which was true and genuine in the
feeling of his particular vocation.   In this is the incomparable
value of his message to be found.   Too closely involved in the
details of his conflicts and his evasions, we saw above all at
this time, what was the human ransom of this message and
vocation.   The essential, the positive, which comes before all
and is the mark of divine predilection was this message and
this vocation.

Several years before his conversion he said one day to Jacques
in the presence of Sorel, who approved : "If Catholics only

knew ! They alone are able to answer the needs of the world ;
they could take the lead in temporal history, nothing could
stand against them ; but they are too dumb for that !"

He who knew what "Catholics" did not "know," considered
too exclusively the work which his prophetic instinct showed
him ought to be done in the world, for temporal Christendom.
He did not know how to balance his very true feeling for his
vocation with the whole of the requirements of Christianity,
and he sacrificed to it the obligations to which all are held ;
he allowed it to drag him into a sort of anti-theological passion (in which he had been preceded by Descartes). No doubt
it was to this that his long delay in approaching the sacraments
was due in the last analysis. This in my opinion is the central
point from which everything should be considered. Nothing
is more false than to make of him a rebel, a visionary, or an
impenitent free-thinker. He was a Catholic of deep faith,
a man of prayer absorbed by the idea of the temporal task of
the Christian, of his own temporal work to be accomplished,
and of his mission in the world of carnal realities, and who was
in a way left unbalanced in the midst of difficulties that were
too great, and by heart-rending conflicts.

### Break and Reconciliation

Péguy's bitterness increased. For the first time, in May
1910, he wrote Jacques a "silly and mean letter" regarding the
admirable essays by Father Clérissac on Jeanne d'Arc (but
which were in the form of sermons) which Father Baillet had
sent him. "I see," Jacques noted harshly in his turn, "I see
that the hatred of 'intellectual formulas' can very well conceal
a hatred of the truth." Péguy's innate anti-intellectualism
was to show itself more and more, whereas the young philoso-

pher was to turn in a decisive manner toward the intellectual realism of Aristotle and Saint Thomas.

Nevertheless Péguy regretted his letter, and when several weeks later Jacques passed by the shop of the *Cahiers* he found a "very amiable, gentle and conciliatory" Péguy who, with almost too great a humility (but was it not then a case of the poor-sinner theory?) hastened to declare that "there was still much to do, that he did not clearly understand the intellectual authority of the Church, that there was in him a bad residue, etc. etc." In reality nothing had changed. It was at the time when a great mutual confidence reigned between Péguy and Jacques' mother. It was the time when both held against us our Catholicism (which, it appeared, was not the same as Péguy's), our poor suffering godfather, and down to Jacques' philosophical independence. In the view of his mother the latter had three clearly indicated models to follow : in politics — his grandfather Jules Favre ; in religion (since religion came into it) — Péguy ; in philosophy — Bergson. The disappointment of Jacques' mother took a long time to heal.

After we settled in Versailles we saw less and less of Péguy. Péguy's motives for the policy of his *Cahiers* escaped us more and more. And when — in May 1912, I believe it was — Péguy published Julien Benda's *L'Ordination* which nothing in any way entitled to a place in the *Cahiers de la Quinzaine*, our surprise and our pain knew no bounds. We did not blame Benda so much as Péguy. Benda meant nothing to us ; we had neither then nor ever admired him in any way. But how could Péguy be mistaken to this point ? Jacques returned his copy of *L'Ordination* to Bourgeois, the manager of the *Cahiers*, asking him in those quite ungentle terms of which he holds the secret and which I refrain from citing literally, not to inflict such books upon us in the future. Péguy, in a fury, claimed and told, that we had withdrawn our subscription — a major crime, but an unjust reproach — and ceased to send us the *Cahiers*. This time the break was real ; * it was to last for nearly three years and Péguy did not spare Jacques in the meantime. Their friendship was renewed, as I have said above, a very short time before the war of 1914, as if Péguy and we had the premonition that a total reconciliation was mysteriously called forth by the supreme illumination of faith in Péguy's soul, and by the tragic events which were to come.

## Péguy's Last Mass

It is not for the purpose of bringing to light our personal relations with Péguy during the last six years of his life that I have written these pages ; it is in order to add to the story of Charles Péguy those things that we were able to know of his religious difficulties. These were hard and bitter to his soul ; but his soul, in the midst of these perplexities, never lost hope — that virtue of hope of which Péguy spoke with supernatural conviction. It was because of this hope that he entrusted his family to Our Lady, and that after his death he obtained their conversion to the Catholic faith ; † it was because of it that he went on a pilgrimage to Chartres in June 1912, to keep a vow which he made when his little son Pierre was gravely ill ; and another time still, in 1912 or 1913, together with Alain Fournier (author of *Le Grand Meaulnes*), also killed in the first World War. This virtue grew in him at the first rumours of war. It flared up in a high flame on the day of mobilization, August 4, 1914. Péguy laid down his burden ; he entrusted his family to God and to Our Lady ; he was leaving, as on that same day he

---

* *L'Ordination* was also the main cause of Péguy's break with Sorel, whom Péguy accused of having prevented Benda from obtaining the Goncourt prize in 1912. See Daniel Halévy's *Péguy*.

† With the exception of Marcel, his oldest son, who became a Methodist.

told Geneviève Favre, "as a soldier of the Republic for general disarmament and the last of wars." (Alas, there will doubtless be no last war until the Day of Judgement !) As a soldier he was to live thirty prodigiously real, luminous and heroic days, until his glorious death at the battle of the Marne on September 5, 1914, where he fully accomplished his destiny.

*
*  *

Péguy therefore left Paris on August 4th. His regiment, the 276th Infantry, was taken east, up to the Hauts-de-Meuse.

On August 15th, for the first time since the days of his childhood, Péguy heard mass.*

The 23rd, his regiment received the order to move west. The day before Ernest Psichari had been killed in Belgium ; he, at least, did not know the anguish of that sudden retreat which on September 2nd brought Péguy back to only twenty-four kilometres from Paris !

On September 3rd, Péguy's company camped at Saint-Witz. On the 4th, the whole regiment was allowed to rest. Joffre decided they would attack on the 6th ; his order of the day was read to the soldiers in the courtyard of a farm at Vémars.

On the morning of the 5th, the 276th got under way. . . "It was not that day a question of attacking, but only of forming the army front which would attack on the following day. . ." But the Germans started an attack "to oblige the French to reveal their strength, and to see what was happening. Thus at this precise point on the front, the battle of the Marne began eighteen hours in advance. . ." † The 276th, then, took its battle formation. The 19th company found itself in the neigh-

---

* See above, p. 54, the letter of August 16, 1914, to Mme. Jeanne Garnier-Maritain.

† Daniel Halévy, *Péguy.* Grasset.

bourhood of Villeroy where Péguy was to fall before the day was ended.

\*

\*    \*

Regarding Péguy's last days and his death there exists, among others, a very valuable eye-witness account, written by one of his companions-in-arms — Victor Boudon — who was in the same battalion with him "from the Lorraine to the Marne," in August and September 1914, and who published in 1916 a book bearing precisely this title.    Here are several passages from it : *

"This thoughtful man," writes Victor Boudon, "seemed to foresee a happy conclusion to the terrible war that was beginning.    Everything about him spelled confidence, and until the end the certainty of final success shone on his countenance. . ."

When the struggle began "the youthful and ringing voice of Lieutenant Péguy directed the fire.    Careless of the shots which grazed him, running from one man to another to speed up the firing, leaning for a moment, in order to catch his breath, on a farm roller abandoned on the road, standing upright, courageous, admirable . . . gloriously mad in his bravery. . . He stood as a challenge to gunfire, seeming to call to himself the death which he glorified in his verses.    At that instant a deadly shot pierced his noble forehead.    He fell upon his side, without a cry, with a dull groan. . . When, several metres farther on, leaping like a madman, I cast a glance behind me, I saw stretched there upon the warm and dusty earth . . . the body of our dear, of our brave lieutenant. . ."

A month later Claude Casimir-Périer, who on the evening of September 5th had taken over the command of Péguy's company, wrote to his wife :

* Victor Boudon, *Avec Charles Péguy de la Lorraine à la Marne, Août-Septembre 1914.*    Preface by Maurice Barrès.    Paris, Hachette, 1916.

"Péguy . . . on the day before September 5th seemed to forebode his glorious end. Everyone who came near him felt it as I did. . . The evening before, he had been quartered with his men in an old convent and spent the night heaping flowers at the feet of the altar of the Virgin."

Daniel Halévy explains that this altar of the Virgin was at Saint-Witz, in a chapel of the utmost simplicity. A placard, which Péguy must have read, he says, was attached to the door and gave the story of the origins of the chapel :

"The hill of Saint-Witz was a place of devotion and pilgrimage from time immemorial." During the Revolution, "a statue of the Virgin, venerated by pilgrims, had been hidden in the hay in a barn, and thus saved from the hammers of the impious. In gratitude this statue was left in the barn, which later was consecrated and made into a chapel.

"We cannot doubt that Péguy saw something symbolic in this combination of circumstances. . ."

The faithful Virgin to whom he had entrusted what was dearest to him in the world, together with his own soul, was coming forward to meet him. The *now* and the *at the hour of our death* were no longer separated, and Péguy, who had long felt it sweeter to pray for the second of these than for the first, could now combine them into one same feeling of total abandon.

"All the desires of the pilgrim of Chartres were fulfilled," continues Halévy ; "the war presented itself to him as an immense pilgrimage, at the end of which he found the Virgin, lodged in certainly the most humble and peasantlike of her dwellings in France, where she was waiting to assist him in his decisive trial. All the elements of a poem which Péguy never wrote seemed to have been assembled here by an invisible hand. He gathered flowers, carried them into the consecrated barn, and when evening came and his men were peacefully sleeping, he returned to the chapel for a night of prayer. . . All those

who slept there that night were to die the next day" * at the
dawn of the Victory of the Marne.

### Jesus Christ Dresses as a Beggar

As I set down these recollections I have on two or three
occasions been accompanied in my happy or sorrowful meditation by the melody of a humble popular song to which Péguy
was greatly devoted, and which two or three times I heard him
sing : "Jesus Christ dresses as a beggar : I beg you, give me
alms. . ."
By what miracle came this musical accompaniment ?
It was no miracle ; but a coincidence which was singularly
moving for us.
Mr. Vernon de Tarr, the carillonneur of the Episcopal
Church of the Ascension — the one possessing such a beautiful
fresco by John La Farge — brings twice daily to the peaceful
neighbourhood of New York near Washington Square the most
exquisite choice of classical, Gregorian and popular airs.   And
for several moments twice daily this pure and soothing music
lulls our anxieties and transforms them into a resigned melancholy ; it is one of the few amenities of our exile in this country
of such warmth and hospitality.
I do not know Mr. Vernon de Tarr, and he knows me still
less.   But I note down this singular coincidence and the feeling of gratitude with which it fills me, in order to remember it
as one of our debts to this great city.
It seemed to me that each time the carillon played this air
— an air I never would have expected to hear in New York —
it seemed to me that Péguy appeared to me and saluted also
with his kind and arch glance this America where he is begin-

* Daniel Halévy, *loc. cit.*, pp. 354 and 355.

ning to be known, and his French and Franciscan soul to be
loved.

\*

\*            \*

Jésus-Christ s'habille en pauvre
Faites moi la charité
Des miettes de votre table
Je ferai bien mon dîner

Les miettes de notre table
Les chiens les mangeront bien
Ils nous rapportent des lièvres
Toi tu ne rapportes rien

Madam' qu'êtes en fenêtre
Faites moi la charité
Ah ! montez montez bon pauvre
Bon souper vous trouverez

Après qu'ils eurent soupé
Il demande à se coucher
Ah ! montez montez bon pauvre
Bon logis vous trouverez

Pendant qu'ils montaient les degrés
Un ange les éclairait
Ah ! ne craignez rien Madame
C'est la lune qui paraît

Dans trois jours vous mourerez
En Paradis vous irez

*Et votre mari Madame*
*En enfer ira brûler.**

\* Jesus Christ dresses as a beggar
I beg you, give me alms
From the crumbs on your table
I shall make my dinner

The crumbs from our table
Are for the dogs to eat
They go hunting and bring back hares
But you, you bring back nought

Madame, up there in the window
I beg you, give me alms
Ah ! come up, come up, poor man !
A good supper you will have.

After they had had supper
The beggar asked for a bed
Ah ! come up the stairs, come up, poor man !
A good lodging you will have

As they climbed the narrow stair
An Angel lit their way
Ah ! be not afraid, Madame,
'Tis nought but a moonlit ray

Three days hence you will die
To Paradise you will be borne
While your husband, Madame,
To hell will go to burn.

# CHAPTER FOUR

## The Mercies of God

### My Father's Last Days

The month of February is often for us the bringer of great trials and of spiritual graces.

Thus, exactly one year after the baptism of Pierre and Léon van der Meer on February 24, 1912, my dear father died, and the last three days of his life were lighted and comforted, for him and for us, by the upsurging of divine grace.

At first confounded and afflicted almost to despair by our conversion to Catholicism, our parents had become resigned to it when they saw us so happy in our new life.

In Russia, when a Jew received baptism, it was always, so far as they knew, to obtain equality in civic rights with other citizens. And for these Jews they had deep contempt. But if a Jew in France passed over to Christianity it seemed to them that it could only be in order to separate himself from his people through anti-Semitism, through a horrible treachery toward his great unfortunate family, and this they could not condone, nor even explain.

It was only when they were able to realize the depth of our religious convictions — and the fact that through these my sister and I began to perceive the greatness and the significance of Israel's vocation — that our parents softened a little toward us, and came to consider in themselves the basic reasons for our stand. Nearly three years had to pass before the faintest signs of any change appeared in them. It was toward the beginning of 1910 that we noticed my father's passion for the organ, which often made him enter a church. Now for a Jew like him to go willingly into a church was in itself a sign that he had

ceased to reject Christianity in principle.   How could I have
failed to understand it then ?   And his growing tenderness
toward us ?   On Holy Saturday of that year mother went
with Vera to Notre-Dame in Versailles.   And on Easter Sunday it was Jacques who took my father to the same church.
But apart from these rare occasions we kept a great reserve.
Discreet allusions came rather from my father, by which he
doubtless wished us to understand that Christianity was not
foreign to his thoughts.   As he often did with me, he would
put it in a humorous way : "Who is a little girl three or four
years old, knowing French, Russian and German, and who's
been married for five years ?"   It was naturally myself, and
this meant that he understood that the life of the spirit begins
from baptism.

There were a few rare conversations about Christianity with
my mother, who always listened to me sweetly.   After all, this
kind of Christianity seemed acceptable to her — not for herself, of course !   She who knew Judaism so well would never
consent to be baptized !   We shall see, thought the God of
the Jews, and smiled. . .

God is patient ; his creatures are much less so.   It happened
that we had sometimes to repair the disastrous consequences of
the awkward eagerness of our best friends in regard to our parents.   Had not Madame Bloy written them at the very time
they were most painfully upset about us : "You have crucified
Our Lord Jesus Christ . . ."   This sweeping style was unknown
to people of my parents' simplicity and they took it literally ;
they were deeply scandalized.

Another time the Bloys were lunching with us ; when the
time came to say grace, which Bloy never omitted, he suddenly
took mother's hand and tried to make her make the sign of the
Cross.   My mother was deeply wounded, and for a long time
we suffered the consequences.   That was because for a Jew
to make the sign of the Cross was to perform a serious religious
act which engaged one's soul and broke with the Torah.

The years passed without bringing anything decisive. In 1911 my parents moved near us, in Versailles. From time to time a few words spoken casually by my father showed me he was thinking of religious problems. I finally decided, trembling for fear of acting at the wrong moment, to give them a catechism in Russian. A little later he asked me questions which proved that he was reading it; he asked me one day what was the meaning of the sin against the Holy Spirit.

February 2, 1912. My father fell gravely ill, and soon the physician considered his case to be hopeless. We lived through days of sorrow and anguish. It was the first time that death was coming to one of those I loved — and how I loved him ! It seemed to me that I had always carried his soul in my soul, as though it were my task to defend one who was so defenceless because of his simplicity and goodness. And now I had to defend him against death, against the shadows and the anguish of death. He was so dear to all three of us ! And he loved us so much ! He loved Jacques with a special love ; he understood as with a prophetic instinct the value of a soul which had still to prove itself. In his pain and sickness did he not depend upon Jacques as he did upon Vera and me for help in the ways of truth and in the face of death ? Did he not have the right to depend on us — we who claimed to know these things ? We felt this obscurely. But what should we say to him ? Was he thinking of baptism — this baptism in which his children had found certitude and joy ? Just what did he believe ? For two weeks he kept a stubborn silence. Perhaps he hoped he would recover. By interfering would we not add to the pangs of death and to the sufferings of his illness ? Must we have such terrible courage ? But perhaps he was already thinking of death, and waiting perhaps for God to give him the strength to face it by giving him faith ?

Jacques put this question to mother, to my poor mother, in her despairing grief. She protested, saying that her husband

would never consent to be baptized.   The following day, I in
turn approached her with the same question ; she answered me
in the same way as she had Jacques.   We both wept and
sobbed, away from the sick-room, in the little kitchen of the
apartment, and through my tears I tried to give her a quick
outline of apologetics.   I tried to make her understand the
meaning of baptism and to show her in Catholicism the fulfillment of the Jewish religion.   But she felt that such an
interpretation was mine alone.   "Nobody believes as you do,"
she said.   We realized that she was not really aware of her
husband's thoughts on Christianity.   We must therefore speak
to our father.   Jacques said a few words to him on the subject.
My father answered that he could not talk of these things in
French ; he would speak of them with me when he was well.

We prayed to all the saints in Paradise — to Saint Barnabas,
our patron at baptism, and especially to Notre-Dame de la
Salette — that our father would recover, that God would give
him the time to understand. . . And how terrible it was to
risk disturbing him when he was so ill !

As we were praying for him thus, there came upon each of us
a feeling of sweetness and hope ; and Jacques understood that
in the order of grace we could ask for anything.

But our father was not to recover.   On February 21st, going
into his room early in the morning, Jacques saw on his face the
signs of death.   He sent word to the physician — our friend
Dr. Legrain.   I arrived in the meantime.   My father was
breathing with difficulty, and there was a dull film over his
eyes.   He appeared to be scarcely conscious.

When the doctor arrived, toward ten o'clock, my father
rallied a little and asked us to leave him alone with him.   We
left the room.

After several minutes Dr. Legrain opened the door.   He
appeared very much moved, and said to us : "Come in, you
have a very good father !"

My father was sitting up in bed, his face grave and calm. He explained what had happened : "I asked the doctor to tell me the truth about my condition. He said to me : Only a miracle can cure you.

"I asked him : Doctor, do you believe also ? He knelt beside me and said : Yes.

"And since he has told me the truth about my illness, I wish to prepare myself ; I wish to be baptized."

He turned toward his wife as if to ask her consent ; he hoped, he said, that he was not causing her grief. My mother, in tears, replied that she was opposed to nothing.

We all believed that death was imminent. Dr. Legrain knelt beside the patient who became his godson and mine ; Jacques took a bottle of La Salette water and baptized him "in the name of the Father, and of the Son, and of the Holy Ghost." He was called Jude-Barnabas. The peace of God descended upon him and us and filled us with joy.

Jacques ran to get Vera. She was not well, and not knowing that things would happen so quickly that morning, we had let her rest. As soon as father saw her, he said, "My little girl, are you happy ?" He was happy and beaming ; there was a gentle light in his eyes, so dull a moment ago. "I am happy," he said to my mother. "It is as though a great weight had been lifted from my heart — an Eiffel Tower." It was Ash Wednesday, the 21st of February 1912.

Thus our intervention which had caused us so much anxiety was justified. There only remained to try every means for his bodily cure. My father's physical transformation was so great that we thought he was going to recover.

Spiritually we asked for nothing more. The gift of innocence was in him, by the grace of God, and we thought that baptism would produce in him for the moment no more outer effects than it does in a child.

But suddenly we heard him say that he wished to receive all

that the Church gave to the sick, and that he wanted to see a priest "who would not let him sleep" and who would talk with him for two or three hours ! He said this playfully. He also wished to have Mgr. Gibier, the bishop of Versailles, come to see him. After that he declared : "Now you must put my medals around my neck !" (He had in his purse a medal of the Blessed Virgin called "the miraculous medal" and a medal of Saint Benedict we had given him a long time before and which he had accepted with kindliness ; we added a little cross and a medal of La Salette.)

He then said : "How do I pray ? I don't know how to read" (in French, he meant). I gave him a leaflet on which I had written in French, but with Russian characters, the Our Father, and the Act of Love. I knelt beside him ; he asked for his glasses and spelled out painfully, with deep gravity, the holy words, while I helped him a little by translating certain passages. I asked him if he forgave his enemies ? "Oh, yes," he replied, smiling.

The little paper containing his first prayers he guarded lovingly, and placed it over his heart. He sought it at night, he extended his hand toward it as he was dying, and dead he kept it pressed on his breast.

Finally, that same Ash Wednesday morning, he asked me to teach him how to make the sign of the Cross. Thus he took his first steps in the Christian life. And we will never forget the grave recollection with which he slowly crossed himself, carefully pronouncing the words, "In the name of the Father, and of the Son, and of the Holy Ghost."

In obedience to my father's wish, Jacques went to find one of the priests at the Cathedral, our friend Father Courtellemont, whom he told of the situation. My father had a long conversation with the priest, and then received the sacrament of penance. On leaving the room the young priest, who was much moved, told us that he found the ill man remarkably well instructed and "in such good dispositions that one could not refuse him anything" ; the following day he would bring him communion and give him extreme unction.

My father passed a rather good day. The day following, February 22nd, he received the Eucharist and extreme unction. And not knowing how to unite himself to the prayers of the Church, and wishing wholeheartedly to manifest his faith, he covered himself with great signs of the Cross all during the ceremony, his hand sweeping from his forehead to his knees and from one shoulder to the other.

My mother was present, and all in tears. Then my father said to her, "I will pray for you, so that you may be with me." And a little later, "The children won't say anything to you." Indeed there was no need to "say" anything ; my father's prayers were doubtless enough ; and my mother's religious evolution took place slowly and gently.

This day again seemed to bode good for the patient. He remained peaceful. The following day, Friday the 23rd, the Bishop of Versailles came to give him the sacrament of confirmation ; profoundly touched by the faith and confidence of the dying man, Monseigneur Gibier wept with us all, and said to him : "You are now a soldier of God."

Thus provided — in three days he had received everything, and was radiant with the light of the sacraments — my dear father serenely entered his last hours, occasionally visited by a mild delirium during which he expressed desires of recovery. Several times he said to us that he was happy and that we should be happy too.

We were all beside him, with mother ; but I went from one room to another, unable to bear seeing him die.

Jacques never left him ; he was right beside him, by the bed. In the very last minutes, at dawn on Saturday, February 24th, a little before four o'clock, he heard him say : "My God, save my life !" Jacques suggested to him gently : "My God, I give you my life," and my father repeated : "My God, I give you my life." Thus he gave his last breath.

His face was beautiful and noble ; the room was filled with sweetness. We were worn out as though after a combat in which all the strength of the body and soul had been strained to the extreme limit ; in our sorrow we were strengthened by the divine peace which filled our father's heart until the end.

My dear Jacques had a splendid funeral for him accompanied by beautiful music, having remembered that it was to hear the organ that my father had first entered a church. The Bloys were there with us ; and our new friends who were as brother and sister to us, Pierre and Christine, and Léon van der Meer.

### Elisabeth-Marie

My father's conversion left mother troubled and irritated with us. This lasted a while, after which all her tenderness for us returned. Living with us from then on, she was closely bound up with our life. Of a very sociable nature, she was happy to see our friends, priests and laity, and she loved them as we did. For many years she heard priests and religious — Abbé Millot, Father Lamy, Abbé Charles Journet, Father Garrigou-Lagrange, Abbé Altermann, Father Vincent Lebbe, Mgr. Vladimir Ghika, Charles Henrion, Father Bernadot . . . speaking in our home of the marvels wrought by God and Mary ; Henri Ghéon reading to us nearly everything he had written since his conversion ; Jacques explaining the philosophy and theology of Saint Thomas Aquinas during the meetings of our Thomist circle. She loved the fervour, the gravity and intention of these meetings even if she was not able to follow the discussions. When the privilege of a private chapel was given us, she attended the masses that were celebrated there. She did not make the sign of the Cross and did not kneel ; she remained respectfully standing, and prayed in her heart in her own way, without separating herself from us. For thirteen whole years she lived with us in this way, and not once during that time did we speak directly to her of religious questions. Our father's words, "the children won't say anything to you," no doubt influenced us. Nevertheless we wished ardently to see her become a Christian and we asked God that this come about at a peaceful time, when she was in good health, at a time when the cruel spectre of death would not be hanging over her. . . This, in fact, is what happened.

It is not my intention to speak at length now of those things that happened so long after the time of our life in Versailles, which forms the subject of this book. But as I do not know if it will be given to me to speak of them later, I wish at present to give the main facts.

The first person who put a direct question to our mother on the subject of baptism was a holy priest, who was probably simply a saint — Father Lamy, pastor of La Courneuve. We had first met him in 1921, on Holy Thursday of that year. Ever since we were living in Meudon, he came to say mass in our chapel on great feastdays. So it was that we had the happiness of having him with us on December 24th and 25th, 1924. That day he confided to us that two weeks earlier, finding himself alone with mother, he had asked when she would become a Catholic, and she had amiably replied, "A little later." My mother did not mention this short conversation to us, and we did not ask her any questions.

Two months later, Prince Vladimir Ghika, who had been ordained a priest only eighteen months earlier, came back in haste from Rome (where he had been called upon a tragi-comic affair about which I may not speak) in order not to miss celebrating mass in our home on the anniversary of my father's death — February 24th. He asked our permission to ask mother the same question that Abbé Lamy had asked her on December 10th. He did so after mass. This time she was touched, and spoke to me about it. Without making any promises she had replied to Prince Ghika that she would do the will of God. After that day mother often asked me about this and that point of doctrine. She had books in the Russian language, the catechism my father had used and the New Testament. She was more tender towards me than ever. I continued not to intervene, unless she wished it. She was in peace, and we also. It appeared that nothing was to happen quickly.

The first binding thing she said was three months later, on May 26th. "I will read all this [she was referring to prayers] because I must prepare myself, mustn't I ?" On Sunday, June 7th, the feast of the Blessed Trinity, mother told me of a dream she had had the preceding night. "The Pope was standing before me, dressed in white. He gave to Jacques, for me, something white which seemed to be *one* bird, but was *three* (she stressed the numbers which I have underscored). And Jacques was to give them to me, and I was very near Jacques." Mother was much affected to learn that this very day was the feast of the Blessed Trinity — she did not know it. Her dream had deeply impressed her, although she had not attached any special meaning to it.

The following days were filled for us with happy events ; it was like the extraordinary flowering of a spiritual summer : the foundation of the *Roseau d'Or* series. The confession and communion of Jean Cocteau. Satie who was very ill had gone to confession and received communion several times before his death on July 2nd. Jacques saw him for the last time on June 29th ; Satie had gone to sleep, and Jacques had remained beside him praying in a low voice. Then Satie had awakened and he had said to Jacques very gently these words : "It is good to be together like this, without saying anything, especially when we think alike."

Finally on July 29th, towards evening, I found mother down-

ELISABETH-MARIE

RAÏSSA MARITAIN

stairs in the dining-room reading the Epistle of Saint James, a happy and peaceful look on her face. Perhaps she was reading these verses : "Every good gift and every perfect boon is from above, it cometh down from the Father of Lights, in whose shining is no change such as maketh the shadow to turn."

"It is very beautiful," she said to me. "Yes, mother, and now you know many things." "Do you think so ?" she said, and then, "So you think I 'm ready ?"

All of us were around her, a little delirious with joy. She told us that for the last few days she had been troubled, but that very day all anxiety had left her and she had resolved to be baptized. She asked that it be by our friend Father Millot, vicar general of Versailles. He was a priest whose simplicity was angelic and who loved the Blessed Virgin in the manner of Saint Bernard. Our mother's choice touched us deeply. And the sympathy between them was reciprocal. Father Millot did not wish her to wait for baptism for more than two or three days ; Jacques would be her godfather and I her god mother, and to her name, Elisabeth, she added the name of Mary. Thus she was baptized on Sunday, August 2nd, at five o'clock in the afternoon, in our chapel on the second floor, while on the floor below were gathered our friends, who had not been warned and who knew nothing of what went on, and who were merely surprised by the profusion of roses in our living-room. With our hearts brimming with happiness we came down around six o'clock, keeping mother's secret so that she would have some time of peace and silence.

She was happy, her health was excellent. God had given a marvelous answer to our prayers ; He had heard those of our father who had said to his wife several hours before dying : "I will pray for you, so that you will be with me." She was now with him in the Church of God ; and for seven blessed years she was to live in the faith and innocence of her baptism, ceaselessly praying for her children.

## ELISABETH-MARIE

Oh se peut-il que se défasse ton doux visage
dans le nuage de tes cheveux d'argent
Et que jamais plus je ne baise tes petites
mains diligentes ?
Sur l'humble royaume de ta maison tu as
régné avec sagesse
Et nous ne fûmes jamais que des enfants
pour ta tendresse.
Tu avais dans ta mémoire les plus beaux
chants de l'Ukraïne
Et des neumes de Synagogue ornés à l'infini
Et dans ta voix passaient des regrets et des
peines
En longs soupirs où s'apaisait la mélodie.

\*
\* \*

Ton grave esprit fit lentement le chemin de
l'Ancien au Nouveau Testament
D'Elisabeth à Marie.
O ce jour enfin où tu nous dis, l'Evangile
ouvert sur tes genoux — je suis prête.
Ton visage paisible brillait, la vie entière nous
parut un jour de fête.
Tu pris ta place à la chapelle comme une
enfant
Silencieuse en oraison ou murmurant des
rosaires
Cœur recueilli de la maison cœur vigilant
Dieu te fit don de sept années de vie et de
prière.

## ELISABETH-MARY

O could it be that your gentle face is vanishing
    in the cloud of your silver hair
And that never more may I kiss your little
    diligent hands?
Over the humble kingdom of your house you have
    reigned in wisdom
And we were never more than children
    to your tender love.
The enchanting songs of the Ukraine
    lingered in your memory
And the neumes of the Synagogue in their infinite adornment
And through your voice regrets and
    sorrows came to us from the ages
In long sighs in which melody grew calm.

*
*    *

Your grave mind slowly travelled the way from
    the Old Testament to the New
From Elisabeth to Mary.
O that day when at last you said to us, the Gospel
    open on your knees — I am ready.
Your peaceful face alight, the whole of life
    seemed to us a feast-day.
You took your place in the chapel like a
    child,
Silently in orison, or murmuring
    Hail Marys
Thoughtful quiet heart of our home O watchful heart
God granted you seven years of life and of
    prayer.

Un matin de mai tout finit, un samedi le jour
    de la Vierge
Et tu parus attendre la dernière onction
Pour dans un baiser d'abandon
Unir tes lèvres et mourir.

*

\*     \*

Dans la robe claire que tu as aimée,
    une mantille sur tes cheveux fins
A tes pieds un bouquet de roses, et le chapelet
    entourant tes mains,
Je te verrai toujours si doucement dormir.
Sommeil absolu, recueillement corporel
Corps immobile et qui diffuse le silence
Présence tout à coup d'une vie totale comme
    un astre
Conclusion du lent travail de l'âme et de la
    grâce
La Sagesse a bâti cette maison — c'est l'évidence.
    Et ce corps est sacré.
C'est pourquoi la paix qui l'environne est si
    douce et si déchirante
Et absorbante comme un gouffre.
Je n'ose regarder la fenêtre de ta chambre
Où tu te penchais pour nous voir dans le jardin
Et le soir quand nous montons il n'est plus
    nécessaire
De baisser la voix pour préserver ton sommeil.
Le bruit que nous faisons nous est toujours
    un dur rappel
De ton absence
Et de ton repos éternel.

One May morning all was ended, a Saturday
    the day of the Blessed Virgin
And you seemed to await the last anointing
So as in a kiss of abandonment
To close your lips and die.

                 \*

        \*        \*

In the bright dress you have loved,
    a mantilla over your fine hair
Roses at your feet, and the rosary
    about your hands,
I shall always see you ever so gently sleeping
Consummate sleep, bodily serenity
Stone-still body diffusing silence,
All at once is present a life whole
    as a compact star
Conclusion of the slow labour of soul and
    grace
Wisdom built this house — this is plain.
    And sacred is this body.
That is why the peace about it is so
    sweet and heart-rending
Drawing one like an abyss.
I dare not look at the window of your room
Where you leaned to watch us in the garden
And in the evening when we go upstairs
    we have no longer
To lower our voices to keep from waking you.
The noise we make is always for us
    a harsh reminder
Of your absence
And of your eternal repose.

# CHAPTER FIVE

## ERNEST PSICHARI

### The Call of the Army

If Charles Péguy's conversion, after a moment of happy surprise and a period of pure joy, was strangely to become a cause of a grievous misunderstanding between us, to the point where, at one time, there remained of our friendship nothing but fidelity — the conversion of Ernest Psichari was to be for Ernest and for Jacques a tightening of those fraternal ties which had bound them since their college days, and was to give us the overwhelming spectacle of the grandeurs of grace working in a magnanimous and simple heart, in a free and chivalrous soul.

I have already mentioned the atmosphere of liberalism and elegance in which Ernest grew up.* The fame of Renan, his mother's father, and the enlightened solicitude of his parents, surrounded him with an atmosphere of easy happiness. He knew almost all of the younger celebrities of the France of that period, among them writers, scientists and political men, who came to the hospitable home of the Psicharis.

Every door was open to him as was every heart; it seemed he would succeed in anything he undertook, and every opportunity was given him to develop the rich qualities of his mind and soul. And in truth he *was* successful in everything, but along the line of other ambitions, expectations and events; in everything he was successful, even in despair and in death. For from mortal despair he arose to life; in his hard and self-sacri-

* See *We Have Been Friends Together.*

96

ERNEST PSICHARI

ficing life he walked in the ways of truth, and through his bloody death he rose to the purest glory.*

*

*      *

Swift are the milestones of this brief, full life. The first rebuff his fate reserved for him crumbled with one blow the entire edifice of his happiness. Despair over his first love — his first and only love — surrounded his heart with dark shadows. He left the peaceful home of his childhood and wandered through the streets of Paris trying to find some manual labour. Having scarcely any money he became familiar with the sordid rooming houses of the poor ; he tried to lose in a life of infamous debauchery the memory of both his happy existence of the past and his pure love. But he could not forget ; disgust added itself to his despair and made him prefer death. He drank a vial of poison. A friend arrived in time to bring him back to life. "But," relates his sister, Henriette, "Ernest, coming out of the night in which he thought he would be engulfed, was seized with a fit of hatred for life. . . He had one more resource, and hastily took from his pocket a revolver. The two young men struggled in the half-darkened room, silently, hand to hand ; the slightest false movement would have caused the weapon to go off as they brutally snatched it from one another. At last it fell to the floor. Ernest saved, but with his strength gone, collapsed into the arms of his friend."

Ernest recovered slowly from his crisis of despair. He passed long months of complete solitude in the country ; he became

---

* I shall have to quote throughout this chapter, and I shall do so without further reference, from the pages of Jacques Maritain on Ernest Psichari in *Antimoderne* ; *Notre Ami Psichari*, by Henri Massis ; *Ernest Psichari, mon frère*, by Henriette Psichari ; *Souvenirs sur Péguy*, by Geneviève Favre ; *We Have Been Friends Together*.

familiar with suffering and learned to live with it. He then considered his future and decided on his destiny. In his mind he separated himself from the elegant existence he had known until the age of eighteen or nineteen, and in which he was threatened with dilettantism. He was now twenty. Without listening to any advice, aware only of a superior instinct in his own mind, he made the only decision which at that time could have been salutary for him. A lone wanderer, he surmounted by his own strength the disintegrating forces which had been devouring him.

"Any other young man, going through such a grave crisis, would have allowed religion to come to his rescue," writes his sister Henriette. "Ernest never thought of it. Ernest knew nothing about religion. He considered it an historical phenomenon . . . in his eyes it was a class-room abstraction ; he still did not know what could be the power of faith."

However, "he desires," as Jacques later wrote, "the reform of his entire self . . . to create within himself an inner order, and to become attached to some accepted order acknowledged by man." He therefore sought a school of discipline, a discipline as foreign as possible to his existence up to that time, and he found it in the army. The matter was settled, his decision was irrevocable. He began by anticipating the draft. In 1903 he became a soldier, the humblest among soldiers, a mere private in the 51st Regiment of Infantry. In 1904, to the astonishment of all his friends, to the scandal of the anti-militarist intellectuals who made up the family friends, he signed his re-enlistment in the 51st regulars. "He became a sergeant, but being impatient for action he asked to be transferred to the colonial artillery as a simple gunner. Soon he was given his stripes as sergeant-major and left on a mission to the Congo under a well loved chief, Commander Lenfant. He returned to France in 1908 with the Médaille Militaire, after a tremendous trip across the basin of the Sangha and the plain of

Lake Chad. . . He then entered the artillery school at Versailles which he left in September 1909 as second lieutenant.
Immediately afterwards he went to Mauretania from which he
returned only in December 1912, after having, during a solitude
of three years, travelled the most beautiful of spiritual itin-
eraries."

So six years passed during which he saw more each day that
his decision was being justified. He had not been mistaken
in seeking salvation through discipline. What sustained him
during all this time and gave him an aim in life was certainly
not just the power of forgetting, and the distraction brought by
rigid regimentation and the harassing fatigue of army life — it
was the intuition he had had from the very beginning of the
formative and spiritual value of discipline freely accepted in
order to serve an unselfish aim. He had foreseen that his
soul would be strengthened in this way ; that his power of
determination would be fortified. "We are of those who
burn to submit in order to be free," he wrote in *Les Voix qui
crient dans le Désert*. For him the ultimate fruit of his obedience as a soldier was liberty, spiritual liberation. The army
was a school of the will, a strengthening of one's free will ; a
school of self-sacrifice also, offering a wide field to the generosity of a great heart. Is not the whole army essentially devoted to the good of something other than itself, to the good
of the country ? (This is not always so — as we know — and
so much the worse for those who, being a part of it, think only
of furthering their own career or renown ; but Ernest never
thought of these vicissitudes.) Ernest looked upon the army
from the viewpoint of a mystic (in the sense in which Péguy
uses this word), that is, he saw it as it should be if the best
of its essence were realized. He devoted to the subject an
enthusiastic book — *L'Appel des Armes* — which is "in praise
of a return to the virtues of the military order, of discipline and
action, of a return to love of France." Ernest, it is true, ac-

cords to the army a slightly more beneficent power than its nature possesses. Later he was to understand this. For the time being the army was his Church. But later he was to acknowledge that this "poor book" dated from the time he was awaiting "the light which heals and saves without doing anything to merit it." However, he could write with all sincerity in *L'Appel des Armes* :

"When the writer of this account took his first steps in the armed service of France, it seemed to him that he was starting a new life. He really felt that he was leaving the ugliness of the world and was passing the first milestone on a road which would lead him to more pure heights."

And later, in *Les Voix qui crient dans le Désert* :

"We know what the submission of a soldier means. We know too that it is a symbol of a higher submission." This truth he began very early to understand.

## The Call of a Friend

In the beautiful and moving book which she wrote about her brother, Henriette Psichari tells how each October when school reopened young Ernest "had already unfailingly singled out from among his thirty-odd classmates the one who was to become his intimate friend for that year. . . The family, accustomed to this procedure, accordingly welcomed the following Sunday the one elected for that year. Only Ernest's father would remark a little critically and sarcastically : 'Well, say, how about So-and-So we used to see so much of last year ?' . . .

"It was no surprise then, when at the beginning of his fifteenth year, Ernest announced that he had met such a 'swell fellow' who was so incredibly intelligent that already after a few days, a truly brotherly friendship existed between them. No one believed him, but it was true. Ernest, proud of his find, immediately introduced his new friend to his parents, and in the evening anxiously tried to find out about the impression he had made. This time he had made no mistake ; all were of the same opinion ; the new friend was perfect."

The friendship which from that day on bound Ernest and Jacques never diminished. Jacques was as enthusiastic about Ernest as Ernest was about Jacques. The latter was a year older and exercised over Ernest "the incontestable right of seniority." Their very different dispositions were absolutely congenial ; their qualities complemented rather than opposed each other. They were alike in an equal capacity for enthusiasm, an equal love for ideas, and an equally non-religious education. From the beginning their affection was very deep. According to an invariable trait in his character, Jacques surrounded Ernest with solicitude ; when Jacques was ill Ernest was beside himself. On one grave occasion he braved the danger of contagion ; nothing could stop him from entering the room where the invalid lay ill of smallpox.

"Boy, you 're sure swell ! But you must beat it ! I 'll write you," murmured Jacques.

As for Jacques, he triumphantly introduced his precious friend to his mother, by whom Ernest was immediately adopted and forever cherished as a son. The happiness of the two friends remained undisturbed during a period of three years in which literary, philosophical, political and social discussions, in addition to their studies, sufficed to fill their lives.

But now they were eighteen and nineteen years old ; Ernest fell in love with Jacques' sister, who could not reciprocate his love, and this meant the shattering of his youthful existence.

Jacques was desperate over Ernest's despair. What agony he suffered, fearing the worst, and not without reason ! With all his devoted strength he tried to help Ernest overcome his dreadful suffering. But what can friendship do against the

magical enchantment of love ?    Helplessly he had to witness
the havoc wrought in Ernest's soul, watch him sink into "those
days without light," watch him withdraw from his influence
and from the affection of his own family.

Once the supreme crisis had been passed, Ernest's decision to
go into the army brought to Jacques if not a great deal of joy,
at least a certain sense of relief.    While Ernest was training to
become a soldier we were living through our own drama.    In
1905 we made the acquaintance of Léon Bloy, and in 1906 we
became Catholics.    Ernest knew nothing of our evolution ;
we had wished to follow our adventure to the very end — alone.
About two months before our baptism, Ernest departed exult-
antly for the Congo ; we ourselves left for Heidelberg in the
month of August.    Since he had begun to live the life of the
Faith, Jacques dreamt of the wonderful help Ernest would find
in it.    He never ceased to pray for him ; and at last he thought
the moment had arrived when he could inform him of the
grace that we had received.    He did this doubtless with the
awkwardness of inexperience.    From Heidelberg he sent Ernest a card which ended abruptly with these words :

"I hope that you will return from your solitude believing in
God."

"It nearly gave me a heat stroke," Ernest wrote to his mother
on February 15, 1907, telling her of Jacques' message, and adding : "I think of you so often in this solitude that it keeps me
from thinking of God as good old Jacques would have me do."
And Henriette Psichari, who quotes this letter of her brother,
adds : "Ernest was to remain in a state of astonishment
and bewilderment for many long months over the fact that
Jacques had become a believer."

Jacques, without worrying too much about his friend's reactions, wrote him again, this time from La Salette, where we
were spending several days in June–July 1907 :

"We prayed for you from the top of the holy mountain.    It

seemed to me this beautiful Virgin was weeping over you, and that she wants you. Will you not listen to her ?"

This letter astounded Ernest as had the first, and did but afford him an opportunity of convincing himself of his own irreligious state. However Henriette states that on the steamer which brought her brother to France in January 1908, "he was dreaming of the mysterious postal card, of the unknown God who perhaps some day would be of help to him. From that moment," she says, "Ernest kept feeling the influence of his friend growing in him."

In January 1908, Ernest came back from the Congo with the Médaille Militaire for which Commander Lenfant had recommended him. Here is the "report of the special recommendation concerning Sergeant-major Psichari," which I am quoting because all of Ernest's principal characteristics are mentioned so concisely in it :

"This non-commissioned officer, the youngest of the mission, was given difficult assignments in which judgement, military aptitudes and manly character revealed themselves entirely to his honour. After having worked energetically to procure supplies for the Nana column he went with the detachment of Boubanjidda from Bouala to Leré. His moral energy, his firmness, his sense of justice and his goodness towards the natives assured the success of this column, which was passing through places populated by impressionable peoples. Entrusted from the start with the Penndé column he led it alone from Lai to Dokoula, showing great initiative, energy, devotion, intelligence and care. Sergeant-major Psichari showed great self-possession when passing through rebellious tribes. Always active and ready to face danger, his courage never faltered during the movement of this very large column which was difficult to defend and was constantly exposed.

"On his return to Sangha, after travelling 3,200 kilometres he undertook two reconnoitring expeditions in the Yanghere country whence he brought back careful surveys as well as documents of real scientific usefulness.

"Sergeant-major Psichari has shown initiative and constant activity during the mission. Always on the alert, he gave without stint of the full measure of his endurance, of his energy, of his keen intelligence, of soldierly qualities, and of personal worth. . ."

In Africa Ernest Psichari started his first book, *Terres de Soleil et de Sommeil,* and finished writing it in France. It bears traces of dilettantism and a tendency to paradox which is especially obvious at the end of the book in a hymn to the violence of war. The equilibrium of his soul showed itself as still unstable. One feels it seething, groping for an entirely sure footing, but not yet able to find it. The book was a great success; Maurice Barrès was enthusiastic about it. Jacques was much less so, for he felt its pages were not on a level with his friend's character. So he simply wrote him as follows :

"On reading your pretty book it seemed that in a dream I could see you returning to that far-off land as a real subduer, and under a different guise than that of a soldier."

It is again Henriette who quotes from his letter and adds :

"Ernest no longer shrugged his shoulders, nor wore a skeptical smile. He could feel the presence of something stronger than himself, a height to which in spite of Jacques' exhortations, he could doubtless never attain. So much the worse for him if he could not climb so high, if he could not be more pliable under the fascination which Jacques' influence exerted on him, if he was not yet ready to receive 'what is best in time and in eternity, the peace of God, that peace which the world cannot give.' " *

Immediately on receiving this letter from Jacques, Ernest read it to Henri Massis while they were walking about the

* From Jacques Maritain's letter of December 31, 1908.

streets of Paris on the night of December 31, 1908–January 1, 1909 and no one knows why they began to talk about God.

"Which one of us spoke of God first ? I can no longer remember, but it was then that Psichari mentioned the name of Jacques Maritain, which until then was unknown to me. . . We were going back down the Champs-Elysées which between the banks of its sidewalks and its double chain of lights resembled a large river over which a cold wind was blowing. Psichari stopped beneath a lamp-post, and drawing from his pocket a letter which Maritain had just written him à propos of *Terres de Soleil et de Sommeil,* he remarked : What a frightful idea good old Jacques seems to have ! He sees me going back there in the robe of a missionary."

Massis adds :

"Whatever admiration he may have had for the 'great idea' that filled Maritain's heart, however troubled he was by the conversion of that rich and rare soul, he nevertheless resisted. He could not but admit this to his great friend. At that time, the beginning of 1909, Psichari was not yet ready to listen to him.

"All that I can express to you at the moment," Ernest then wrote to Jacques, "is my attraction toward that beautiful dwelling of the spirit which you would have me enter. Your thought, my dear Jacques, is of so precious an essence that it holds a real fascination for me. I cannot tell you the sensation of delight and refreshing joy that comes over me in reading you or in listening to you. But I must confess to you that it is mainly a physical sensation. I am drawn toward your dwelling, but I cannot enter."

This attraction remained static for the time being. During the eighteen months that he spent in France, before his departure for Mauretania in October 1909, Ernest above all came to a full realization of his military vocation. He was helped by the powerful influence of Péguy for whom he had a pro-

found affection and to whom he dedicated his second book —
*L'Appel des Armes.* But when it appeared in 1913, this book
too indicated a period which had already been passed, one
which was already nearing its end when he began writing it in
1910, at the beginning of his sojourn in Mauretania.

"Psichari was quite soon to realize," writes Jacques, "the
absurdity of seeking in military 'mysticism' the equivalent of
religion, and all that is necessary to man in order to live and
to die. Nevertheless, in view of his own personal history,
it is easy to understand why he had to go through this phase,
and why his apologia of the soldier should not be judged from
the positive and surface standpoint of political and social
realism, but from the standpoint of a realism of the soul, from
the standpoint of heroism and the conquest of an inner harmony."

It was during the three years of his sojourn in Mauretania
that Ernest was to succeed, if not in achieving perfectly this
conquest, at least in becoming receptive to God's gift, to an
invasion of His grace. He gives an admirable account of the
approaches which led to truth within his soul in *Les Voix qui
crient dans le Désert* — which is his own story of his experience ; and in *Le Voyage du Centurion* in which his spiritual
itinerary is recounted in the third person : here it is no longer
*I* who speaks, but Maxence, his prototype.

In order to finish this story of his quest for God, I will resort,
in addition to my personal reminiscences, to the confidences
of Ernest Psichari himself which we find in *Les Voix qui crient
dans le Désert.*

This book describes a double journey : that of the soldier
who at the head of a camel corps rode across the desert of
Mauretania in order firmly to establish French possession and
to win over to his greatly beloved France the support and confidence of the nomads ; and the spiritual journey — the only

one of which I shall speak here — whose point of arrival was the conquest of faith.

## The Call of God

Nevertheless, at the beginning of 1909, nothing seemed to have yet stirred Ernest's thoughts toward any religious preoccupation whatsoever. In the month of October of the same year he left for Mauretania to all appearances quite unchanged. But four or five months later the first pages of *Les Voix* . . . , which dated from the month of February 1910, testified if not to religious stirrings in him, at least to a very significant moral preoccupation. Arriving on February 18th at the outpost of Aleg, where the French flag was floating, Ernest, struck with the beauty of the place, exclaimed : "A magnificent picture . . . which from the very first gave us the key to Africa. I realized that it was to my soul that she would speak rather than to my senses. And here I was vowed by the pure symbol of all that is noblest beneath the skies, to the noblest of spiritual lives.

"What is necessary above all," he adds, "is that this rediscovered land of Africa give me useful counsels. . . I have no stronger desire, no firmer purpose, than now to go across the world, watching myself carefully, decided to conquer myself by force. I will not cross the land of all virtues as a mere tourist, but at all hours I will ask it to give me strength, uprightness, purity of heart, nobility and frankness. . ."

These words give us the key ; give us the tone of that life which would develop within Ernest's soul in the African soil. In that land he felt a singular gravity "to the point of sorrow," in which nothing incited irony or even a smile. "O, no ! I did not laugh in Africa. I know well that I shall not remain a skeptic in it, that I shall *choose*, that every day I shall want to choose. I am not among those who wish to conciliate everything, to love everything. The sensitive souls may leave! Those who are frightened by rough feeling, those who are offended by too great an honesty of heart may quit forever this land of strength and virtue. All who hesitate, all who tremble before too brutal a truth, let them not come to partake of the coarse food of Africa! Here one needs a steady outlook on life, a pure outlook that goes straight before one, an outlook that is youthful, frank and altogether clear."

In speaking of a military post which had been assigned to him on the edge of the cliff of Moudjeria, where he stayed from May 24 to June 12, 1910, he said : "It was there I knew my first hours of real solitude, there that for the first time I reverently listened to the hours falling on the eternal silence of the desert. In this dead land where no man had ever made his dwelling it seemed that I transcended the ordinary limits of life and advanced trembling with dizziness to the edge of Eternity. During the crushing heat of day, while my companions slept beneath their familiar sun, I remained in my tent, my chin on my knees, my heart beating, and with a feeling as of a mysterious expectancy."

At this same period he began to grow suspiciously sensitive, — which seems strange for an unbeliever — with regard to France's reputation as an irreligious country. Whenever anyone seemed to forget in his presence that France was a "Christian power" he was seized with the desire to re-read the histories of Sire de Joinville and to learn once again how the latter conducted himself "in that sweet pilgrimage of the Cross."

A strange thing : it was Moslem contemplatives who made him remember Christianity.

"The rough life of these men of the brush, the austere existence of their contemplatives," he says, "is not so removed from us as one might be tempted to think."

He read a book by Coppolani on the religious brotherhoods of Islam : "Nothing is more interesting than to follow with Coppolani the different stages which lead to mystical perfection, beginning with poverty which is the initial state. . . So many lofty dreams, so much mysticism flourishing in the midst of the twentieth century on the most inhospitable soil in the world, can very well stir us . . . but in the last analysis it is ourselves we find again.   So we prick up our ears when Coppolani quotes the reply of a Sufi to whom a rich man offered money : 'Are you trying to take my name from among the poor at the price of ten thousand drachmas ?' — which he compares to the words of Saint Teresa : 'They have shorn us of the poverty which was our treasure.'   We are here in a familiar land, we are at home."

Had he not covered much ground who, scarcely a year before, had been so troubled by his friend's conversion ?  How did he come to know suddenly that poverty is the basis of Christian perfection, and that contemplation is its living heart ?   The example of the contemplative Moors, the immensity and the emptiness of the desert, the rigorous simplicity of his life as a soldier purged him of all vain thoughts and took him into the ways of divine truth.

He writes : "The great helps to meditation provided by this spiritual land have been utilized by the Moors and they give to this arid soil admirable ornaments.   Why, by transforming such forces to our own measure . . . do we not also try to enrich ourselves, or rather to win back our lost treasures ? . . . We are worth more than the Moors."   He quotes from Gobineau one of the essential maxims of Islam : The ink of scholars is more precious than the blood of martyrs, and he exclaims : "One shudders to imagine what we would be and what France would be, if the theologians of the Occident had proclaimed such a truth.   We are worth more than the Moors. We are worth more than ourselves.   But we need to be warned.

. . . Then, plumbing certain depths, we act like a diver caught in the weeds who, extricating himself with a vigorous kick, rises to the surface, his arms reaching toward the light of the world."

Toward the light of the world. The light which is Christ. From then on, Ernest never ceased to rise toward it from the depths of his wretchedness, although not without moments of weakness, not without feeling again the terrible weight of all these thicknesses of body and soul through which he had to pierce from top to bottom. But He who was drawing him to the light was never again to abandon him until He had brought him as close as possible to His heart in life, and a short time afterwards in death.

And now we come to February 1911. Ernest, who had received orders to leave for the Adrar, arrived at the border of the Tagant and saw the immense plain strewn with rocky reefs which led into Adrar. "On the threshold of new lands I felt my heart swell with the dawn, and like the sound of a gigantic wing I heard life itself in flight."

A young Moor who bears one of the finest names of Islam — Mohammed Fadel Oued Mohammed Roulam — who had a cultivated mind and was eager to learn, accompanied Ernest during the long journey to the Adrar. The conversation always came back to religion. "Ours preoccupied him greatly," said Ernest. "One day he asked me with real anxiety if the French believed in only one God or in three." The two companions were equally serious. "Besides, who could smile in such a country? . . . Day by day our journey prepared us gradually for the Adrar. . . Already at El Argoub the terrain was so rough that it seemed out of harmony with the human form. Nothing is tolerated there but lofty thoughts of glory, virtue, and pride. Even they do not seem sufficiently rarefied. There should be music, and it should be coming from heaven rather

than from the earth. . . So here we are, preparing to cross the
threshold of the Adrar, that district of the purest grandeur. . .
We are entering the very heart of this strange bulge of granite
where silence and death reign as master . . . where there grows
not even a tree or a blade of grass. . . One's heart is wrung and
drowned in sadness before these brutal masses from which
life seems to have forever fled. . . And all is still — save the
wind which blows from one year's end to the other. . . This
wretched land, where we ourselves are so wretched, yet has a
singular virtue of excitement. One feels one is rising above
one's self. . . This is the land of the mystical aura, which
makes us tremble a little. . . Look at it : it's a perpetual
groan, an endless lamentation. It is mangy, cleaned, washed
and washed anew, scraped to the bone by the wind. . . As we
approach lands we do not know, we discover great unexplored
regions in our own hearts." Ernest noticed that in this destitution he was at home, that he was at ease in this desolation.
"This absolute simplicity . . . this absolute ruggedness are
virtues which we love, and in which we love to move." There
Ernest felt that he knew the meaning of fidelity : "We are
not rebels, we even love these familiar gentle chains" which
bind us "to the grandeurs of the world."

But then suddenly he thought : "Why have we abandoned
so much, been guilty of so many betrayals . . . why should
we reject the Church ?"

In his long conversations with Mohammed Fadel he wanted
to remain "French" and quite naturally, and with the same
impulse he spoke of Christ as a Christian, "and I should have
felt the greatest shame," he said, "not to have done so." He
recalled those conversations "as the strangest thing in the
world. I did not have the faith and I spoke as one who believed, and yet I did not have the feeling I was lacking in sincerity. For the first time I realized how Christ bound me to

Him, as though despite myself and without my knowing it."

How quickly day began to break in this sincere heart "swelling with the dawn" !   From then on Ernest was without ceasing to progress in Light.   Was it not the seed of supernatural truth, given to him by his long-ago baptism received in the cradle, which wished to live, forcing itself toward the sun of grace that had been lost ?

However, he continued on his way in the desert, magnificently carrying on his calling as a soldier.   "In the nameless regions where I am going, the immensity is swept by evenly-blowing winds.   All wish to teach me what is known on this earth about the infinite."   *The spirit of God is borne upon the waters.*   These words kept coming back to him as he "swayed monotonously on his camel during the long hours of the day," and he thought, when seized with dizziness during the sand storms : "The spirit of God is borne upon the sands. . ."

He also meditated much during those indescribably peaceful hours of morning, on "the Roman centurion Christ praised the very day He entered Capharnaum.   *In Israel I have not found so great faith. . .*   Thus a modest lieutenant of the Roman legions surpassed in love those of the race chosen among all others !"   And one feels the joy, the pride with which he said :

"We also are centurions.   We have a hundred men under our orders. . . We also command, and we obey.   Nothing is changed — unless it be true submission, which we do not have, unless it be humility and love. . . Perhaps we shall never know the happiness of the centurion of Capharnaum.   But we know that we shall offer no resistance and that God will enter under our roof when He wills."

Plunged in profound meditation he found himself in Capharnaum with the centurion.   On leaving his tent in the evening he was seized with dizziness :

"The immense horizontal stretch of the Tijirit already looked like black velvet, but the sky straight up to the zenith was marvelously clear. . . Assuredly great things can happen beneath a sky like that. Its very silence makes us hurry. The evening hour spurs us on. It enjoins us to return within ourselves, I mean in that part of ourselves which is pure spirit and where we shall find again *even that which is not ourselves*. It frees us from the evils of selfishness and yet it demands that we take full possession of ourselves. It projects us beyond time, beyond space, into a region where human experience seems paltry, and yet where what we discover within ourselves is inexpressibly beautiful.

"I have a feeling that beyond the last lights on the horizon there are the souls of all the apostles, virgins, and martyrs, the endless army of witnesses and confessors. All of them take me by violence, take me by main force toward a moral region loftier than that in which I live today. This evening we desire with all our love their purity, and humility, their compassion, their chastity, their wisdom, their strength, their knowledge, their piety. We can understand how one can aspire toward their perfection.

"When I ponder the problem of faith, none of the difficulties raised by modern exegesis succeeds in impressing me. The so-called 'contradictions of the synoptic Gospels' serve only those who from the very first and without examination have decided to deny the supernatural. As ignorant as I am, I know well that such miserable discussions could never make anyone convinced of anything whatsoever. In fact — and here lies the whole question — it is a question of knowing whether one desires a certain moral foundation, a certain rebirth of the soul, a kind of innocent purity. It is a question of knowing whether one has an instinct for heaven, or not ; of whether one desires to live among angels or beasts ; whether one has the will to uplift and ceaselessly to spiritualize one's self. There is the question.  To every argument can be opposed an argument, and thus appears the futility of all arguments.  So if there is no desire to enlarge one's heart, if this instinct for God does not exist, no proof can be usefully furnished, and no argument is efficacious.  But if one wishes to consider that anguish of the Christian which is but the desire for perfection, if one does not fear the absolute, but on the contrary feels his heart is large enough to contain it, if one is perspicacious enough to desire something other than natural morality, however beneficent it may be — then one is not far from saying as did thunderstruck Saint Paul :  'Lord, what wilt thou have me to do ?' "

*

*        *

In the desert, two persons never ceased to grow in the purified vision of Ernest Psichari : the human person, of which each of us becomes aware, together with a sense of his responsibilities, and the person of France.  He knew that in the task assigned to him, "a single man represents for thousands of beings the whole of France.  We realize that here we are men held in high esteem.  We *must* succeed.  If we are beaten, it is we who will be in the wrong.  If we are beaten morally, that is to say, if we build on injustice when we should have built on justice, we will be in the wrong even more.  No matter how humble we may be, we nevertheless have a mission to fulfill."

This mission to make France and her justice loved was what in the first place made the knight Psichari set forth on the road in search of absolute Truth.  It was first the love of France which brought him to defend the spiritual honour of his country, and it was there that he discovered Christianity.

Now, he was the Centurion in quest of the cure for his soul, searching for spiritual liberty : "We are of those who burn to submit in order to be free."  Had he not already shown this when, in order to reconquer his soul, he gave himself up to

army discipline ?   And now he says : "What a master must
we not have at this time !   It is the Master of Heaven and Earth
whom we call to us.   We know what submission means to a
soldier ; we appreciate the greatness of it.   But we know also
that it is only the symbol of a higher submission."

Within himself, in his inner life, he clearly saw that he
should concentrate all his energy to "deserving God," to per-
fecting himself until he could "force grace upon himself," yet
that without God he could do nothing.   "Grace is God's part,"
he would say, "the desire for grace is my part."

From then on, until his return to France in December 1912
(and a little later), he remained in the same state of mind :
he knew where the truth and life which he so desired were to
be found but he could not attain them by his own strength ;
he was like the paralytic on the edge of the pool whose waters
could cure him.   And he bewailed not having the faith to
which he aspired.   "O, how well I could have used it," — this
land of Africa which had already proved so healthful to his
soul — "if only I could have come as a Christian !" Psichari
exclaimed.

In July 1911 he passed through the city of Chingueti, a city
of scholars and priests.   "Deep in the desert, in the midst of
desolation, a city of prayer arises ; a city of God, beaten by
every wind that blows and which, rejected by the gardens of
the earth, has gone to rejoin Heaven."   What astounded Psichari was "the heavy sadness on all faces . . ." and he thought
that the frightful weight on the mind of these men of God
came from their belief that Heaven is closed to the prayers
of men.   "They are dying from never having heard that blessed
phrase from which alone a little joy spreads over the earth :
*Ask, and it shall be given to you . . . knock and it shall be
opened to you.*"   But coming back to himself he adds : "We
are not even as good as these great dreamers who at least adore
the real God, even if they do not adore Him in truth."

A painful feeling of the heavy responsibility which weighed upon him and upon young Frenchmen in general, overwhelmed him : "We are aware it is upon us that the salvation of France depends, and therefore the salvation of the world and of civilization. Everything is staked upon our heads." Psichari wrote that exactly three years before the First World War. Was not this young man of twenty-seven, who in three years would have ceased to live, at the very heart of reality ? Faced with the task which France must accomplish under pain of death, he trembled as he thought of the mediocrity of the intellectual and political leaders of youth : "All our dignity, the moral greatness which has reigned over twenty centuries of history no longer exist — drowned as they are in the sea of mediocrity that is submerging us." He was remembering what his friend Jacques, who was taking his first steps as a philosopher, had written a short time before, in 1910 : ". . . One can easily see that modern thinkers prefer first and foremost and without any hesitation, ten errors coming from man to one truth coming from God."

And he who already loved that which he could not yet *believe*, wished at least, by speaking and acting like a Christian, to contribute to the strength and to the salvation of France. Is not this of far greater importance than personal salvation ? he asks himself. "What does a particular vocation matter when the election of a whole people is in question ? Even if I do not walk in the paths of grace, I still have the satisfaction of knowing that I am acting in a certain way, that I am continuing a great Christian action of the past and that I am participating in a great Christian action of the present. . . In no way claiming a place among the elect myself, I participate nevertheless in the election of the French people. What is a vocation in comparison with election ? What is the salvation of the individual in comparison with the eternal salvation of France ?" This thought comforted him, but if through his generous as well as sophistic arguments, he had thought however little to smother the voice that cries in the desert : "Make straight your paths !" he failed. For the question is not to know who is among the elect — how could anyone know this with certainty ? — but to know what we should do. "Lord, what do you wish of me ?" Saint Paul cried out as soon as Faith had opened his eyes. Ernest tried to escape from himself in the intoxication of wide spaces, or in the repose during the brief halts. But what did rest or the intoxication of space mean "for him who feared above all to find himself face to face with the quagmire of his own soul, for him, in short, who would not stop until he had found the perfect order and delightful harmony of truth ?"

What made Psichari's experience in the desert so astounding a testimony of the ways of God, is that he was still pursuing a life of sin while at the same time receiving the most illuminating graces. It would seem these graces were all the more penetrating in that they were still unstable — but with what invincible force they attracted him ! They preserved him from anxiety and gave him the assurance that Another would heal him ; they tended first and foremost to infuse him with faith.

And he thought with his whole heart, a little nostalgically, of "those well-ordered French lives, always taken up with prayer and honest work, well established in purity and peace of heart. Back there are souls who do not seek the exhilaration of travel because they have found their haven . . . in incomparable beatitude.

"Instead of that we are cast upon the world, in sin. . . Fear slips into us. It is not possible, some unknown voice tells us, that life be there — in all this rancour, in this despair that is sin. It is not possible that this road which leads nowhere be the right road ; it is not possible that the Saints do not prevail over us, and that purity does not prevail over impurity."

But for this human ethics cannot suffice. "They are power-less to give you peace," says the voice. . . "Take the most righteous of pagans. Think of the most admirable Stoic. He quickly reaches the limits of his perfection. Having reached this point, he stops, looks himself over and, if he wants, writes the *Meditations* of Marcus Aurelius or the *Encheiridion* of Epictetus. Take now the humblest of the Saints. Natural morals seem very little to him ; because what is easy is not enough for him. . . Up to his death he is anxious for perfec-tion. . . Thus his life is a perpetual springing forth, a perpetual movement, a glorious ascension, it is like a scaling of heaven which allows no rest. . ."

So once again we see the saints giving to a soul filled with desires the desire of Him who is the author of all sanctity.

Ernest now thinks wholeheartedly about Christ and about those of His commandments which seemed to him the most op-posed to human reason. "Must I really believe that this bread is Your Body, and this wine Your Blood ? This is the impos-sible requirement. And I say like Your very disciples on the morrow of Your teachings at Capharnaum : This is a hard saying, and who can listen to it ?"

And yet, because of the mysterious faith acting within this soul so filled with the "humble desire for Truth," Ernest could see in this "hard saying" a truth which goes beyond our natural means of knowledge and leaves to our assent the privilege of being freely given. If he could not attain this *mystery* of faith it was because he was sick and could not stir of his own accord. So whether he believed or did not believe — he himself did not know, but God knew — he asked to be healed :

"O my God, deign to see my misery and my trust. Have mercy upon a man who has been ill for thirty years !"

Not until three years later would he be thirty, on the day of his death. He must hasten ; God must hasten to perfect the faith of the Centurion.

Bravely he went on with his calling as a soldier. He went on suffering the fatigues of long journeys in want, in hunger and thirst, in the torrid heat and in the sandstorms.

"O God ! We are tossed about in the midst of Your elements. Here we are, with bowed heads, in the blowing storm. We are afraid. We tremble with fear of not answering Your call on that day when it will please You to come to us. At that hour, O my God, make us see You clearly, and give us the strength to say in our turn : 'Lord, what wilt Thou have me to do ?' — without arguing, without hesitating, without disputing the hour, that hour which You have chosen from all eternity."

To this good will, God replied with the gift of joy and of a greater security :

"What bliss to awaken when the morning is young, and to go to sleep when the evening is young, younger one's self and more confident, without fearing to acknowledge the Absolute, but on the contrary calling it to us with our whole heart that has at last been healed ! Twilight of beatitude — it is to you we owe this feeling of still being able to adore and to await like Israel the coming of the Lord : *From the morning watch even until night, let Israel hope in the Lord.* . . And now let us also pray — we who are little and sincere before His Face :

"O my God, I shall no longer be afraid of Thy Light, now that I have seen this light, and I shall no longer fear myself since I know Thou art within me. I did not know Thee because I desired proof of Thy existence, and now I know Thee because I can no longer prove Thy existence. And while I knew Thee not, Thou wert nevertheless within me, and while I neglected Thy Sacraments during that long night, Thou wert nevertheless preparing the coming of this supernatural light.

"I know Thee, O my God, because it pleased Thee to make Thyself known. I know Thee by that which is unknowable in Thee. I know Thee by Thy unknowable mysteries which are the Holy Trinity, the Incarnation, the Redemption. Those are the proofs which Thou hast deigned send me.

"O my God! Forgive me the great lie in which I have lived, since I was well aware of this force within me which guided me through life, and which I did not wish to refer to Thee. Forgive my ingratitude for not having restored to Thee that in me which belonged to Thee, and because the sail that swelled with the breath of the ideal did not set out toward Thee. Forgive me my cowardice in having believed in love without believing in Thy Love, and in law without believing in Thy Law, in goodness without believing in Thy Goodness. Forgive me the felony of having contemplated the ocean of light and not to have ventured on it, and of having hesitated at the edge of the eternity which Thou hast given me. Forgive me my great pride in having wanted to study Thee before loving Thee, and of having wanted to know Thee, which in a way was to cease to know Thee."

What could be lacking now in the faith of this desert man of meditation, of this beggar for Truth? One day when his companion Sidia said to him: "I know that *Issa* (Christ) is a great prophet," Ernest did not hesitate a second in replying to Sidia:

"*Issa*, my friend, is not a prophet, but in all truth, He is the son of God. . . He is the son of the Virgin Meryem who conceived Him by the grace of the Holy Spirit"; and he told him all the holy story of the Incarnate Word, and in ending, added: "Learn that to serve this master we would willingly give our lives."

He himself realized the strange state of mind he was in at that moment: "I did not believe that Jesus Christ was the son of God . . . yet I was speaking from the depths of my conscience. . . At that moment I knew perfectly well I was lying, but I knew also that I would have lied much more if I had not confessed the truth about my God."

Later he was to weep "delightful tears in memory of those confused hours which preceded the coming of Grace." If he had not been sincere these tears would have been bitter, not delightful. The "confused hours" were those when intermittent graces of light instructed the soul while they were active and left it in darkness again when they disappeared. Or else his state of mind which had already received in its depths the beginnings of Faith remained divided, while the conscious faculties of intelligence, will power and memory had not yet been instructed by it, nor corrected of their errors, nor modified or transformed by conscious and reasoned acquiescence. *Rationabile est obsequium nostrum.* So Ernest acted and spoke from the uprightness of his heart in spite of the incompleteness of his Faith, and even because of this incompleteness ; and perhaps he did not himself know to what degree he was sincere !

\*

\* \*

And thus graces followed one another in his soul. At Christmas time, in 1911, while he was meditating on the hope of future battles, he realized that "he who is thirsty for heroism rapidly becomes thirsty for the Divine. He has embarked in the Absolute — whether it be earthly or heavenly — and he can do nothing more than submit humbly to all that is imperishable in the world." Then he called to his aid the "God of Armies" and begged him to reveal Himself to him. Once when he had ventured quite far he went through one of those moments in one's life that can never be forgotten. In the ever dry bed of the river Oued, a rather thick tree invited him to rest. "All was so melodious, so drowsy, it seemed to me as if

I were on this earth as in a cradle. When I got under the tree I sank to my knees. It was the first time in my life — but it seemed as if this gesture so new to me had been ordered from on high, and to struggle against it would have been impossible." He felt infinitely at rest in this frail shelter, and to "the power" that made him bow he revealed with utter frankness the needs of his own heart. "I realized with absolute certainty that these needs would be satisfied and these wishes granted, and even more. I was sure that some day I would be a Catholic, and I felt only a kind of impatience without nervousness at the thought of the happiness which was promised me." Such at that moment were his desires and the prayers of his heart. He emphasized this : "I did not pass through any 'crisis' while in Mauretania. There was no inner drama, no inner struggle or anxiety. Just a period of calm waiting." He cursed the disorders of his life and immediately added : "In that also will I be healed." He trembled for fear of being abandoned in life, but immediately he exclaimed : "One day a hand will be stretched out toward me. . . And my heart beat as if it would burst when I thought what that day would mean to me. . . I could see beauty only in Christianity, nor could I conceive that beauty could lie anywhere else except in truth."

Still only a short time must pass, scarcely a year, and the loneliness of the Centurion would be ended and the desires of his heart fulfilled. The year 1912 was beginning — the year that would see him return to us. We were passing through the great ordeal of the illness and death of my father. At this same period Ernest, in the desert, was drawing up an account of what "two years of uninterrupted wandering in misery and in joy" had meant to him. Here are some of his meditations at that time :

"1) The heavenly Father : 'How much I shall love Him once I have become a Catholic !' The Blessed Virgin : 'How

humbly I shall be at her feet when I am a Catholic !' And
again : 'How I shall love when I believe !' Yet, as I have said,
I never doubted that Faith would some day be given me. . .

"2) I know nothing, but I am not afraid. . . At bottom I
do not know where this venture will lead me. . . I shall regret
it perhaps but I should regret it still more if I stop on the way.

"At my age it is quite a hard step to take. But no, I shall
do nothing ; it is Jesus who will do everything. It is He who
will care for me and be preoccupied over me, whereas I shall
be carefree and at peace. . . O my God, I know that Thou
hast said : 'Ye have not chosen Me, but I have chosen you.'

"3) Sin. 'I speak of Thee, Lord, and not a day passes without my offending Thee. . . *After my conversion* I will stop.'
[Doesn't he talk like a sick person who says : I will work when
I am well ?] 'Will I be sufficiently strong ? I have the assurance of this. . . 'I felt remorse — like everyone else. Because at bottom there is nothing funny about sin. Vice does
not amuse anyone. . . I felt remorse — a dull, pinching remorse, but I was not afraid. . . I did not quite know what
would happen. But I knew that on the day I became a Catholic, at that precise moment everything would change, and all
difficulties would be surmounted.

"4) The people whom at bottom I love most in this world
are the pious . . . those who are really pious . . . men of
scrupulous fidelity, men of exactitude and unction . . . the
obedient and the peace-loving. Why do I not join my real
friends ? Absolutely the only thing lacking is that tiny spark
of Grace. . ."

While waiting for Jesus to light this fire in his soul, Ernest
never ceases to yearn for "*the Truth* . . . the plenitude of
truth, a thought not of fiction but of reality. . .

"For days and years we have bathed in the unity of the world,
and we have slept beneath the stars. Solitude — divine solitude has thrown us back upon ourselves, and what a wealth

of riches we have found : dreams of the Church, the promises of Israel. . .

"The great silence of our seclusions prepared the way for Grace. . . And we walked confidently, having forgotten our cities. But less fortunate than the pilgrims of Emmaus we were continually awaiting the 'breaking of the bread.'

"*That God whom they did not recognize when Jesus expounded the holy Scripture, they recognize when Jesus breaks the bread.* 'They *knew*,' said Gregory the Great — 'and it was Jesus who had taught them this lesson ! — and yet they remained in the dark. The breaking of the bread was necessary in order for them to recognize Jesus, that is to say, the whole Truth.'

"It seems to me that we *know*," Ernest adds. "Do we thus lack nothing more than the true sign of recognition, the pledge of certitude : The BREAKING OF THE BREAD ?"

We come to April 1912. Ernest never ceased to meditate on the light which little by little appeared to him, and also on the natural means which go toward awakening in us the desire for God. "First silence . . . then poverty. For we are poor and this poverty has been sent to us. Now nothing can make us advance so much in the spiritual life as living on a handful of rice a day with a little salt water. . . Quite naturally thoughts of the eternal arise in a heart from which all that is ephemeral in life has been driven away, which has no desire other than the cross of its God. . .

"*He hath filled the hungry with good things.* This is the motto of the Sahara. . . Already, through nothing but misery . . . as through . . . silence we feel carried very far, as far as we can be led by natural means. We are truly on the threshold of God. . .

"O my God, the very land of the Infidels becomes an instrument of Thy mercy. . . O helpful land. . .

"O let us profit jealously of these hours of meditation that are sparingly allotted to us. Let us use like misers these pure moments of liberty."

While Ernest was taking his first steps towards evangelical perfection, helped, according to his own avowal, by the virtues of the desert, which are silence, solitude, deprivation and destitution, another great Frenchman was taking his last steps toward sainthood and martyrdom. Ernest never met him — either in France or in Africa — as the abode of the hermit was in the northern part of the Sahara — but in passing, he mentions the "venerable and celebrated Father de Foucauld," without suspecting that soon they would both be leaving the desert and solitude to take their places in the innumerable multitude of the heavenly armies. It was indeed at the beginning of the First World War that the French hermit was assassinated by order of the Germans.

Now, from May 16th to July 18th, Ernest traveled over the Zoug. Certain days were "monotonous and idle." However they passed by quickly in talks with the Moors. How did it happen that these talks made him think of Durkheim and Saint Thomas ? Ernest had not broken his ties with his friends in France. Péguy's letters would have spoken of the sociologist and Jacques' of the theologian. Of the Moors he thought that their simple, barren life had nothing in common with the "return to simplicity," and the "naïveté of the early ages" of which so many of our writers dream. "There's a good one !" exclaimed Ernest. "Some agreement ought to be reached as to who is simple and who is naïve — Mr. Durkheim or Saint Thomas." . . . As for the Moors "when one considers the point they have reached in their inner life, one finds that they know better than we how to safeguard themselves against lack of culture and vulgarity. . . In my estimation the country of the Zoug does not lead back to simplicity.

"We are clearly warned that we must return to something,

raise ourselves up from those depths within us.   But it is not
a question of simplicity.   Saint Paul and Saint Augustine were
not simple ; and nothing is more contrary to the French tradition than the faith of the coal-heaver. . . What makes the
backbone of the French tradition is a strong faith — that of
the Catholic, apostolic and Roman religion — resting on a
wide culture or parallel to a wide intellectual culture." It
therefore has nothing to do with seeking simplicity of mind ;
and as for the Moors their simplicity is that of their customs,
which are "in inverse ratio to simplicity of mind."   And if he
prefers the lesson of the desert to "that of the intellectuals,"
it is not in the sense of a "return to nature and to naïveté, but
rather to intelligence which is," as he states so admirably, "in
a certain sense, the greatest of all the kinds of simplicity."

*

*        *

It is during this period that Ernest wrote Jacques the letter
which overwhelmed us by giving us the certainty of his forthcoming entrance into the plenitude of faith.   This long letter
sums up nearly all I have quoted from *Les Voix qui crient dans
le Désert*.   Here are its main passages :

"Zoug, June 15, 1912

"My very dear Jacques,

"I received with pleasure and read with profit your precious
letter and the two pamphlets which you kindly enclosed.

" — 'Although philosophy in the desert must be cultivated
but little, and must be hardly diverting,' you write.

"No doubt, and yet the nature of the Sahara, so extremely
purified and rid of all ornament, clothed in silence and solitude,
soon inclines one to meditation, and in a way can serve as a
cloister. . . If I sought in reason reasons for which to believe
— and indeed : *The assent of faith is by no means a blind*

*movement of the soul* — I feel that my starting point would be your discussion on the Bergsonian theses of nothingness, of order and finality.

"But as at this time I had more need of love than of light, you will not be surprised that I took more pleasure in the first essay which is more fervent and passionate — at least in its form — than the second. . .

"All attempt at 'liberating' one's self from Catholicism is an absurdity, since whether we like or not, we are Christians — and it is also wicked since all that we have of goodness or greatness in our hearts comes to us through Catholicism. We cannot obliterate twenty centuries (and behind them a whole eternity) — we cannot obliterate twenty centuries of history, and as science has been founded, as you so rightly remark, by believers, all that is great and lofty in our morality also comes from this unique and great source of Christianity from the abandonment of which flows false morality, as also does false science.

"And I believe that these are for us the real reasons to believe. While still maintaining the text of the Vatican Council which, by the way, you singularly illuminate in your apologia of the intelligence — and without desiring it to be a 'blind movement' which carries us toward faith, one can indeed say that we are living at a time when the danger of barbarity and impiety is so great that there one no longer has leisure to stop at theological arguments. Besides, the *Summa Theologica* cannot be grasped by everyone. What matters before anything is to destroy this 'intellectual' gang, and all that clique of mediocre people who dominate us — novelists of adultery, worldlings, free-masons and radical socialists who give to our time its aspect of anarchical confusion, so striking as soon as one sees it from a distance, as I can. . .

"Now, my dear Jacques, I have told you enough to dare to go to the end of my confession.

"With all this, I do not have faith.  If I may say so, I am this absurd thing : a Catholic without faith.

"I was thinking of myself with a certain sadness in reading this beautiful page :

" 'It seems that in these times truth is too strong for the human soul. . .'  And I was wondering whether you might be holding my impiety against me.  Yet it seems to me that I detest the same people you detest and I love those you love, and that I differ from you only in that grace has not yet touched me.

"Grace !  That is the mystery of mysteries !  You are going to warn me not to fall into the error of Jansenism, and that man is free, and capable by his works if not to force, at least to attract grace (I do not know if I say this correctly).

"But no !  I feel that having come to the turning point where I am, there is nothing else to do now but wait.

" 'Dull your wits,' says Pascal to me.  But it is impossible. One can no more dull one's wits than one can make one's self intelligent.  Should I read and learn ?  But the disciples of Emmaus did not believe after Christ's teaching : *That God whom they did not recognize when Jesus expounded the holy Scripture, they recognize when Jesus breaks the bread.*  This phrase of Saint Gregory causes me to ponder endlessly.  So, in no way like the blind man who did not ask to be healed, I call loudly to God who does not wish to come.

"Has all this really great importance ?  It is only after all a question of my individual salvation.  If I loyally serve the Church, and her eldest daughter, France, will I not have fulfilled my entire duty ?  In regard to the Church indifference is not possible.  He who is not with Me is against Me.  And I take sides with all my heart.

"Now, after that, I believe that the working out of my salvation interests no one since, with all the great things there are to do in this world, this question scarcely interests me.  I take everything from religion except my own salvation.

"When I think, my dear Jacques, of the terrible difficulty of tying together again a lost tradition, I understand better the lesson given me by the Moors, with whom I have been living for over two years.  Here are pure, simple people who preserve their faith as they have received it from their fathers !  But above all they are great because a rotten civilization has not stifled within them the vital power of meditation.  Must we then come here to see the faces of the last mystics and ascetics ?

"A few days ago I was passing through Port Etienne.  I was showing the wireless installations and the distillation apparatuses to one of my Moorish companions, my faithful Sidia . . . and I was saying to him :

" 'Can't you see that the Moors are crazy to want to struggle against such a rich and powerful people as the French ?'

"Sidia remained thoughtful for a moment, then spoke as follows — I translate more or less litcrally :

" 'Yes, you Frenchmen, you have the kingdom of carth, but we Moors, we have the kingdom of heaven.'

"So this is the esteem in which the Moors hold us after five or six years of contact with French officers !

"I sent this remark to Monseigneur Jalabert, Bishop of Senegambia, in a letter in which I expressed to him my desire soon to see a great and beautiful cathedral built in Dakar which would show the Moslems that we too have our God and our Faith !  But this God, alas, is very little in our hearts, and the anecdote proves it ! *

"You were not being deceived, my dear Jacques, when you were told I have written a novel.  I even attempted a few other short essays aiming at setting up some life-buoys to which I could cling and hold tight.  But if I decide to publish some of these manuscripts I am quite certain that the 'intellectual clique' will not claim me as one of themselves !

"You, too, will not wholly approve, but at least you will

* Ernest's wish was granted, and this cathedral has been erected in Dakar.

recognize my good intentions and this will console me for the fury of the others !

"Please give my respects to your wife to whom I send my most respectful condolences in her loss, and believe in my great affection which remains always the same.

Ernest"

Certain of Ernest's deep sincerity, we were persuaded that his period of waiting would not be in vain, because God always responds by the gift of faith to the good will of those who seek Him, because He it is who causes us to seek Him.

In the summer of that year, the last he was to pass in Africa, and the one in which he underwent the worst period of hardship he had ever experienced in Mauretania, there came to him, as he states in *Les Voix* . . . "the sweetest thoughts regarding the consolations" which he knew were in store for him.  In that rough life of a soldier deprived of every comfort, he suffered from hunger and thirst and from the extreme climate.  "In spite of my destitution I started to live in a most extraordinary exaltation. . . In this condition in which I felt forsaken by everything, certain virtues of which I had scarcely thought seemed to me the loftiest that could enrich one's soul. But all of these were virtues peculiar to Christianity : renunciation, humility, detachment from the world, the spirit of penance, asceticism and chastity — not that of the body, which is of a lower order — but that of the spirit itself.  I felt an infinite happiness in inhaling for the first time the sweet odour of Christian virtues. . .

"And I turned to the Saints . . . and could not deny that they were the highest examples of humanity which were ever seen in the world.  So, after looking with love towards Paradise, I could not believe that this desire for the sweetest virtues could be forever forbidden me."  And he asked : "Can a religion which proclaims such morals be false ? . . . No, the

Catholic religion is not false. Doubtless there are many difficulties in it, but none are insurmountable ; on the contrary,
if one surmounted them everything would appear perfectly
beautiful and harmonious in our hearts as in our minds."

For us also the holiness of the Saints had been the determin-
ing argument. . . And much later, after a long examination
of morals and mysticisms, did not Bergson also recognize in
the Saints — the Christian mystics, the only ones "who hit
the mark" — the highest summit of humanity ?

If we accept Catholic morality — this morality "which nothing can equal, . . . almost immediately," says Ernest, "a miraculous light reaches into the darkest nooks and crannies of
our souls." Having arrived at this point in his reflections, he
blessed not only the God of Saints but also his own wretchedness, because it was in the midst of it that he had discovered
"the infinite treasures contained in the Gospel."

Ernest had now accomplished his mission in Africa, and it
was time for him to return to France. On October 15th when
he left the camp of Agoatim he felt his heart being torn. "A
great dark hole was being dug behind me. A heavy twilight
was weighing down upon my years of misery.

"But also the dawn was breaking, a dawn of youthfulness
and purity — and a celestial clarity lit up the horizon before
me. This time I knew where I was going. I was going toward
the Catholic, apostolic and Holy Roman Church. I was going
toward the dwelling of peace and blessing, I was going toward
joy, toward health ; I was going, alas, toward my cure. And
then, thinking of this true mother who for so many years had
been awaiting me, back there across two continents . . . I
wept with happiness, love and gratitude.

"Yes, it was a magnificent truth which was calling me back
there in my gentle homeland. The whole Christian order
appeared to me in a rejuvenated atmosphere ; an immense and

majestic temple — founded on solid rocks — a temple of Reason and divine Wisdom stood before me, and all the lines of this temple were so straight, so pure, so united that in its presence one could desire nothing more than to live eternally in its shadow, far from the enchantments and the vanities of this world."

All those who with a sincere heart cross the threshold of the Church have this vision at one time or another.

While the Angel of Temptation makes us climb the mountain of concupiscence and, by lowering our glance shows us and offers us the kingdoms of the earth — the Angel of Conversion leads us through the vale of humility and tears, and, drawing our gaze toward the heights, shows us coming down "from beside God, the holy city, the new Jerusalem, clothed like a bride attired for her bridegroom." And then we feel the truth of what is said to Saint John in the Apocalypse : "Behold the dwelling of God with men, and He shall dwell with them ; they shall be His peoples ; and God Himself shall be with them. . . Write, for these words are faithful and true." *

This inspired, real and mystical vision, if once seen not with the eyes but with the soul and spirit, might later pale away ; but the splashings of human mud on the walls of the heavenly Jerusalem shall never again be able entirely to hide the brilliance of its eternal light ; we shall never lose — unless by mortal faults of infidelity — the knowledge of the essential goodness of this protecting mother of souls, of this city "shining with the glory of God." †

This inner revelation of the Church preceded Ernest's conversion by a very short time. His last words in *Les Voix* . . . as he left Africa, tell us that he was no longer disputing with God ; "confiding in Him and resting in Him, after so many

* Apocalypse of Saint John, xxi, 2–4.
† Apocalypse, xxii, 11.

journeys and efforts, I on the contrary awaited in peace and joy to know to its magnificent fullness the sweetness of the name Christian."

## The Centurion's Reply

On December 8, 1912, Ernest embarked at Dakar ; three weeks later he was in France, in Paris, among us.  Our hearts were beating like his with anguished hope.  What we were expecting was so great, infinitely surpassing the power of all desire, that we dared not count on it with complete certainty ; did not the gift of God depend on God alone ?  And would not Ernest — having left the African wilderness far behind him, drawing near to the land that was the mother of his culture and noisy "with the controversies and discussions of philosophers and scholars" — wonder whether, in the silence of the desert wastes, he had not been a victim to a mirage of the mind ?  This indeed happened ; the demon of illusion tried to convince him of it, and to turn him away from the goal toward which his strong and faithful soul was really reaching out.  This always happens before a conversion : God tests us under conditions where all natural exaltation falls away.  Only then can we see to what point our will is really involved in our desires ; only then do we become open to divine Grace.

So for several days Ernest went through moments of darkness and doubt — but how brief they were !  In less than six weeks all would be accomplished.

At our first meetings he declared that he was "a Catholic without grace" to whom service to his country was enough. "He was sincere," wrote Jacques, "but how keenly one felt that he was not telling the truth."  No, service to his country was no longer enough, and this truth did not long delay in becoming apparent to him.  In the diary of his innermost

thoughts — published by his sister Henriette — he wrote on
January 10, 1913 :

"Come to me, my Lord, my God . . . and help me achieve
in purity of heart and mind the task I have started with Thee."
And on the 16th : "That love could not fail to come."

Jacques and Ernest saw each other every day, either at Versailles or in Paris, where Ernest came by for him after class
at the Collège Stanislas, and they analysed and discussed endlessly together the dogmas and doctrines of Catholicism. But
conversations were not enough, they also wrote to each other.
And Ernest put down in his notebook sometimes his own
words, sometimes those of Jacques. Jacques wrote to him
on January 23rd : "What I beg God to do is to have you enter
His Church through the royal door of Peace and Light, and
without any delaying of His grace."

And Ernest wrote to Jacques, when it seemed to him Jacques
was exasperated by his slowness :

"It seems to me impossible that I should continue much
longer to regard the adorable Christian thought as a stranger,
and I tell myself that having been deprived of so many sacraments, it is not surprising that the hill is so hard for me to
climb up again. I implore you, my dear Jacques, do not abandon me, and try not to become disheartened, however sad the
opinion you may have of me. You alone can support and
guide me. Take into account my immense good will. . ."

On January 21st did he not write in his notebook :

"Today I begged Jacques to introduce me to a priest who
would be able to understand. . ."

For a long time we had known just who this priest would
be. Ever since Ernest's departure from Mauretania, Jacques
had never stopped speaking of him to Father Clérissac, that
man of great faith and strong intelligence who now knew Ernest
almost as well as did Jacques. But even so, what agony we

again endured ! We were in that precious and delicate domain of sympathies and friendships ; of the meeting of one soul with another, and with God. Would not an awkward move on our — Jacques' and Raïssa's — part spoil it all ? Already, we happened to know, Ernest had been shocked at certain outer manifestations of our faith : the portrait of Pope Pius X in Jacques' study, the little oratory with the statue of Notre Dame de la Salette ; and a certain conversation we had, in which hardly anything was discussed, it seemed to me, except Mélanie and Saint Hildegarde, both extraordinary prophetesses, one of the nineteenth century, the other of the Middle Ages. . .

But whether it be cleverness or awkwardness — could this make any difference there where God acts ? Would He be stopped by my foolishness, I who prayed for the soul of my friend ; or by a moment of irritation on the part of this soul so dearly contested between God and the Prince of Falsehood ? Was not this a case where our infirmity and helplessness were our greatest strength before the Author of grace ? And had not that hour of grace sounded for Ernest Pischari ?

On January 31st he met Father Clérissac for the first time. Here are his impressions as he entered them in his notebook on that date :

"Passed by Stanislas for Jacques. We went to Versailles and found at his place Father Clérissac of the order of Saint Dominic. This man has a magnificent head, fiery eyes, a bitter mouth and a face that shows suffering and faith. One feels him to be a man of ardour, of a stable mind, a large heart ; one feels he is an enemy of weakness and stagey religiousness, and yet filled with a glowing inner fire. He is highly educated, and has a refined culture. . . He and I went for a walk together in the Park, and I told him of my immense desire for confession and the feeling I have of my unworthiness. He helped and encouraged me with an enlightened goodness that went straight to my heart."

Their second interview took place Monday, February 3rd. Ernest and Father Clérissac lunched at our house. There was perfect harmony and poignant emotion, because a grave decision was at hand which would bind an entire life, and because we knew that "the love of God is without mercy." *

After lunch Father Clérissac took Ernest into the Park. They stayed for two hours during which time we never ceased praying. At last they came back. Everything had been decided. Ernest was to go to confession the next day and be confirmed that same week, and on Sunday he was to make his first communion.

Days marked by great and immaterial acts were to pass quickly, reminding us on this anniversary month of baptism, of the illness and death of my father, and the great days illumined by the grace of his conversion.

So the next day, Father Clérissac and Ernest came together at about four — into our little oratory decorated with flowers, and where candles blessed at Candlemas were burning. Ernest Psichari, kneeling before the statue of Notre Dame de la Salette, read in a forceful voice the profession of faith of Pius IV and Pius X. Father Clérissac, who sponsored him before God, stood listening. Jacques and I, trembling witnesses, were on our knees. After this reading we went out. Ernest then made a general confession and received absolution. Then Jacques and I were called again. Before us stood a new man. His face and his eyes were new, washed by water from heaven. I recalled the pure shining eyes of my father after his baptism ; miracle of the "renewal of images," images of God that we are, and whose colours are effaced by sin.

"You are looking at a man who belongs entirely to God," Father Clérissac said. We felt that a mutual tenderness, paternal and filial, had sprung up, by grace of the sacerdotal

* Words of Mélanie Calvat, shepherdess of La Salette.

sacrifice of Christ and His priest, between these two souls,
equally heroic in their different destinies.

Ernest came back to Versailles the following day, February
5th, to receive the ashes at the Cathedral.

The 7th he wrote in his notebook : "Eve of my confirmation. I take the firm resolution to live in God and for God."

He was confirmed Saturday, February 8th, at Versailles by
Bishop Gibier : "It seems to me I have another soul," he said
to the Bishop after the ceremony.

He noted in his diary : "Through providential chance, today
was the feast of Saint John of Matha who, in 1198, founded
an order to buy back the Christian slaves . . . and often went
to Morocco."

The 9th he made his first communion, again at Versailles,
in the chapel of the Holy Childhood, from the hands of Father
Clérissac who said the Mass. We were alone, Jacques, Vera
and I, with Ernest and Father Clérissac. Admirable silence,
ardent recollection of our souls.

That entire day was for Ernest "a magnificent day of sun-
shine, full of pure light, certainly *intentional*." During these
days of grace we had indeed the feeling that God was thinking
only of us ! And it was true. God acts within each one of
us as if we were alone in the world.

On February 9, 1914, the only anniversary of his first communion which he ever celebrated, in thinking of this day when
he had recognized Christ "by the breaking of the bread," Ernest
wrote us :

"Yet is it not true that just a year ago we were kneeling in a
little chapel at Versailles and you, my dear friends, were help-
ing me as I entered into the incomparable light of the Eucharistic life, and bent beneath the long-desired yoke of Jesus
Christ. . ."

The same morning of February 9, 1913, Father Clérissac,

Jacques and Ernest went on a pilgrimage to Chartres, to the favourite cathedral for our devotions, the one which played so great a rôle in the conversion of Péguy and in our own. . . Péguy ! How close he seemed to us in those hours ! How greatly we had desired for him the fullness of joy and peace which from now on would be the viaticum of this young man who was so dear to him, and who so passionately admired him. Should not Péguy have been with us on that day ?

On the contrary, as we have seen,* it was on that very day that there began the disagreement which up until then had affected only Jacques and me, and from which Ernest in his turn was to suffer.

*

*     *

Altogether different from Péguy's, who attributed the change in Ernest to "the clerics," was Jacques' point of view concerning his friend's conversion. "It is," he writes, "a magnificent testimony rendered to the reality and efficacy of grace and to the supernatural essence of Faith." Indeed, "the act of Faith is an act of the intellect, but of the intellect commanded by the will which has itself been righted and directed toward God. And where can this redress of the will, so indispensable to the genesis of the act of Faith, where can this abduction, this carrying up of desire to substantial Beauty, be seen more strikingly than in the Centurion of the Adrar ? It is a supernatural act of which grace alone makes us capable ; and where is this need of rescue by grace and this helplessness of nature before the insupportable mystery of the Deity more marked than in the holy waiting of Psichari ? 'Perhaps we shall never know the happiness of the centurion of Capharnaum,' wrote Psichari, 'but we know that we shall offer no resistance and that God will enter under our roof when He wills. This is the founda-

* Cf. above, p. 67.

tion : not to resist truth, whatever it may be.  Just wait, wait
patiently. . .'

"The act of Faith," continues Jacques Maritain, "is in itself
a mystery, properly speaking . . . and it is only by analogy
that human or natural belief can help us to have any idea of
it."  Indeed to believe, humanly speaking, is much less than
to know ; but to believe by supernatural faith is much more,
incomparably more, than to know in a natural way.

"This school where God is heard and teaches," said Saint
Augustine, "is very far removed from the senses and from carnal
knowledge.  We see many coming to the Son because we see
many believing in Christ ; but where and how have they heard
or learned this of the Father we do not see.  For this grace is
much too profoundly mysterious. . ." *

---

\* *De Praedestinatione Sanctorum*, M.L. t. XLIV, col. 970.  After quoting
this text, Jacques Maritain continues thus in *Antimoderne* :
."Doubtless a preparation of prudence and a valid foundation of apologetics
are necessary for the theological act of faith.  But the *formal motive* of faith
does not rest upon human argument, faith is not a scientifically or rationally
acquired conclusion on which a supernatural mode meritorious for salvation is
superimposed "like gold plating over copper," faith is *essentially* supernatural
*quoad substantiam*, and it has its root principles not in the human truth of
apologetic demonstrations, but in the very revelation of the first Truth which
is, at the same time, *that which* we believe and *that by which* we believe, just
as light is at the same time that which is seen and that by which one sees ;
and this faith rests formally on a supernatural illumination and inspiration, on
a grace infused from on high which causes us to receive within us the testimony
of God.
   " 'Adhering to the testimony of a creature — angel or man,' says Saint
Thomas, 'cannot lead *infallibly* to Truth except in so far as it is the testimony of
God speaking which one considers in them.  That is why faith must make man's
intelligence adhere to the truth peculiar to divine knowledge itself, transcending
the truth of the human intellect (*De Veritate*, 14, 8). . .'  There are three
things which lead us to the faith of Christ : natural reason, the testimony
of the Law and the prophets, the preaching of the apostles and their successors.
But when a man has thus been led as though by the hand to faith, then he
can say that he does not believe for any of these preceding motives ; neither
because of natural reason, nor because of the testimony of the Law, nor because of the preaching of men, but only because of the first Truth itself. . .
It is from the Light infused by God that faith draws its certainty.  (*In Joan-
nem*, IV, lect. 5, n. 2.)
   "And lastly the beginnings of Faith, and even the desire to believe — *pius*

To this grace "which is from on high and descends from the Father of Light" * Ernest was to remain faithful unto death — to which, alas, he was so near. He lived with holiness the eighteen months which separated him from it, continuing his life as a soldier.

While stationed at Cherbourg, his concern was for the soldiers whom he instructed, the poor whom he visited, God Himself whom he carefully tended within his soul, watchful to serve Him lovingly.

What rejoicing for his friends when he came back to Paris, to Versailles ! We will always remember Christmas 1913 and Pentecost of 1914, when he was among us with Father Clérissac. What life, what joy were in him ! How he sang, how he

*credulitatis affectus* — by which the soul affectionately trusts in God, who saves from sin, and wishes to attain God and to love Him and hope for Him and believe in Him without yet categorically believing — all this is a gift of grace and comes to man through the inspiration of the Holy Ghost. And was not what the Centurion lived through in Mauretania first of all that *initium fidei*, those supernatural tremours and first illuminations of grace, that whole vast movement of the intellect and will which the theologians call 'the intention of faith' ? After this there came 'the election of the faith,' which supposes the prudential examination of the reasons for belief, inspired and supported by Divine help. But it is still the supernatural light which at the end of this second stage, can alone cause the judgement of 'credentity' : *we must believe* (a judgement preceding the act of faith itself), that *credo* which Psichari was definitively to say after his return to France.

"It was not that the Centurion lacked a reasonably valid apologetical foundation or motives of rational credibility. But they did not present themselves as separate arguments, and were not of a scientific and philosophical nature, or let us say, purely speculative. Should this surprise us ? Who would ask the same muscular effort of an invalid as one would ask of a man who was well ? Among many of those who have grown up in the atmosphere of the modern world and who are, by very reason of their intellectual ardour, saturated with its miasma, the intellect — however brilliant and scintillating it may be — is encumbered by obstacles that cause it to lose some of its natural vigour ; it is much weaker and more sickly in reality than is imagined by certain philosophers who do not know, thank God, the wells of the deepest bitterness. The health-producing action of grace was first required before such an intellect could grasp the whole value of purely rational demonstrations. From the beginning Psichari realized this, and he stated it forcefully in the letter I quoted a short time ago.

* Epistle of St. James, I, 16–18.

laughed ! Yet he was passing through a difficult period ; he was much worried about his mother ; his father was leaving her and remarrying. "She was nothing more," to use Ernest's moving expression, "than a poor old abandoned woman."

Naturally he had found again Jacques' sister in Paris. She too was separated from her husband, and like Ernest, converted to Catholicism. She was free — but only in the eyes of the world. She was still bound in conscience by a marriage which had none the less been destroyed.

The age difference now would not have been an obstacle to a union desired by both of them. Jeanne had scarcely grown older in those ten years. For Ernest, on the contrary, his years in Africa had counted double for him. What separated them now — terrible persistence of misfortune — what separated them was their very faith, the faith in which they were spiritually united. And only in this union was the tragedy of their double destiny to be unfolded.

It was in the spring of that year of 1913 that L'Appel des Armes appeared. Henri Massis tells that "among all the trials which during these painful weeks had overwhelmed Psichari with sadness, the publication of L'Appel des Armes was not the least painful." "My novel disgusts and nauseates me," he came to say (to Massis) one evening at the printing press of L'Opinion. "All this no longer fits in with my life as a Christian. . . Think of this fearful thing : a whole book in which the name of Our Lord is not even mentioned. How shameful ! I don't want to have it published. . ." "Father Clérissac had to put him under obedience before Ernest would consent to publish L'Appel des Armes in a spirit of humility . . . and out of a regard for truth. . ."

\*

\*　　　\*

Ernest was moving toward the religious life in the Order of Saint Dominic. On October 19, 1913, he entered the Dominican Third Order. He always followed with fervent fidelity the directions of Father Clérissac who had given him, as a rule of life, to behave at all times "as if the following moment he were going to communion — or to die." He awaited in peace the divine decision. It came with the war.

## The Death of Psichari

Henriette Psichari was given many an account of her brother's death and of the battle of Rossignol. She herself refers to the work of Colonel Grasset.* In addition, when Henri Massis was finishing his own book *Notre Ami Psichari*, she passed on to him the account which Massis cites, of the man who was Ernest's last companion — Adjutant Galgani, a gunner of the 2nd artillery regiment. I will therefore refer to all these sources in the pages that follow :

Mobilized on the second day of the war, Ernest Psichari left Cherbourg with his regiment.

On August 20th, he was in the East in the neighbourhood of Montmédy. A slip of the merest chance and Péguy and he would have met.

On the 21st began the tragic errors of the brave as much as misguided military leaders, whose orders finally brought the 2nd regiment of colonial infantry to face alone an entire German division. Against all evidence these generals were convinced that they had before them nothing but a "curtain" of German soldiers.

So on August 22nd, Ernest's regiment found itself in a

* *La Surprise d'une Division. Rossignol — St. Vincent.* Berger-Levrault, 1932.

desperate situation. Ernest and his men knew it by noon. They put up a heroic defense against the enemy, and the death throes of the regiment began.

"While the envelopment of the colonial corps was in progress, the regiment obeyed up until the end the order that General Raffenel kept reiterating : 'Rossignol must be held at any price, while waiting for reinforcements that will come without delay.'

"But they, the soldiers, knew the reinforcements would not come. . .

"The village's last defense was assured by Ernest's two cannon, which Captain Cherrier never left, and by a few machine-gun squads. . . Ernest went on firing — anywhere. Was there any sort of common goal, any cohesion in this hell ? All was useless, but the detonation of his ordnance helped keep the men reassured." *

"At five o'clock," Galgani relates, "the Germans came into the town . . . Lieutenant de St. Germain came to tell Lieutenant Psichari that by order of the Colonel he was to leave his gun. Our lieutenant replied, turning toward me : 'Why return to die back there ? Let 's stay here.' But as Lieutenant de St. Germain insisted, Psichari answered : 'All right, then. Come, follow me. . .' We took refuge in a small garden, and we had not been there a minute when he said : 'Did you unpin the gun ?' 'No,' I replied. We went back together and I put the cotter-pin in my pocket . . . and we had just come on the road completely uncovered when our lieutenant made a gesture with his arm as if to tell me to cross in a hurry, that the place was dangerous. I heard him cry : 'Gal — ' he did not finish. He turned about on himself and fell to the ground, his arms out in the form of a cross. . . Lieutenant Psichari had been shot in the temple. . .

* Cf. Henriette Psichari — *Ernest Psichari, mon frère* — pp. 228 *et seq.*

"With Lieutenant de St. Germain and the few men there we carried his body to the side of the road." *

"Ernest," wrote Henriette Psichari, "was placed in a temporary grave with three other comrades, but he was quite recognizable for he wore under his clothes the Saint Dominic scapulary.

"His Médaille Militaire which he won in Africa and which he so treasured remained attached to his tunic. . .

"The men who buried Ernest, and who were his fellow-soldiers made prisoners, noticed also a thin gold chain around his neck at the end of which hung a small cross. It was his baptismal cross. . .

"An elderly nun was kneeling there beside him, a humble woman who came to pray for the dead and to help the soldiers in their dismal task.

"What did the young officer with the features that were so pure, still so childishly young, have around his left wrist? Turning back his cuff the nun discovered a rosary of black beads over which his now livid lips had murmured so many prayers. Ernest had kept it wound around his wrist during the horrible battle. . ."

\*

\* \*

We learned of the death of Péguy and Ernest at the same time. Thus it was that our greatest friends began leaving us, and the dearest ones were the first to go. Father Clérissac who was Ernest's guide as well as our own soon followed in death his heroic spiritual child. He passed away November 16, 1914, not many days after learning that Ernest had fallen at Rossignol.

* Cf. Henri Massis, *Notre Ami Psichari.*

# CHAPTER SIX

## On Some Who Were Young in 1912

### Henri Massis and the Agathon Inquiry

At the beginning of 1913, Sunday, January 5th, Psichari came to see us with Henri Massis, one of his friends we had not yet met; he brought him to our solitary retreat in the Rue de l'Orangerie.*

They had lunched that same day in Versailles with Péguy, and spent many hours listening to him talk with his peculiar rich eloquence of his refound faith, of the rôle he would play in the re-Christianization of France, and of the ways in which his activity differed from Claudel's : "Claudel lacks simplicity," he said to his young friends, "he seeks the extreme . . . there is something provoking in his Christianity. . . I myself am not a man of the mountain-tops, I am a man of the plains. . . I walk with the foot-soldiers, I follow the road of everyone else, I stay with everyone, with all those people who live — this is a case to say it — of the grace of God. . . And, for my salvation, I do not have any other arms than they have, and these are contrition, hope, prayer. . . I pray, I pray all the time." †

When Péguy left them — "Psichari then took me by the arm," Massis relates, "and pulling me along, said : 'Now come with me to Maritain's !' "

Massis was the youngest of the three young men thus brought together for the first time. Of medium height, thin and nervous, he scarcely looked his twenty-five years. With

* Regarding the date of this visit Henri Massis makes two mistakes in his book *Notre Ami Psichari* ; on page 134 he puts it down as Sunday, January 25th, and on page 144 as the 3rd of January. It took place on Sunday, January 5th.
† Henri Massis, *Notre Ami Psichari*, Flammarion, Paris.

his lively and intelligent face, he appealed to us from the beginning, despite the rather too Barrès-like lock which hung across his forehead.

Ernest and Massis spoke to us of Péguy whom they had just left ; then without idle preamble the conversation turned to Catholicism and the Church. "We could only speak, Psichari and I," wrote Massis, "of our solitude, our exile, for we no longer had any objections." And the one and the other declared themselves "Catholics without faith."

Jacques said little, listening to the voice of their souls. Vera and I said still less. We were awkward (we still are). We had no idea of the world. From the Sorbonne we had gone directly into the Church. We had no outside shell and our hearts were completely open — which is the worst awkwardness. About the conversion of souls we knew nothing except our own and that of our father. We confidently expected Ernest's conversion. But Ernest was so close to Jacques that with him we were not outside our intimate circle. Massis was the first who came to Jacques from the outside world. Jacques was not airing any arguments. Jacques had no opinion of himself, and did not compare himself to anyone. He desired only the truth for souls, and he loved all those whose lives were motivated by the search for truth.

I am grateful to Massis for having felt all this and for having written, in recalling this first meeting : "He looked at us both as one prays. . . And we felt drawn about us an invisible net, one woven only of the threads of love."

Since Ernest's departure for Mauretania three years before, his evolution and that of Massis had been pursued separately, but they had led to the same desires, the same anguish : "By what truly divine coincidence did this young officer just returned from Adrar, vibrant with action," wrote Massis, "confide in me the same need which I had given up hope of satisfying in the sad materialism of the modern world ? . . . We

were putting the same pressing, decisive question to life, and
we refused to believe that there was no direction to our destiny.
We could not do without an ethical absolute. . ." Our own
story was being re-enacted in them. "Without confessing the
Catholic faith, both of us already perceived the radiance of
eternal beauty in the Church. . . Our intelligence had nothing to oppose to its dogmas ; even more were we persuaded
that there alone lay the truth."

This was already faith ; or at least it was soon given to them.
A month later, as was seen above, Psichari was received into
the Church.  Massis did not delay in joining the one he had
always considered as the model and young leader of his generation.

Massis also spoke to us of the inquiry which he and G. de
Tarde had conducted in 1912 among the young intellectual
élite of France with regard to its main tendencies, the results of
which were published in L'Opinion under the pseudonym of
Agathon.

The conclusions from this inquiry were later collected in a
book,* accompanied by the testimony which had given rise
to them, and by the letters it had called forth.  There were
things in these conclusions which moved us.  They showed
us that we were no longer isolated or those strange animals to
whose condition we had resigned ourselves.  The way which
we had followed five or six years earlier, finding no one at that
time among our companions who understood us, was now being followed by many young people, disappointed in the same
way as ourselves, animated by the same exigencies, ending up
with exactly the same decision regarding religious faith.  It
seemed to us a natural — although unhoped-for — reaction of
the spirit ; and for the severe battles that were to come, as we
knew, we were happy to lose some of our peculiarity and to take
place among the humanity of our day.

* Agathon, Les Jeunes gens d'aujourd'hui.  Paris, Plon, 1913.

Massis and Psichari were themselves profoundly impressed by this convergence of thought. In general Agathon had found among boys ranging from 18 to 25 years of age in 1912, a love of action which some of them opposed to intelligence, others only to Epicureanism of thought ; a certain optimism opposed to the "disillusionment" of the "uprooted" of Barrès' generation ; a realistic sensitiveness "joyfully consenting to be taken in by life," a generous love for their nation not yet side-tracked, as it was later to be sidetracked for many, by a nationalism of the Maurras kind ; a taste for classical letters and the humanities too often mixed with a naïve indifference with regard to science ; and sometimes an ultra-Bergsonian anti-intellectualism, sometimes an aggressive intellectualism inspired by Maurras — oscillation of the pendulum of the intelligence to either side of the immaterial line of truth.   And these various tendencies were summed up in general "in the traditional and avowed form of Catholicism."   The religious sentiment of young men "needs a clear-cut and definite armature in which to put its living richness ; it reaches out toward discipline to assure its liberty ; it accepts the traditional attitudes because they seem to offer a marvelous frame, broad and supple enough to accept and organize present-day discoveries. It is love for life which guides them toward the faith. . . Is not the sense of the divine," added Agathon, "in a certain sense a superior form of the sense of the *real* ?"

According to Agathon, whose conclusions were recognized as correct outside Catholic circles — for example by a Socialist professing atheism, like Marcel Sembat — all the university youth of the first decade of the 20th century — those of our higher institutions of learning, of our most "intellectual" *lycées* such as Condorcet, Henri IV, Louis-le-Grand — then seemed to be taken up by Catholicism, and the science students even more than the "literary" ones.   The Ecole Normale, for instance — that cradle of university intelligence — which in

1905 numbered no more than three or four Catholics (who were called *talas* because they went to mass),* had forty in 1912, that is to say, close to a third of the Ecole.

At the Sorbonne "students of philosophy, departing from the sociological methods of Durkheim and Lévy-Bruhl, were seeking their inspiration from a Catholic, Victor Delbos," or Emile Boutroux, "whose speculation led them to the threshold of religious life." From that time on Bergson exercised the same influence. Claudel, Péguy, Francis Jammes and Léon Bloy — the latter known still to only a few — henceforth had their ardent readers and followers.

Another remarkable fact was that the young believers of 1912 were almost always converts : "Their search had not lasted long. One or two years at most, then one saw them submit-. ting faithfully to the Church," wrote someone who was to become one of our greatest friends, himself being at that time a convert of recent date, and of whom I shall speak later on.

I do not believe that it is without interest to go back to this far-off inquiry which in its day produced so profound an impression. If I do so, it is because the state of mind it brought to light and which caused Bergson to say : "The evolution of present-day youth appears to me as a kind of miracle," † did not pass away like so much smoke. Nothing was lost of the tendencies of that time ; all its seeds of truth or error produced abundant fruit.

*

*    *

The most fervent of these young men who in the first part of the 20th century affirmed their refound faith, persevered in it and fulfilled their promises after themselves making disciples in the generations which followed, and this in every sphere —

* Allaient *à la* messe.
† Inquiry made by the *Gaulois*, June 15, 1912.

among manual workers as well as intellectuals. The number
of influential Catholics has not ceased to grow in France in
the last thirty years which have been marked by famous conversions. Many of those in whom high hopes had been placed
fell in the First World War : Péguy, Psichari, Léonard Constant, Lotte, Alain Fournier, Pierre Villard, of whom I shall
speak in the third volume of these memoirs, and many others.
But their ideas inspired the young Catholics of today who have
participated with heroic fervour in the French resistance.

What did the young intellectual élite of the beginning of our
century oppose, and to what were they dedicated ? We could
not fail to be passionately interested in this.

Believers and unbelievers were both turning away from what
is now known as the dilettantism of Renan ; some because
Renan offended their faith, others because they were attracted
to action, and action imposed the choice of and a strong and
persevering love for the object of that choice. Nevertheless
no human course is ever entirely interrupted, and the influence
of André Gide, aided by the prestige of art, was later to succeed
that of Renan.

The fact remains that those Frenchmen who were young in
1912 had no liking for a passage from Renan like the following
from his *Saint Paul* :

"We would like to think of a skeptical Paul, shipwrecked and
abandoned, betrayed by his own, alone, subject to the disillusionment of old age. It would please us if the scales had fallen
from his eyes a second time, and our gentle incredulity would
have its little revenge if the most dogmatic of men had died
saddened and in despair, or let us say tranquil, on some shore
or road in Spain, also saying : '*Ergo erravi.*' " By which one
sees that dilettantism is quite a light word, which can conceal
resentments of singular bitterness.

Neither did the young Frenchmen of those days have any

liking for that kind of "cult for unbelievers" which seemed to be the ideal of Renan's *Patrice*.

"We would like to use our most precious perfumes to embalm Christianity and place our lachrymatories upon its tomb, if it would seriously consent to considering itself dead." Such perfumes, mixed with such tears, would have quite an odour !

The same cultivated youth which rejected dilettantism also turned away from the anti-patriotism made fashionable by the preceding generation. This youth which had not undergone the humiliation of the defeat of 1870, had found again a healthy love for its country, faith in France, a consciousness of her vocation in the world — a vocation not for domination but for liberation. This youth was ready for the sacrifice it could see was coming, as well as ready for action.

In this restoration of natural feeling Péguy and Maurras played a great rôle, and continued to play it ; the first in the sense of a very pure patriotism, mystical and moral, the second in the sense of amoral politics. The partisans of one and the other tendencies played their beneficent or nefarious rôle in martyred France.

Regarding the eclipse of French patriotism toward 1890, Agathon recalled some writings which today seem strange and incredible : Rémy de Gourmont named one of his articles in the *Mercure de France*, "The Bauble of Patriotism," and declared, "If we must state the matter clearly in a word, here it is : We are not patriots." A certain Léon Bazalgette wrote in *Le Problème de l'avenir latin* : "A man who is really human should not refuse to imagine the possibility of his country's ruin." Since then France has had occasion to see some of these "truly human" men show of what they were capable.

"In their absurd belief in historical fatalism some of our elders," added Agathon, "went so far as to consider it a good thing for primacy to pass to the Germanic race 'in which all was pure and great.' " These too had their heirs — who venerated the force rather than the "purity" of the conqueror.

## The Generation of 1905

"The advent of the new generation" was then dated from 1905. The German menace was again present, and our entire youth was ready to oppose it. It was indignant at the contemptible formulas I just recalled, and at the statement of one of their professors, who spoke of patriots as "pure sentimentalists." The idea of war became familiar to it, and the conviction that "France needed heroism to live."

Ernest Psichari was the very young forerunner of these young men — he who for ten years, since he was eighteen, had belonged to the army by free choice.

On his return from Africa he had wished to add his testimony to Agathon's inquiry. He had written :

"We have a feeling of frightful responsibility, and drag with us everywhere, as if riveted to us, the certainty of a crushing obligation. Our generation — those of us who began their manhood years with the century — is important. It is in it that all hopes have been placed, and we know it. Upon it depends the salvation of France, therefore the salvation of the world and of civilization. Everything turns on us.

"It seems to me that young men feel obscurely that they will see great things, that great things will be accomplished by them. They will not be amateurs, nor skeptics. They will not be tourists across life. They know what is expected of them."

Jacques, at the request of Massis, wrote to Agathon concerning the orientation of French youth toward Catholicism a letter in which he insisted upon those truths which seemed to him most in danger of being misunderstood :

"Will the movement toward conversion among contemporary youth be limited to a cultured élite ?  Does God will finally to send to His poor the apostles of the later times, proclaimed by Notre Dame de la Salette and by Blessed Grignion de Montfort, and who will separate for Him those He will have chosen ? . . . Here in any case is what reason and experience permit us to affirm : the tendencies in question will lead to nothing solid or durable if one is not firmly resolved to allow oneself to be radically informed by the *ecclesiastical* spirit, which is the Holy Spirit.  *As you are unleavened.*  God wishes us entirely renewed ; it is the Church alone which can make us over.

"But for this, piety alone is insufficient — doctrine is necessary.  *The lamp of thy body is thine eye.  If the light within thee becomes darkness, how great will become the darkness !*  However little the doctrine becomes impaired in us, we allow ourselves to be corrupted.  Do not Christians belong to the Truth, to the second Person of the Blessed Trinity ?  If they scorn Intelligence, it is the face of their God, whose light is sealed upon them, which they deride, at the same time exposing themselves to the vilest failings.  To keep oneself intact from the least stain of error and to have one's eyes turned toward God — this is Catholic purity.  It has its source in the intellect, which discerns essence and maintains integrity. . .

"Doubtless the 'simple' do not need to study theology.  But 'a poor peasant woman' when she knows her catechism, knows exactly the theology of which she is capable.  It is right that the 'civilized élite' know as much — in proportion — as this poor peasant woman. . .

"The Christian vocation is a contemplative vocation.  It is through the intellect that we will have our beatitude in heaven : *joy from the truth*. And here below, if merit depends upon the will, it is still the intellect which rules the will. And above all we are called, from the time of our regeneration by baptism, to taste in this life an anticipation of our end. For Martha adds the active life to the life of prayer, but she is not deprived of the part of Mary, since this part is necessary and the only one necessary. That is why the desert Fathers, according to Cassian, made contemplation the normal end of every Christian life, to which all the rest, even the virtues, was subordinated as a means. Assuredly it is charity which is the principle and the end of contemplation. And the saints teach us that in contemplative union the natural processes of the intellect should give place to the darkness filled with light in which God makes Himself known through experience. It is none the less true that the intellectual faculty is the condition and the instrument of contemplation, and that doctrine — acquired by study or infused by extraordinary grace — is the indispensable foundation of the house of the soul.

"Thus it is that from the illiterate to the most erudite, Christians are, properly speaking, *intellectuals* ; and the greatest crime of the pseudo-intellectuals of the modern world is to have brought about, among many, the confusion of intelligence with their madness."

Thus Jacques took his position concerning problems which appeared to him thenceforth as essential. At the same time he sought to work out a line of thought which could be independent and authentically Christian in the midst of the warring currents of this period.

I should like to stress somewhat the confusion of ideas from which a section of youth suffered at that time, and which has not yet exhausted its effects. I quoted above the page in which Agathon explained how the religious emotions of youth needed a "clear-cut and definite armature" and how they accepted — at least some of them — "the traditional attitudes," guided toward faith by "love for life."

There was much of good in this, mixed with great risks : there was danger of seeking "clear-cut and definite armature" in an order more apparent than real, and a false rigour which would harden the mind in a negative and bitter attitude. There was danger of accepting "the traditional attitudes" as a frozen image of the past to which one clung in order to apply true principles in the wrong way.  Jacques could see the danger of these human traditions weighted down by too many impurities and errors, and he felt that the only way out was to cling to the only tradition in which there was no risk of error — the purely divine tradition of the Catholic faith.  But he was hardly beginning to perceive the demands made by such a determination ; and he had not yet had time to learn by experience how necessary it was to go about alone discovering these things.  How greatly he later regretted not having separated himself at once from that odd and unfortunate group which Massis was to "launch" under the name of "the party of the intelligence" as if the two words could be joined, and as if the first did not do wrong to the second.  He was also aware of the renewing power which tradition as he understood it implied and demanded to be put forth boldly, but he was only beginning to discern the ways in which it had to be exercised.

At this period a section of youth, rightly attracted by all that was evangelical in the social aspirations of modern times, gave in at the same time to a sort of sentimental irrationalism in the philosophical realm.  Another section of youth, reacting vigorously against this irrationalism, hardened itself against all evangelical influence.  So that many of those who were (theoretically) Catholic in spirit ran the danger of becoming pagan at heart ; and many of those who were Christian at heart ran the risk of becoming heretical in spirit (the heresy of those days was called "modernism").  Jacques, who was interested in those days only in metaphysics and theology, was struck especially by the latter danger. He was to realize several years later that they had to be faced both at the same time.

It is difficult to imagine today to what state speculative reason was reduced in many persons by an exclusive love of action, and by an anti-intellectualism which debilitated in them the sense of truth. Bergson's influence had passed from the philosophical field to the field of religion and dogma, under the action not of the master himself — he kept the strictest reserve in this matter — but of his disciples who made the most intemperate usage of Bergson's theses. Among these disciples many young priests and seminarians — weak philosophers and superficial theologians — carried on the most unbelievable talk. Bergson's young followers thus made the position of religious modernism rest upon a seductive philosophical basis. The Agathon inquiry had revealed the tendencies of an important group of Catholic intellectuals who fervently embraced the doctrines of Le Roy, of Laberthonnière and of Maurice Blondel. *L'Action,* a famous book by Blondel, had an important influence on young Catholics and delivered them from the taboos of pseudo-intellectualism which prevailed in official teaching, but it lent itself to doubtful theological interpretations. One of the most remarkable contributions published by Agathon, that of a young student of twenty, expressed this tendency very well :

"We are no longer religious in the manner of our ancestors, and yet we adopt in full good faith the same formulas and the same dogmas. Each of the words we use expresses an idea which is new, or at least which has lived and been enriched ; but whereas these ideas have changed, their relationship has remained immutable, and these are the same dogmas which express what we believe in with our whole being. Thus, as Pascal wished, we speak as the common man, but 'with a hind-thought.' . . . It was Bergson who opened up a new road which we followed in the wake of Le Roy, Blondel, and Father Laberthonnière.   Our reason is thus able to grant to our emotions those religious effusions which they need. . ."

The lack of logic and the danger of such a position were evident : one wondered how, if "each of the words we use expresses a new idea," their relationship could remain unchangeable.   New ideas normally mean new realities, or those newly known.   Why would these realities remain in unchanged relationship to one another ?   And if their relationship changes at the same time as the real content of knowledge, how can their dogmatic statement — which this group of Catholic young men declared they did not renounce — continue to denote the same revealed truth, the immutable object of Catholic dogma ?

Bergsonian anti-intellectualism, accidental at least in part, since with Bergson himself it was first directed against the errors of rationalism, before putting in question the true nature of the intellect, was thus aggravated by the new or old defenders of modernism in being applied in the field, which Bergson himself had not considered, of the dogmatic statement of revealed data.

The young Catholics of fervour and good will who believed themselves disciples of Bergson were opposed to other fervent young Catholics who by an even graver error, or through carelessness, attached themselves to the rationalism of Maurras. Anti-intellectualism and rationalism which could only be efficiently and rightly combated by the metaphysics of Aristotle and of Saint Thomas Aquinas.

### Responsibilities

Massis spoke much later of his first visit to us on Rue de l'Orangerie in a touching and generous way, in *Notre Ami*

*Psichari* : "Can I ever forget," he said, " — no matter how opposed our political ideas may be — what meeting them meant to me ?"

Neither have we forgotten what a friend Massis was for a long time to us, his desire for truth and intellectual integrity — his confidence. And it is with great sadness that I think of the fate that has conspired against him. Why was it that he had to develop in the least generous direction of his nature, that he had to become the victim of the hard hearts and false minds who have too long dominated a notable part of the youth of our country? If Ernest Psichari had lived, this doubtless would not have happened. Massis was much closer to Ernest than to Jacques. Ernest would sooner or later have freed him.

I will refer further on to the responsibility we felt toward him in those far-off days of which I am speaking. The fact remains that thereafter he closed his ears more and more to the advice of the friend from whom Father Clérissac told him never to separate himself, and that he refused — not only regarding political ideas but also regarding positions which involve the entire life of the spirit — what Jacques, in the midst of the stormy controversies of the time, tried to make him see as he himself was discerning it more clearly. This all was to end in a stupid cabal to which Massis lent himself, and in which those men who hated the author of *La Primauté du Spirituel* * tried — this was not the first time nor the last — to carry up to Rome calumnies which would satisfy their resentments as well as their political combinations, and through which, this time, they turned into account the doctrinal zeal of one of Jacques' former pupils, imagining they could use him in order to have Jacques "condemned." This attempt failed miserably, and Massis no doubt regretted having taken part in it. But even more than this personal incident which might have been overlooked, it was — well before the present war —

* Translated into English under the title, *The Things that Are Not Caesar's.*

Massis' political orientation and his attitude generally opposed to that of Jacques' on questions of universal interest which put an end to their friendship.   If these lines happen to fall under the eyes of Massis I should like him to know, however, that we remember that friendship and that I do not wish to have said anything that would wound his soul.

At the time we first met him, on the eve of the First World War — on the threshold of the Apocalypse, according to Léon Bloy — Henri Massis was still politically free and independent of the Action Française.   He himself bore witness to this independence in *Les Jeunes gens d'aujourd'hui.*

One of the characteristics which he pointed out as common to the youth of those days was that "realism," very varying in quality to be sure, in which democrats and monarchists shared alike.   Agathon wrote that democratic youth "is the most numerous and if not the most restless, doubtless the most truly realistic."   Such youth mistrust "the purely rational order" of Maurras, and "the formal perfection that scorns interior perfection."   The youth of the Action Française "admits the individual disagreements which separate them ; they declare they are content with the practical concord of their action" which is easy for them because "complete moral skepticism inspires their doctrine."

Agathon notes the fact, moreover, that it was "from the Action Française group — from Charles Maurras and his young disciples in the *Revue Critique des Idées et des Livres*" that he met with "the fiercest objections. . . M. Maurras termed us 'doctrinaires of enthusiasm and of the faith.'"   M. Clouard wrote Agathon a letter warmly defending Maurras' position.

Another fervent partisan of Maurras whom the latter later treated with choice ferocity, was surprised that Agathon found the methods used by the Action Française "too dry."   "There is not," he wrote, "now at the beginning of the 20th century a more passionate movement than the Action Française." This remark was no doubt exact. But what sort of passion animated these enemies of romanticism ?

"You see, the young men who have just entered life," said the same correspondent, "and who have a sense of political and social realism know that love does not reign upon earth . . . and that man's first care is to be always ready to fight. I imagine that when they see in their midst a child who thinks only of love they say : 'The fool ! He will be beaten by life.' "

These naïve people "who thought only of love" were in the opinion of Maurras' followers, the disciples of Marc Sangnier who made up the Catholic group, the "Sillon." Neither charity nor good will were lacking in this group, but firm philosophical and theological doctrines. For these reasons the position of the Sillon was condemned ; nevertheless its members' loyalty to the Church appeared in the alacrity with which they immediately declared their rejection of the errors pointed out in the document denouncing them, and submitted to the decisions of Pope Pius X.

For a long time the partisans of the Action Française claimed they had had an easy triumph over them. But the day came when their school of thought was also condemned ; in 1926 they too were denounced by the Church and held outside its communion until their submission, made with great difficulty in 1939.

*

*    *

It was after 1918, if I am not mistaken, that Massis connected his activities as a writer to the Action Française group. From then on he continued in the general attitude — intellectual and political — of the partisans of Maurras.

In the beginnings of his development in this direction Father Clérissac and ourselves played a part — the measure and sig-

nificance of which I am not able to estimate, but it was enough
to add a feeling of responsibility and a particularly poignant
regret to the memories we have of our naïveness and thoughtlessness in those times.   Father Clérissac passionately admired
Maurras ; and in his disgust for the modern world, his pure
enthusiasm for the metaphysical notion of order, he trusted a
movement then developing under the aegis of "violence in the
service of order," the spiritual dangers of which he did not discern.   Maurras' school had at that time a certain appearance
of intellectual vitality, and had not yet hardened in its worst
aspects ; this partly explains Father Clérissac's illusions.   His
advice and influence absolutely prevailed over our minds, and
dispensed us from examining questions which, in any case,
seemed to us then without importance.   For Jacques attributed importance only to metaphysics and theology, and I —
lost in the unclouded bliss which came then to me from
prayer, and from meditation on the Treatise on the Trinity in
Saint Thomas' *Summa Theologica* — felt completely foreign
to political problems.   In any event, I had by instinct an in-
superable apprehension toward anything concerning political
activity, in which I saw — and still do — the domain of what
Saint Paul calls the evil of time ; a domain reserved to those
called to bring about the triumph of some great idea by means
of the circumstances at hand, but entirely inappropriate for
the action of a man of thought, which is carried on above time,
and seeks to persuade and not to conquer.   When in this
story the sequence of our life's events obliges me to touch on
this domain I do so unwillingly, and in order to give an idea of
the painful problems in which Jacques found himself involved.

Of ourselves we should not have dreamed of taking the
slightest interest in the movement of which Father Clérissac
spoke so sympathetically to us and to Massis.   As I said, our
preoccupations were purely of a speculative and religious order.
Besides, our allegiance was and always has remained on the

side of those who wish more justice on earth, who respect the human person and who are indignant over the destitution to which such great masses of men are reduced. We could not take seriously the monarchical restoration preached by Maurras and desired by Father Clérissac. Order, old or new, was not for us an unconditional absolute ; we thought that it too should bear the spiritual mark of truth and charity.

But we were scarcely emerging from that deep disorder of the spirit from which God had rescued us through the gift of faith and Saint Thomas by the rigour of a doctrine in which the Church herself finds inspiration.

We felt that we owed the peace and equilibrium which followed in our souls to our godfather Léon Bloy and to Father Clérissac — two men of perfect integrity of conscience. For us their example carried considerable weight, and fate decreed — fate, which is a little blind providence — that these two patrons of our youth were equally * anti-democratic and anti-republican. These tendencies awakened an instinctive antipathy in us, but aware of our inexperience and ignorant especially of the rights and limitations of spiritual direction, we considered it our duty to go against our inclination.

Father Clérissac pitilessly mocked our democratic leanings and the socialistic ideas that remained dear to Jacques' heart. In his eyes all these things were remains of the old man which should be sloughed off. When Jacques went on Péguy's behalf to Appuldurcomb, the Father Abbot, Dom Delatte, had swept away with a wave of the hand the questions Jacques asked him candidly on the subject of the "legitimacy of interest-bearing loans," and which fifteen years later another religious, our dear friend Father Vincent MacNabb, was to receive in an entirely different way.

Jacques willingly admitted that his stock of political and

* Although in a very different way : Léon Bloy never sympathized with the Action Française.

social ideas, or rather tendencies, which had been neither sub-
jected to criticism nor elaborated, were not much good ; these
ideas dated from the time when mankind held for him the
place of God, and it was not yet a question of establishing a new
social doctrine. . . Deeply engaged in the criticism of theological liberalism, he was inclined to consider real the fierce criticism which the partisans of the Action Française made of "liberalism" in every domain, and all the more so since he saw the
official democracy of that day ally its cause with that of all the
anti-religious myths.

In an untimely effort of docility he put off too long examining the value of an anti-liberalism which in reality confronted
one error with another error ; he reproaches himself with having passively accepted an influence and direction which was on
this point outside the spiritual order, and with not having himself made at that time a serious study of Maurras' religious and
political ideas.   We contented ourselves with reading his articles which in those days were always favourable to the Church,
but we did not guard against the fact that it was the Church
only in so far as she was Roman, and not in so far as she was
Apostolic, whom Maurras so praised and admired.   Neither
did we take the trouble to read his books until the day when
our attention was violently drawn to them by Pope Pius' condemnation, in 1926, of his whole school of thought.

We knew that many young people had gone from the Action Française over to Catholicism and we also thought Maurras himself was tending in that direction.   Moreover — and
this contributed further to complicate matters — Jacques'
philosophical positions, despite his early declared anti-Carte-
sianism, were soon accepted by a certain number of young Catholics of the Action Française.   Later on several of them were to
persevere in "Thomism" (as they understood it) longer than
they did in obedience to the Church.   But at the time of
which I write it was the Sillon which the Church con-

demned. And certain of Maurras' young partisans who frequently came to see Jacques were true Christians, whose interior life was very pure and lofty. One of them who had been arrested and imprisoned for his zeal as a *camelot du roi* became after his conversion a truly evangelical priest. Thus all we saw about us led us to consider correct the optimistic views of Father Clérissac as to the religious future of the Action Française.

Less than three months after the death of Ernest Psichari another terrible blow befell us ; we heard from Angers, where he had retired for several months, of the death of Father Clérissac. It was the time of the *"union sacrée"* ; being entirely absorbed by the drama of the war, we were less interested than ever to study Maurras' position seriously. After the war and the peace treaty we should have examined it. It was then, starting from 1920, that our responsibility was involved without our having thought of it — up until the time of Jacques' noisy break with the Action Française, of which I shall speak in another volume. I will quote here two recent pages in Jacques' diary in which he looks back upon these incidents of the long-distant past.

"At that period the partisans of the Action Française still had in my eyes the prestige of their patriotism, and I presumptuously imagined I could help them extricate this patriotism and the healthy ideas it contained from the positivist system of Maurras and from a nationalistic idolatry the danger of which I was perceiving more and more. The parliamentary *mores* of the Third Republic seemed to give reason to the criticisms of the Action Française which blackened them at will with the complacent acquiescence of Republican officials who no longer believed in anything. Maurras' deep atheism, the cult of violence and the intellectual regimentation which raged among his disciples, his increasingly odious polemical procedure (up until the day it became apparent to me in its falsehood and cynical use of calumny, at the time of his ferocious campaign against Georges Valois) — I closed my eyes on all this in the ingenuous hope of Maurras' forthcoming conversion, which many of his Catholic disciples heralded in France and in Rome, and for which so many sincere souls were wearying heaven with their prayers ; and in the absurd hope of bringing about a doctrinal reform and the establishment of a Christian political philosophy in a school whose political principles suffered from irremediable errors, a fact I did not then realize as I had only the most superficial ideas in this field.

"Later on, after the publication of *La Primauté du Spirituel*, Dom Florent Miège — the holy contemplative who invited me at that time to visit him at the Chartreuse of Valsainte and whose incomparable friendship was superabundantly to compensate me for all the hate which rose up in the ecclesiastical Action Française circles — tried to tell me that God puts to use even the mistakes of those who love him and that my relations with the people of the Action Française had permitted my testimony at the most critical moment to aid and enlighten souls of good will, in spite of that I will always accuse myself with having put some faith, for a while, through unpardonable thoughtlessness, in a movement whose political sophisms have as their basis a contempt for the Gospel. Today more than ever I bless the liberating intervention of the Church which, in 1926, exposed the errors of the Action Française, following which I finally examined Maurras' doctrines and saw what they were worth. There began for me then a period of reflection devoted to moral and political philosophy in which I tried to work out the character of authentically Christian politics and to establish, in the light of a philosophy of history and of culture, the true significance of democratic inspiration and the nature of the new humanism for which we are waiting. Thus, at least, for what will soon be for twenty years I have been able without respite to combat the ideas and the men whose wickedness I had seen at close hand, and who were finally to seize power with the defeat of the fatherland, and to betray the soul of France."

There were many causes for the illusions with which Jacques reproached himself in these pages : first, his youth at the time all this began ; the inexperienced docility I have spoken of with regard to the guidance, even in merely human matters, of the spiritual father he so greatly venerated ; the indulgence or enthusiasm so many great theologians were then showing with regard to the exponent of "organizing empiricism" ; and the general attitude of the Church herself during those years, and of Pope Pius X who showed forbearance, waiting for Maurras' conversion. . .

The fact remains that although Jacques never belonged to any organization or institution of the Action Française, and although he always guarded his independence as a philosopher, it was possible to reproach him with an attitude for which his negligence was responsible, as well as with his several years' collaboration on the *Revue Universelle,* which was edited first by Jacques Bainville, later by Henri Massis.

The tenor of Jacques' articles was philosophical and not political ; nevertheless from time to time there appeared, among other quips, an ironical note regarding democracy, the last vestige of the political influence of Léon Bloy and Father Clérissac in a field to which the young philosopher's personal thought had not yet systematically applied itself. Above all, the political positions of one section of those who believed themselves to be his disciples risked creating intolerable misunderstandings and deforming the meaning of a way of thought which was always above party lines, and which, when applied to social and political problems, was to raise against the prejudices of the Rightist parties and the self-righteous a bolder synthesis — but one doctrinally well founded — than the aspirations of the

19th century "liberal Catholics," which were unfortunately overburdened with error.

It was to do away with all misunderstanding as well as to set down precisely for himself the principles of practical philosophy that Jacques Maritain left the field of metaphysical speculation and undertook his works on political philosophy, of which the first was *La Primauté du Spirituel*, published in 1927.

Then several of the young men who had followed him up to that time, turned against him and were obliged to choose between *Politique d'abord* (Politics First) of Maurras and *La Primauté du Spirituel* which had always been, implicitly or explicitly, Jacques' teaching.   But new friends and new disciples were to come who have been — and are — his joy, and among them has numbered the heroic youth in whom we never lost hope during the darkest days of the war ; it was this youth who, according to an expression which has become dear to Jacques, "prevented France from losing her soul." *

## Concerning Spiritual Direction

What I said above concerning our docility in all matters regarding Father Clérissac's advice, and of the way this advice involved Jacques in a bias favourable to the Action Française with which he was to reproach himself so sharply, presents a problem which Jacques and I have often thought of since.

There was in this an inadvertence on the part of our guide — and an error on our part — because this element of a temporal order should never have been proposed by him in the context of his spiritual directions, nor accepted by us without examination.

* *France be careful not to lose your soul* is the title of the first number of the "Cahiers du Témoignage Chrétien," a clandestine publication of the French Resistance.

In this inadvertence of a man of such rare rectitude of judgment and character there doubtless appear the inevitable "limitations of the created" which the Father had mournfully pointed out to us in the actions of the best of men.

If I thus allow myself to formulate a judgement which might appear presumptuous in regard to an admirable priest to whom we owe an immense debt, I do not do so with a light heart or without confusion. If it were only a question of myself, in my own narrow limits, I would silently keep to the examination of my conscience ; but it is a question that concerns truth itself in a certain practical order, and here neither our insignificance nor the greatness of a holy guide could prevent the statement of a fact. A bias which in the case of Father Clérissac was accidental to the essence of his own spiritual life and to his spiritual advice — combined with our confidence in him and our inexperience — resulted in grave consequences for us and for some of those who uncritically followed with us the lead they received from him.

Since then we have often met with errors of this kind, in various connections, and have observed their regrettable consequences. It is therefore in an altogether general way that we can point out a certain risk inherent in the direction of souls, and speak of it here. Whatever criticism I may risk in this, I write these lines fearlessly, feeling it to be my present duty. In every life a time comes when it becomes natural to fear only the God one loves and from whom one expects light and salvation.

Naturally I do not place in doubt for a single moment the general usefulness of spiritual direction. We ourselves experienced how necessary and beneficial were the spiritual guides sent to us by God's grace, and our gratitude toward them will never end. I also know what Saint Teresa and other saints have taught on this great subject. If Father Clérissac himself

made fun of those directors who advise their penitents on the
colour of their hats, or who claim to lead them to heaven "in
an armchair," he still was persuaded, in the line of Christian
tradition, that souls, especially when they have started in the
spiritual ways, have the greatest need of the advice of a wise
and experienced man, and cannot without temerity place confidence in themselves alone. The words "spiritual fatherhood"
would perhaps be more accurate here than "direction." The
moral authority of a father, the education he gives, are as necessary in the spiritual as in the natural order. How otherwise
can the soul sift out the illusions of self-love, prevent itself
from being deceived by inclinations which are inherent in its
individual nature, or escape from the ambushes and mirages
along its way, and learn little by little to form the judgement of
its conscience in that "peace of God which passeth all understanding" ? The Christian soul knows the incomparable value
of total confidence and simplicity by means of which a light
is received that nothing in the world can replace.

The observations I wish to make here are remarks in the
margin of these great truths. And they concern at one and
the same time the prudence of the director and that of the
person directed. Experience has shown us the point to which
the direction of souls demands in the director the purest discrimination between those things which are God's and those
which are Caesar's. To be truly spiritual this direction requires that the director himself distinguish in himself what is
of the order of grace, faith, theology and perfection, and what
is only of human heritage, of time-honoured customs, family,
race or caste prejudices, or of the order of individual inclination, preference or taste. This angelic discrimination doubtless does not exist in its perfection : even the saints, detached
from everything, carried some appurtenance of their times.
Nearly always something remains which dims ever so little the
transparency of vision of the most scrupulous director, and

mixes in with his spiritual directives advice or guidance of another order.

It thus happens, because of psychological entanglements which are very difficult to avoid, that entirely human opinions come to hold in the mind of him who should practice "the art of arts" almost the same rank as those certainties touching upon supernatural life, and are set forth nearly on the same ground as those things which are required for the soul's perfection.

The problem I refer to concerns not only the rôle of the spiritual guide and the restricted number of persons who have recourse to a director. It also concerns, under different conditions and on another level, the ministry of a priest in relation to the mass of the faithful. How difficult is the position of a priest! He must teach and guide. And even when it is a question of the things of the earth he must teach and guide for heaven, not for earth. It is a great misfortune that the faithful sometimes receive, mixed in with religious, dogmatic and moral teaching, advice which adds to eternal truths prejudices and passions of a temporal, social and political order. Yet the Church as such does not occupy herself with things in this domain except with regard to their highest principles, those which touch on the order of morality and whose application has varied throughout human history and can prove sound in various analogous ways.

When the necessity of such discrimination is not clearly recognized, the influence of the priest — which should be purely spiritual and moral — approaches the regions of political contingency, and one is confronted by the case where ecclesiastical personalities use their authority in good faith to direct the faithful in the ephemeral and deceiving ways of the politics followed by a given country or prevailing for but a day. And sometimes this happens, as we saw in the affair of the Action Française, in defiance of the directives and orders of the Pope himself, and without fear of drawing into formal disobedience religious souls who, without this sad confusion, would have recognized the legitimacy of obedience.    Thus it is that schisms come about — much more often because of questions of temporal order than because of questions of religious and theological order.

As for the one who is directed — to returned to our first consideration — it is evident that his own good sense and prudence, hence his responsibility, are involved in the matter.    Many errors would be spared him if he knew clearly from the beginning that however rough-hewn or deficient in virtue his conscience might be in the beginning, it is up to it — after receiving the enlightenment of wise counsel — to carry before God the judgement upon which depends the morality of the free act : because spiritual direction has for its object to teach us to form wisely, and not to elude, the judgement of our conscience.    The accidental danger I have pointed out nevertheless remains all the greater for the one directed in that the spiritual direction he has accepted is the more sure ; the authority of a spiritual father who is admired and venerated then overflows almost inevitably into all the advice that he gives to a soul already inclined to filial docility.

Such souls must endure a hard schooling.    Happy are they in whom by dint of experiences, errors, sufferings and divine purifications that discrimination takes place which they did not find in the mind of their director.    Their spiritual way is simplified in the measure that it has thus been purified, and it tends to conform itself more each day to the simple way of charity, of love of God and neighbour, in which consists the whole Law and the Prophets.    This is truly evangelical simplicity, the most difficult to attain of all the kinds of simplicity, the name of which is synonymous with perfection.    These are the souls which, by the virtue of Christ, compensate for our faults and errors in the bosom of the Church.

# CHAPTER SEVEN

## GIFTS FROM HEAVEN

### The Rude Shock of Conversion

"Blessed are those who die in the Lord," and at the very time grace has touched them and converted them to God. They will not accumulate the faults and errors which lie in wait on life's road for those who have received the rude shock of conversion, those to whom is suddenly given the superhuman precept to live "as not living." Was it not to the first Christians, all of whom were converts, that Saint Paul said :

"Know ye not, that as many of us as were baptized unto Christ Jesus, we were baptized unto His death ? We were buried therefore with Him through this baptism unto death. . ." *

Every Christian is essentially a "separated" being, separated from the world by the shroud of Christ's death ; but for the convert, it is by a sudden blow — which tears apart his bonds with himself and with others — that he is separated from the world ! In one instant, at the hour of grace, all values have been moved about for him. And he becomes a strange being in the eyes of his neighbour whom he loves or tries to love "as himself" — but who does not love or understand him, and looks with a surprise not unmixed with distrust upon this bizarre inhabitant of a city infinitely removed from the roads known to this world. The world is without shame because it is animal, but the Christian must bend his efforts to becoming a spiritual man. The world respects greatness of quantity and strength, the spiritual man must glorify God through humility and poverty.

Eternity has descended upon a soul devoted until then to

* Rom. VI, 3.

passing time ; it has struck it like lightning. The divine storm
has laid waste our disorder, and charity has only begun to order
within us our different loves.

The intention of the convert from then on hangs suspended
to the immutable and eternal truth, perceived within the faith,
and the convert must now put to rights all the objects in a house
made topsy-turvy by the invasion of grace ; what is passing
must be reconciled with what remains forever, we must live
at the same time according to the eternal and according to the
temporal — the disproportion is infinite. How can we adjust
our activities between these two extremes ?

While still rapt in the vision of spiritual things, we are again
set down on the earth, and we go stumbling forward. We
fall ; we err in our judgements, we are unjust, are partial with a
divine partiality — with an all too human clumsiness.

An equilibrium must be established, our vision of worldly
things must become clear again ; but this must not happen too
quickly, it must not come about at the expense of the spiritual
reality known through faith. We must — but this is exactly
what we do not realize until later — we must make this land-
ing gently and without bumps, so that little by little the most
humble things of everyday life are assumed into the spiritual
vision — things, people, the works of men. Little by little we
shall become accustomed to the light and learn to judge with
equity.

This adaptation is difficult ; God must help us and we must
help God. He will work all the good in us ; and we shall have
to let Him act if we are to avoid evil, and to do with Him what
little good we shall not have prevented.

God arranges the events that touch us, which are independent
of our will, and which unfold themselves in time. He acts
also upon our will, from within, because He is more intimate
with us than we ourselves, and because He is the author of our
free will.

The saints respond to His action with perfect abandonment, absolute confidence, with that gentleness and humility which make every deed righteous and wise.

But he who has only just been born to the life of grace — the poor convert — begins his spiritual life as the child begins his natural life : he is at once supplied with and bereft of everything. Life is present and that is *all*, essentially speaking ; but experience is lacking, except that experience outside of time which faith has given him. Wisdom which orders everything with the order of love is present only potentially ; and perfection is but a far-off goal, desired but not yet reached.

Difficulties then arise, on account of our wills which have not yet learned to bend before the demands of grace, and on account of the disproportion existing between the light of the régime of grace and that of the régime of reason. They are not opposed — they are only separated by the infinite distance of natural life from supernatural life.

The convert learns only little by little to know his real powers. He may begin by framing purposes out of all proportion to his real capacity. A holy and learned guide is necessary to him (and more learned than holy, says Teresa of Avila). This guide, if one is so fortunate as to find him, will judge of the solidity and resistance of one's soul ; will prevent activity inspired more by presumption than heroism, and will moderate it to avoid the collapse of a physical and moral energy insufficient to nourish great but premature desires.

But for a long time still, while progressing toward that interior equilibrium which is given by God, the soul of the convert — making its way among the vicissitudes of nature and the adventures of grace, held by the invisible hand of Another who leads it there where it does not will to go — will make of itself for ill-adjusted activity : for too much boldness or timidity, too much pity or too much hardness ; it will wound itself all over, until it finally perceives the true measure which is self-dispossession and freedom.    And blessed be those wounds that are made by the pricks of Christ in poor Adam's flesh, and are of greater worth than the false peace of the world and self-satisfaction.

\*

\*      \*

Many unbelievers who were converts or who were on their way to being converted to Catholicism were to be found among our friends at the time dealt with in this book (and later). Conversions to Catholicism were indeed very numerous in France at the end of the 19th century and thereafter.    These conversions often took place around great believers like Léon Bloy and Paul Claudel, even around such unbelievers as Maurras and André Gide, among their closest friends and disciples. In Gide's circle they were remarkable because of the important artistic and literary rôle and the intellectual quality of those who learned from him how to free themselves from him, and who later understood better than he the parable of the Prodigal Son.    I am thinking of Dupouey, of Ghéon, of Francis Jammes, Copeau, Jacques Rivière, J. P. Laurens, Charles Du Bos, Gabriel Marcel, René Schwob, of Jean-Pierre Altermann, who became a priest and whose action brought back so many souls to God.    One of Jacques Copeau's daughters is a missionary religious, Rivière's son and daughter are a monk and nun in the order of Saint Benedict ; one of Francis Jammes' sons is a priest. . .  Among those I have just named we count several very dear friends whom God gave us without withdrawing them from André Gide, because God loves faithfulness.

But doubtless I am wrong in calling André Gide an unbeliever ; he certainly was not one in 1916–1919, when he wrote in *Numquid et tu* . . . dedicated to Charles Du Bos :

". . . It is not so much a matter of believing in the words of Christ because Christ is the Son of God — as of understanding that Christ is God because His words are divine and infinitely above all that has been proposed to us by the art and wisdom of men.

"This divinity suffices me. My mind and my heart are satisfied by this proof. What you add to it obscures it.

"It is because Christ is the Son of God, people have said, that we must believe in His words. And others came who no longer took His words into account because they did not admit that Jesus was the Son of God.

"Lord, it is not because I am told You are the Son of God that I listen to Your words ; but Your words are more beautiful than all human words, and it is in this I recognize that You are the Son of God." *

It seems Gide always believed in Christ's divinity, even at the time when it was the least concern of his friends and disciples.

Today it would be otherwise if we are to judge from his latest book, *Attendu que* . . . (as in *Numquid et tu* . . . the elliptical points which form a part of the title doubtless also have their meaning), and by the lines which Henri Hell delightedly culls from it in a review.† "Quoting Christ's last words on the Cross : God ! My God ! Why hast Thou forsaken Me, Gide writes : 'How is it possible not to see in these tragic words, not an abandonment or a betrayal by God, but this : that Christ, in believing and making others believe that He and God were together, deceived Himself and deceived us, because the One He called "My Father" had never recognized Him as His Son, that the God He represented — Himself — was only as He sometimes said, "the Son of Man." It is this God alone that I can and wish to adore.' "

I shall not add, as does the author of the article : "O, how one loves this Gide !" I shall say: How can the Gide we love

---

* André Gide. Quoted in his *Journal*, p. 588.
† *Fontaine* No. 32, pp. 220–1, Algiers, 1944.

think and write these paltry and unreasonable words ! "Abandonment, betrayal by God . . . making others believe He and God were together." To adore and to be able to adore only Him who "deceived Himself and deceived us. . . It is this God alone that I can and wish to adore." But such a God would be Satan himself, who deceived himself and deceives us, "liar and father of lies" whose weapons remain falsehood and illusion.

The day Gide wrote this passage which is exactly opposed to the one I quoted from *Numquid et tu . . .* , he must have been drunk with despair and unaware of what he was doing.

It is the duty of the least among believers to speak the truth infused in their souls, without timidity before the great things of the world, no matter how great or admired they may be. Because, through a reversibility that is the inverse of that which carries back to Jesus the good which is done to the least among us, the evil which is done to Jesus — an error put forth in regard to Him — is visited back upon our poor selves in spiritual wounds. In taking on our human nature Christ wished to identify Himself with all human misery ; He is the poor man who is hungry, thirsty, and naked ; He is the sick, the stranger deprived of his country, the man deprived of his liberty. He said so Himself : "When the Son of Man cometh in his glory" and will judge the living and the dead, he will say to those on his right hand : "Come, ye blessed of my Father . . . for I was hungry and ye gave me to eat . . . I was a stranger and ye brought me within. . . Amen, I say to you inasmuch as ye did it to one of the least of these my brethren, ye did it to me." *

He identified Himself with the sinner, much more, with sin itself. The eternal stigmata He received upon the Cross are the wounds made upon Him by sin, which he took upon Himself in its entirety.

* Matthew, xxv, 31–40.

For this reason He is also first among the abandoned ones : God, my God, why hast Thou forsaken me ! But that is the cry that befits the Saviour of our souls ! How does Gide not see this ? To this point He loved us — to the point of taking upon Himself that abandonment which would be our eternal portion if He had not come to save us.

Should this cry scandalize us as it did the Jews who shook their heads on seeing His distress and reproached Him with His claim of saving the world — He who could not save Himself and come down from His Cross ? They did not understand that at this supreme hour when our salvation was being accomplished, the identification of Christ with powerless and sinful humanity was so complete that as a result the very all-powerfulness of His divinity was bound, remitted entirely by the Son into the hands of the Father. This was the hour when Lucifer was vanquished by the absolute dispossession of the Son of God : in which the crucified Word made manifest that not only in His humanity but eternally in His divinity He had received everything from the Father, the perfect source of the procession of the Son, and the Holy Ghost.

## A Great Friend in God

Among the young people whose coming or return into the faith in the first years of this century began to forecast a Catholic renaissance in France, there was one particularly dear to our hearts whom we came to know through Agathon's book. This book contained many valuable documents signed with names that were later to become familiar to us — that of Robert Vallery-Radot, of Jacques Copeau, at the time editor of the *Nouvelle Revue Française*, that of Henri Hoppenot. It contained in particular a letter signed Ch. H. (Charles Henrion), and Jacques' letter which I mentioned earlier.

It was through these letters that Jacques and Henrion realized their congeniality, and because of them that they sought to meet one another.

Here are several passages of Henrion's letter which clearly show the principal tendencies of one who was later to live in the desert in the same way as Father de Foucauld :

"I wish to speak here especially of the Catholic adolescents of today whose distinctive trait, it seems to me . . . is a need of total truth.

" . . . They are in need of the stability, the depth, the inexhaustible riches of religion. . . This thirst for a completely religious life carries the more resolute of them into the seminaries, even after they have finished their studies. . . The number of vocations has only increased under persecution. Many among them come to fruition with the priestly life ; a still greater number seem set apart by God to carry on in the world a kind of apostolate which reminds us not a little of what the Virgin of La Salette and Blessed Grignion of Montfort said of the 'Apostles of the later times.' "

Speaking of modern literature, Charles Henrion wrote : "We expect and we desire ardently religious writings — yes, one might as well say writings of saints . . . in which grace underlies the words, in which nothing touches us save the burning presence of love," . . . for we are only made "for those things that further our union with God."

"For us religion is no longer a 'discipline,' as the literary men of yesterday used to say : in its fullness it is a life. We should strongly insist on this, for it is the heart of our heart ; it is what ought to be explained to all our young people, and what we ought to be helped in bringing about. . . It has been said that we are moralists ; would it not be better to say that we are mystics ? Let no one be surprised ! Certainly not those extraordinary beings who live in ecstasy and special ways. The

fact is we live in the world and everyday labours. Our deep
and secret tendency is to unite ourselves closer every moment
with the 'God who gives joy to our youth' not for purposes of
enjoyment but to be more assured of serving Him in a world
where we no longer have a guide and where there is nothing
to teach us the truth. . . But people do not know that the best
fuel for our fervour comes to us from precise dogma, as Saint
Thomas sets it forth. . . It is difficult for us to understand
more outward activities, politics for example, inclined as we
are to believe they will not save us and that God will not give
us the government we need until we are converted and until
souls have first come back to Him."

There was not one among these lines of Henrion that Jacques
would not have signed himself ; but what perhaps most struck
them both was the mention they made — and they alone —
of Our Lady of La Salette and of Blessed Grignion de Montfort. Léon Bloy had made known to us the writings of the
latter ; Henrion had discovered them by himself.

When Jacques and Henrion met, their mutual sympathy was
immediate and a great friendship sprang up between them ;
and the years of war which almost immediately separated them
from one another did not interrupt its development.

Charles Henrion's friendship is one of the most precious
graces of our life ; we have always found in it extraordinary comfort and profound spiritual joy. He had been greatly helped
in his religious evolution by Claudel. After his conversion and
until in 1914, he led in the Vosges, where his family lived, the
life of a contemplative and lay apostle, preaching about the
countryside upon the Gospel and the teachings of Pope Pius X
who, at that time, was urging Christians to frequent Communion. He had thenceforth a devouring passion for the
theological knowledge of mystical ways and contemplation,

he read Saudreau (who should be credited with reviving interest in mystical theology), and going back to the sources studied the works of Saint Teresa and Saint John of the Cross.* The pressing and insistent questions with which he pursued Father Garrigou-Lagrange in his letters undoubtedly counted for something in the great studies on mystical theology to which the latter was to devote himself, and to which we owe his admirable work on *La Perfection chrétienne et la contemplation.*

Mobilized in the first days of August 1914, wounded on the battlefield, taken prisoner by the Germans, Charles Henrion was then interned in Switzerland until the end of the war. There he became a theological student at the Dominican University of Fribourg (where he knew the eminent Father Del Prado) and it was at this period that we had an important correspondence with him upon questions of the spiritual life.

When the war was ended, impatient to carry out his vow of a solitary life, he retired to his family's country house in the village of Thuillières, desiring only prayer and union with God, not wishing even to continue his apostolic action of before the war, and, like a faithful disciple of Francis of Assisi, humbly fleeing even the honours of the priesthood.

Our attachment for him was increasing despite separation. Jacques and he gave themselves more each day to the study of Saint Thomas Aquinas and Saint John of the Cross. And when finally circumstances permitted them to meet (Charles Henrion came to see us in the village of Vernie, and had later to make several more or less lengthy visits to Paris), we found ourselves bound to him by deep affection and by complete confidence in the spiritual paths he was following.

* Charles Henrion has published an invaluable résumé of Saint John of the Cross : *Abrégé de la doctrine spirituelle de Saint Jean de la Croix.*

### Eve Lavallière

I cannot give here the long story of this precious friendship
without going considerably beyond the period covered in the
present book.  I will simply say that God did not permit
Charles Henrion to abstain from all outer activity, and his
beloved solitude of Thuillières was precisely the place where
his spiritual action was to begin.

It was there, indeed, that one day the priest of the village
came to ask for his help.  There had fallen from the heavens
an extraordinary lady-parishioner, a recent and zealous convert who required spiritual direction which appeared to the
humble priest as a task beyond his power.  He therefore asked
this layman to take over the direction of that exceptional soul
sent him by God.

It was Eve Lavallière, a celebrated actress beloved by Pari-
sians, who, suddenly touched by grace and enlightened and
strengthened by it, had broken all her contracts and cast aside
what remained of her wealth.  Keeping only for herself what
was necessary for a life of poverty and deprivation, she also
had retired (with Leona, her dresser at the Variétés, who was
converted at the same time) to the village Charles Henrion had
chosen as a perfect retreat.

Although he was extremely apprehensive at even the idea
of having a soul in his charge, he could not refuse the interview with Lavallière requested of him in the name of spiritual
charity.  And from that day on he willy-nilly became the guide
of the new convert.

Married to Fernand Samuel, director of the Variétés, a
perspicacious Gentile who had taken the biblical pseudonym
of Samuel in order to succeed, Eve Lavallière had also played
at the Mathurins, the Antoine theatre and the Vaudeville, with
ever-increasing fame.  In the spring of 1917 she had signed a

EVE LAVALLIERE

contract for a tour in America with Lucien Guitry. But she
went first for a vacation in a Touraine village, to a house she
had rented for the season from the local priest. In the course
of a visit paid her by the latter, in talking of the cherries in
the garden which she wished to pick, she spoke jokingly of
the devil, and the priest replied gently : "Madame, if you knew
what hell is, you would not speak of it so lightly." The priest's
grave tone touched her suddenly. Once alone she burst into
tears on thinking of her own life. The following Sunday she
went to Mass, still thinking only of paying a courtesy call on
the good priest who had permitted her to gather the cherries
from the orchard ; but the impression she received was deep.
She read a few books. . . Thus her conversion began. The
idea of God took place in her heart and eclipsed everything
else. She left everything for Him. Soon she announced the
change to her companions, left the theatre, broke her American
contract and departed for Lourdes.* There she learned something of the sufferings of poverty — of voluntary poverty which
was her first impulse and which constantly drew her until her
death. It was winter. With joy she came to know cold, the
existence of which she had forgotten in her luxurious life. She
rejoiced to find reality in poverty.

* In his interesting reminiscences, M. Louis Verneuil (*Rideau à Neuf Heures*
— Curtain at Nine O'Clock — pp. 296–8) suggests the hypothesis that Eve Lavallière's premature retirement can be explained by the lack of success of the
two last plays she had acted in, and in support of this opinion he recalls a
conversation he had with her in the presence of Feydeau on May 6, 1917, in
which she refused a rôle he offered her in a new play, declaring that Paris no
longer loved her and she no longer wished to be in the theatre. I am sure
that Feydeau saw the thing more exactly when he attributed this reply to a
moment of temper and nervous excitement, and said to M. Verneuil : "In
two weeks she will have forgotten *Carminetta* and will be busy with her next
rôle." And as a matter of fact she planned to go on a tour of America after
her vacation in Chanceaux. Had her suffering as an artist unconsciously disposed her to turn back upon herself when she was touched by the goad of
grace ? That is entirely another matter. In any case, she herself declared to
us several times that it was not a disappointment which made her leave the
theatre ; she was indignant at this interpretation which was already being
bruited about, with many others, among her former companions. M. Ver-

A little later she settled in Thuillières with her faithful Leona
— divinely led without knowing it toward the best guide who
could be given her.   It was there she died on July 10, 1929.
For her epitaph she wanted these words : "I have left everything for God.   He alone suffices me.   Thou who created
me, have mercy on me." *

Charles Henrion wrote us several times about her.   First to
tell us of his confusion at the task which had so unexpectedly
been laid upon him ; later to let us know of his joy and wonder
at the generosity of a soul so perfectly forgetful of self, so absolutely abandoned to God.

Finally he wished us to know her.   We met at Violot, a
little village in the Haute-Marne where the saintly Abbé Lamy
awaited us, so we might all make together the pilgrimage to
Notre-Dame des Bois.   Notre-Dame des Bois !   Another of
God's marvels, another beautiful story among the most beautiful of France, but which I am not able to touch upon here.

Jacques, Vera, and I came from Meudon :  Charles Henrion
with Eve Lavallière and Leona came from Thuillières.   We
were all very much moved at this meeting, the indication of so
many of God's graces.   But immediately we were upon very
simple terms.   Was it not perfectly simple that God had converted us, given us a new name, and that He no longer remembered our faults ?   To tell the truth we would never have
known Eve Lavallière, we had never gone to any of the theatres
where she appeared with such success.   She who came was
Sister Eve-Marie du Coeur-de-Jésus — her name as a tertiary

neuil is mistaken when he says : "She stopped acting, and it was long after
that she entered the paths of repentance and piety."   Did not he himself
say only a few lines above that she left for Chanceaux in Touraine "the day
following" the conversation he had with her ?   And that it was here "that
one day, talking with the priest of the village, she for the first time felt herself touched by grace" ?   When she settled in Thuillières in 1919, it had already been two years since she had "entered the paths of repentance and
piety."   The simple truth constantly declared by Eve Lavallière herself was that
she left the theatre to consecrate herself to God.

* Cf. Omer Englebert, *Vie et Conversion d'Eve Lavallière.*

of Saint Francis ; humble and fervent, poorly clad, with no studied effect — not even of simplicity. Her face still had the beauty of pure and regular features ; but being left to itself, without any kind of make-up, it was in no way striking. It was no longer the face which Eve Lavallière had known as her own, and she suffered whenever she noticed it.

Her humility was very great and she was a severe judge of her past life. "One thing only helps me to keep my balance," she said, "it is total abandonment in love ; I forget everything, the past, the present ; scruples fly away and I am drowned in a deep joy made up of peace and trust." And she would add : "Don't think I 'm being humble in all this ; I am being true." — Which is exactly the same thing. From the first moment she gave the impression of perfect straightforwardness. Her natural charm became a sort of courtesy toward suffering as she advanced among the very bitter trials which were not spared her. Since her conversion she had wept a great deal from compunction and love, and her eyes were impaired and gave her much pain, but she could not stop her tears. She suffered from this until the end.

### Mercédès de Gournay

The experience of the spiritual good he was able to accomplish in those years at Thuillières no doubt was a factor in the decision finally made by Charles Henrion to bow to the advice and pressure of his friends and to become a priest. The solitude he so greatly desired was granted to him for only a short time. God indeed destined him for the desert, but not alone.

He was ordained a priest by Mgr. Lemaître, archbishop of Carthage, and retired to the desert to join another convert, ex-Admiral Malcor, who had preceded him there by a short time. Upon ground purchased by Father Malcor, over which passed nomads and cobras, the two priests began by building two cells and a chapel.   There they lived like the Desert Fathers of whom Cassian speaks, on little food and many prayers ; and they also gave medical care to the Arabs who passed by. Another priest came to join them a little later ; and then a short distance away was formed a small community of women contemplatives who cared for the Arab women.

We knew several of these contemplatives ; their modesty and perfect effacement do not even allow me to give their names. But of one, at least, I can say a few words, because for a long time she has been safe from this world — and lives with God in eternal life.

I should like to speak in particular of the admirable Mercédès de Gournay.   For a long time she had been seeking her way; she wrote some very beautiful poems.   But God was holding a larger and larger place in her heart.   Finally one day at our home she met Charles Henrion — Father Charles ; she heard him speak of the desert and of the young women who were leading a life of contemplation there.   She burned her newly published book of poems and left for Africa to join the little community.   Her time of happiness was brief.   She contracted typhus from an Arab woman she had nursed and cured, and died on February 18, 1932, from this act of charity, attended to the end by Father Charles.   She was thirty-four years old. Hers was the first place in the little cemetery of Sidi-Saad, where the Arabs make pilgrimages to the tomb of this saintly Christian.

Mercédès de Gournay, admirable daughter of France, who wrote upon the African soil the most beautiful poem of love !

### Friends and Poets

In the course of his first conversation with Jacques, Charles Henrion incidentally mentioned Louis Massignon.   Henrion himself did not know him, but he had heard him spoken of as a legendary person.

Henrion and Jacques met Massignon a little later. I recall with what emotion Jacques spoke of him to me. Early in the summer of 1914, Henrion, Massignon and Jacques found themselves together at the home of Robert Vallery-Radot, a reunion at which several other friends, among them Dr. Louis Pichet, were also present. That day was like a spiritual watch before the battle ; together they made great plans for the kingdom of God, even though they felt catastrophe coming, for the First World War was at hand. So far as I can remember all those who were present at this reunion, or nearly all, were to remain steadfast in the friendship which united them on that day.

Louis Massignon is one of the great French Orientalists. At an early age he was appointed to the chair of Islamic civilization at the Collège de France. He too is one of those converts of the beginning of our century, and an ardent faith has directed his whole life.

When as a young scholar he was preparing his doctor's thesis on the great Moslem mystic Al Hallaj,* he was smitten by grace during a dangerous expedition through Syria — and in his case one can speak literally of the road to Damascus. Thenceforth, burning with heroic zeal, his great desire was to join Father de Foucauld in the desert ; but he humbly followed the counsel of his spiritual advisers and remained in the world and married. He came to see us a little before his marriage and told us himself of his conversion. Since then and up to the day the present war made all communication impossible, he and Jacques always kept in touch with each other regarding the main directions of their activity in the religious sphere. During the many years preceding the Second World War constant communications, based upon deep mutual affection, were ex-

* Louis Massignon, *La Passion d'Al-Hosayn-ibn-Mansour-al-Hallaj, martyr mystique de l'Islam*, 2 vols., Paris, Geuthner, 1922.

changed between them and Father Charles, even though accord was not always perfect — nor could it be — between men of such different and pronounced temperaments. In particular, disagreements which arose between Father Charles and Jacques in the years preceding the Second World War regarding Jacques' attitude in political matters did not alter their friendship, but were a cruel trial for them both.

*

*    *

In summer Father Charles generally left his hermitage and came to France where for about two months he lived either with his mother in the Vosges or with us at Meudon. Here in 1925 he met, among many more of our friends, Pierre Reverdy and his wife Henriette, and other poets — Jean Cocteau, Paul Sabon, and Mercédès de Gournay.

After seeing him once or twice Pierre Reverdy, at that time recently come to Catholicism (owing to dear Max Jacob, that scapegoat of genius, who played so great a rôle in the poetry of our times, and who has just died, not in his old retreat at Saint-Benoît-sur-Loire, but, according to the underground paper *Libération* * in the abominable concentration camp of Drancy) Pierre Reverdy desired with all the violence of his nature to retire, if not to the desert where his wife could not follow him, at least to some place near a Benedictine monastery. He quickly carried out his wish and settled in Solesmes where we saw him again in 1939 ; he was then cultivating a beautiful garden — and it seems that his wife, who had only regretfully followed him to his Solesmes retreat, found the place even more propitious than he for the development of her religious life. (Such was the case, at least, at the end of 1939.)

How heartbreaking and strange is the memory of our conversations during those dark days with this admirable poet more

* April 7, 1944.

than ever afire with a powerful inner flame ! The village of
Solesmes lay about us carrying on its daily life, the Abbey of
Solesmes rose more stern and forbidding than ever in its silence.
Anxiety filled our hearts, weighed down with the heaviness
which precedes the storm. Reverdy's words burst forth in
flashing images, and in answering him Jacques was constantly
thinking of his approaching departure for America, called there
by engagements made prior to the war and by a desire to try
to serve there the cause of France. And he was painfully de-
bating with himself whether he should take Vera and me with
him despite the danger of magnetic mines and German sub-
marines. For Vera and myself there was no problem.

Father Charles also played an important part in the conversion of Paul Sabon, an exceptionally gifted young poet, who
however lived too brief a time to reach the measure of his
talents. He had gone to André Breton as he would have gone
to Poetry in person and to freedom of the soul — with all the
generosity of his nature. Ill satisfied by the bitter fruits of
surrealism, broken in body and soul, it seems he was first vaguely
disturbed by Catholicism upon reading Delteil's *Jeanne d'Arc*.
This book, although far from orthodox, is inspired by a sincere
admiration for Jeanne d'Arc. Was this the first time that the
heroism of sanctity came before the eyes of the young poet ?
He wrote to Delteil and Delteil sent him to Jacques.

He gained our affection by his moral uprightness and the
loyalty of his attachment. It took him several months to be
cured of the despair in which he was submerged, and several
months more to understand that spiritual liberty is bound not
to arbitrary will but to truth, and depends upon the presence
in the soul of virtues which come from heaven.

When he met Father Charles at our home he recognized in
him the one who would put an end to his last hesitations. But
he did not receive the sacraments until after the death of his

friend, André Grange, who had also recently parted with surrealism. A short time before being seized by the violent illness which was to cause his death, Grange had found the road of divine surreality in reading the excerpts of Saint John of the Cross compiled by Father Charles. To Jacques who saw him several hours before his death he told of his joy in having received the sacraments and in possessing the certainty of faith, adding : "It was Saint John of the Cross who did everything." To Sabon he said : "I am happy, I know now — do as I have done."

*

*          *

The impression that Father Charles could produce on first encounter was described in a striking manner by Jean Cocteau in his *Letter to Jacques Maritain.**   Cocteau wrote :

". . . You were starting a collection with Plon. . .†   One evening several of us gathered at your place to discuss it. . . You had announced a possible visit from Father Charles.   I knew nothing of him except that he wore Father de Foucauld's cassock and lived in the African desert as a hermit.

". . . A heart entered the room ; a red heart surmounted by a red cross in the middle of a white form that glided about, bowed, spoke, shook hands.   This heart hypnotized me, distracted me from the face, beheaded the Arab's robe.   It was the real face of the white form, and Charles seemed to hold his head against his breast like a martyr.   For the head, burned by the sun, seemed a reflection of the heart, a mirage in all that African light.   The cheekbones and the chin outlined the mirage's relief and the tip.   Then I distinguished a glance badly focussed for short distances, and the hands of a blind man ; I mean hands that see. . . I, stupid, groggy, as boxers say, was

* Stock, Paris, 1926.
† *Le Roseau d'Or.*

looking through a thick pane at the white object moving in
the depths of the sky.

"I suppose your wife and guests must have noticed ; room,
books, friends, nothing existed any more.

"It was then, Maritain, that you pushed me.   Pushed me in
the back by a blow from your soul . . . pushed me head first.
All saw that I was losing my balance.   Nobody came to my
rescue, for they knew that to help me there would have been
to lose me.   Thus I learned of the spirit of this family with
which Faith endows us instantaneously, and which is not one
of the least of the graces of God.

"A priest struck me with the same shock as Stravinsky and
Picasso. . .

"The morning of the feast of the Sacred Heart of Jesus, in
your chapel, in the midst of some intimate friends, Father
Charles gave me communion. . ."

And Jacques replied to Cocteau : *

"God kept on pressing you.   Reverdy and I could feel the
time coming when you had better see a priest.   To whom
would you turn ?   It was then you met Father Charles.   If
there was conspiracy, it was of the angels.   A telegram warned
me of his arrival on the very day you were to die at Meudon.
When he entered we knew at once, by a great eddy of silence
in our souls — which lasted until the end — that he came only
for you.   This heart that you draw at the bottom of your letters,
he was wearing over his chest, but with a cross planted in it.

"Solitude was sending you a contemplative ; contemplatives
and poets understand each other : a man accustomed to the
ways of Heaven was at ease with your invisible. . ."

*Remain free* were the precious words Charles bequeathed Cocteau at the hour when the poet's soul had been purified by the
sacraments and was filled with the love of God.   Cocteau has
not always borne in mind the sense Charles gave to these words,

* James, 1, 25.

which is the sense of the *ama et fac quod vis* of Saint Augustine. Love — God — and do what you will. In this love your will will take the form of the will of God itself, and you will accomplish it freely in the perfect love of freedom, as free men . . . and as servants of God.* All commit to some degree the error derived from a lack of love, and we offend the real liberty of our souls when we forget the demands of that love.

Of the disappointments and sadness that came to us later I do not wish to speak; it is enough to allude to them. And who of us has always been perfectly faithful to our friends, and has not at one time or another, by acts or words, in a false freedom of judgement or conduct, brought harm to those invisible treasures which should have been guarded in common ?

*

\*          \*

I have again got very far away from the main period covered by this book, because of Charles Henrion who came to us in those years, and all the precious memories his name brings up. But these incidental pages are too short for the reality they tell, and I intend to come back to them if it is granted me one day to continue the recital of God's mercies of which we have been the unworthy witnesses.

* I Peter, II, 16.

# CHAPTER EIGHT

## A Philosopher's Beginnings

### Early Endeavours

I now propose to speak of several domestic events and of Jacques' early work, and this obliges me to go back a little.

As I said, we took up our residence in Versailles in October 1909, Rue de l'Orangerie, and we lived there until 1913.

From 1909 to 1913 Jacques, in addition to his personal work, devoted himself to the compilation of a "Dictionary of Practical Life." * Although he and his collaborators were late, even with the extensions of time successively granted him, he finally reached the end of this irksome labour, but abandoning along the way his author's rights to the sale of a masterpiece which he always had difficulty in recognizing as his own.

As for his philosophical work in these same years, it was in part devoted to a thorough study of Aristotle and Saint Thomas and to the reading of contemporary scholastic authors, and in part to his first writings and lectures.

In 1909 he had written a study upon "Neo-Vitalism in Germany and Darwinism," in which he used the materials collected during our two years' sojourn in Heidelberg, and which was published in 1910.†

He thus acquitted himself of the obligation he had incurred as recipient of the Michonis fellowship. In this study, in which he reviewed the work of the principal representatives of a peculiarly uneven philosophico-scientific movement, he stressed particularly the research work done by Hans Driesch. He con-

* See *We Have Been Friends Together*, pp. 201 *et seq.*
† *Revue de Philosophie*, October 1910.

sidered the latter's method as sound and conclusive, and he believed with Driesch that no combination of differentiated parts constituting a purely physico-chemical whole — no machine — can behave in the same way as those embryos of sea-urchins which have been divided into all kinds of fragments, each of which loses no time in recasting itself into a whole so as to develop into a complete sea-urchin. Jacques dreamed of continuing these experiments, but life offered no more opportunities to his vocation as a biologist than to his vocation as a painter. He admired the analyses in which Driesch showed the necessity of an extra-spatial factor ("entelechy") in the development of the living organism, as also those in which he showed that the behaviour of animals cannot be explained without a "psychoid" factor (the expression greatly amused us). Jacques, while regretting that Hans Driesch left his laboratory for a rather uncertain metaphysics, has always retained his esteem for a man whose intelligence was so penetrating and whose heart so generous. Later he wrote the preface for the first volume of the French translation of *The Philosophy of Organism*, a collection of Driesch's Gifford lectures.

*
* *

In 1910 Jacques wrote his first philosophical study, *La Science moderne et la raison*. It is quite an affair, that first article in which a young man proposes to bring his thought before the public. Jacques put into it all his intellectual passion and that desire to "break window-panes" and annoy the reader which befitted a godson of Léon Bloy — and which was moreover justified by the obstacles that had to be overcome. The article was presented to M. Trogan, secretary of the *Correspondant* and was instantly rejected as being incompatible with the restful subjects which that calm periodical liked to set before its readers. It appeared several months later, in June 1910, in

the *Revue de Philosophie,* directed by Father Peillaube.* It
was a reprint of this article which Ernest Psichari read in the
desert.

Jacques here described something of which he had a very
lively and painful intuition, namely the tragic state to which
reason had come — "it seems that in our times truth is too
strong for souls, and that they are only able to feed on diminished truths. . ." — and the confusion which, in enfeoffing authentic science to an unavowed pseudo-metaphysical system,
turned the science of phenomena, in itself essentially dedicated
to truth in a definite domain, into an instrument of debilita-
tion of the intellect with regard to the truths of another order.

"Thus bound, not by nature, but by the circumstances of
its birth . . . to intellectual pride and rationalistic vanity,
'modern Science' has become in the end that crude divinity
which is adored in the grade schools, that fortress of the worldly
spirit, that storehouse of confusion and false ideas which constantly furnishes error with weapons, that thick and heavy
wisdom according to the flesh which threatens to crush the
human mind." I have quoted here the conclusion of the
article ; its violence made it appear to those who did not read
it carefully that Jacques was taking sides "against science,"
which would be a pure absurdity, a kind of suicide of thought
— when all his efforts on the contrary were and have always
been to purify the notion of science (and in the same way,
every kind of knowledge) of the parasites which disfigure it,
and to return science to *its* own truth.

Father Peillaube, who was sympathetic to the young philosopher from the first, was himself engaged at this period in great
intellectual struggles at the Institut Catholique of Paris where
up until that time instruction in philosophy came under the
auspices of the Faculty of Letters and was given by a single

* This essay forms the first chapter of *Antimoderne* (1923), in which Jacques
assembled his early articles.

professor, Abbé Piat. By his perseverance and artful obstinacy
Father Peillaube brought about the creation of a special Faculty
exclusively devoted to philosophy, in which the study of Saint
Thomas was to hold the first place. Jacques has always retained a deep gratitude for Father Peillaube's personal affection
as well as for the philosophical battle he has constantly waged.
Father Peillaube had founded the *Revue de Philosophie*, which
was published by Marcel Rivière. The latter was also the
publisher of Georges Sorel and ran a socialist bookstore. Sorel,
who was on the alert for all indications of new currents in
thought, had one day said to him : "Keep an eye on those
Thomists of whom no one seems to be talking yet and who are
agitating to restore Catholic intellectual life — they have a
future. . ." It was in writing book reviews for the *Revue de
Philosophie* that Jacques came into contact with Father Peillaube, and later with some of the Marist Fathers around him.

### Bergsonism as a System and
### Bergsonism of Intention

In 1911, at the request of Father Peillaube, Jacques wrote
for the *Revue de Philosophie* * a long article *L'Evolutionnisme
Bergsonien*. This article outlined the criticisms which the
Bergsonian system called for from the viewpoint of Thomist
philosophy.

A year later Jacques, who hoped that his criticisms would not
be confounded either with the bitter zeal and the partisan spirit
of those a little later called "integral Catholics," or with the
ferocious and empty aggressiveness of Mr. Julien Benda, published in the *Revue Thomiste*,† an article *Les Deux Bergsonismes* in which he distinguished, according to a distinction

* September–October 1911.
† July–August 1912.

which has always remained dear to him, "Bergsonism as a system," against which he was very severe, from "Bergsonism of intention," the spirit of which he admired, and which he regarded as being rich in valuable seeds of truth ; according to him the "system" had betrayed the vital "intention." And he concluded thus : "If ever one were to try to isolate and set free this Bergsonism of intention, it seems likely that, passing to the act, it would liberate and order its powers in the great wisdom of Saint Thomas Aquinas."

It was singularly audacious thus to set the greatest philosopher of our times in opposition to himself. But were not the illustrious man and the bold youth before all else friends of truth ? We found out that although Bergson was chagrined, he thus understood it. (As far as Saint Thomas is concerned, Bergson wrote a few years before his death that although he was little familiar with Saint Thomas, yet each time he had come across one of the latter's texts, he had found himself in agreement with it, and that he readily acceded to having his philosophy placed in the stream of continuity flowing from Saint Thomas.)

Many years later, after the publication by Bergson of his long-awaited work : *Les Deux sources de la morale et de la religion* — encouraged by our friend Georges Cattaui (one of those beloved and admirable Cattauis taken captive by Christianity) who often saw Bergson and who told me that the philosopher remembered his old pupil, the young girl who attended his lectures on Plotinus — I brought myself to pay him a visit.

I spoke of this visit in an article published by *The Commonweal.** Of what Bergson said to me I wish to quote here only what referred to Jacques' article on *Les Deux Bergsonismes.*

"Bergson spoke of Jacques, and of Jacques' work. He said to me : 'You know, when your husband set up my philosophy

/ * *The Commonweal*, January 17, 1941, New York. Cf. *ibid.*, August 29, 1941.

"of fact" against my philosophy "of intention" as containing
certain virtualities which were not developed, he was right.'
And he continued, while my heart filled with gratitude and
admiration : 'Since then we have moved toward each other,
and we have met in the middle of the way.'   And I thought to
myself that they had met in Christ, who is the Way, as He is
also the Truth. . ."

Léon Bloy, to whom Jacques had given a copy of the *Revue
Thomiste*, consented for once to read a philosophical article.
He wrote in his diary : "Everyone knows my lack of enthusiasm for philosophy, in my eyes the most boring way of wast-
ing life's precious time ; besides its Hyrcanian jargon discourages
me.   But with Jacques it is all singularly different. . . I did
not expect to see so strong an arm come forth from the tattered
outfit of philosophy.   The arm of an athlete and the lofty voice
of a bewailer of olden times.   I felt at the same time something
like a wave of sorrowful poetry, a powerful tidal wave coming
from a far distance." *

*

*          *

An important religious event in our lives took place in the
autumn of 1912.   Jacques, Vera and I travelled to Holland, to
the Benedictine Abbey of Oosterhout where we became oblates
on September 29th, and where new names were given us, under
the patronage of Saint Placidus — who is not only honoured
in Benedictine annals for his fall into the Lake of Subiaco from
which he was miraculously rescued by Saint Maur, but also for
the great affection borne him by Saint Benedict whose faithful
assistant he was at Monte Cassino ; of Saint Agnes, whose
youth and martyrdom are cherished by the Church — going
to her death as to her nuptials she encouraged her executioner,

* Léon Bloy, *Le Pèlerin de l'Absolu*, October 17, 1912.

saying : "Strike without fear, for the bride gives offense to the
Spouse if she makes Him wait" ; — and of Saint Gertrude for
whose spirit I have always had a great liking.   We were received by the Abbot of the monastery, Dom Jean de Puniet,
and without any merit on our part were made participants in
his merits and those of his sons.   He had left France to found
in Holland a branch of Solesmes which was quickly elevated to
an Abbey.   He died during the Second World War before
he had the joy of seeing the liberation of France.

At this period, yielding to a deep attraction, we decided to
turn our lives more definitely toward the work of contemplation, and to sacrifice to this quest many of those things and
hopes that are normal in the life of the world.   For several
years, at a time when our lives were not yet troubled by outer
activities, and when we were able to dispose in large measure
of our time, the three of us were to live like a little religious
community, in which the study of spiritual things was given
first place.

\*

\*   \*

In October Jacques began the first year of his philosophy
courses at the Collège Stanislas, which he entered upon the
recommendation of Father Peillaube.   He ceased without regret his labours for the Maison Hachette.   That is not to say
that the beginnings of his courses at Stanislas were easy.   He
had decided to make the philosophy of Aristotle and of Saint
Thomas the centre of his teaching.   But Thomism seemed to
the administration of the college, to the students and their
families as singularly dangerous for the ultimate success of
candidates for the *baccalauréat* degree, to which they limited
every intellectual ambition (after the *baccalauréat* came one's
career, far more important than philosophical convictions).
The director of the College, Canon Pautonnier, looked upon

Jacques with a worried eye. It was Canon Pautonnier who said to him with smiling insistence : "It will pass, my friend, it will pass, this neophyte's ardour. . ." "It has not passed," wrote Jacques several years later in the foreword to *Antimoderne*. "On the contrary, it has become with time more tenacious and more determined although it has lost — at least so I hope — the useless harshness of youth and inexperience."

But there was something worse than his Thomism : from the first day Jacques undertook to begin his class with prayer — an *Ave Maria* followed by an invocation to Saint Thomas ; this "neophyte" took seriously the "Catholic" status of the College and of his students. Such was not the custom at Stanislas, especially in the classes of the philosophy students, who were no longer children, you understand, and who followed courses in "worship," as it was called, but who felt religion had nothing to do with the real classes — those which prepared for the examinations. The system of "air-tight compartments" then prevailed. . . A large boy, who became one of the best students in the class, and to whom Jacques grew very much attached, got up the first day and declared he could not recite the prayer "because he had passed the modern *bachot* and did not know how to pray in Latin." "Good," replied the professor, "leave the class and don't come back until you know enough Latin to say the *Ave Maria*." The student and his parents complained to the administration which began to fear losing its pupils. . . Nevertheless, Jacques won his case. His accounts of these incidents gave my sister and myself a slightly anguished joy.

Jacques was very happy to have to give a complete course in philosophy ; he learned a great deal in preparing it. He read a great deal and meditated even more, and tried not to leave unsolved any question dealt with in the course. Yet he did not think he should give a ready-made solution to his students ;

the solution should in each case emerge from the discussion as a new discovery, and curiosity, the urge to explore the unknown, should be constantly stimulated.   How tormenting it was suddenly to fall upon an unforeseen difficulty, and to have to find the answer before next day's class ! Jacques passed nights working on such things.

He bent all his energy to setting forth in the light of the principles of Saint Thomas the subjects on the program and the problems of contemporary philosophy.   And in the end, contrary to unanimous fears, the percentage of students who passed their *baccalauréat* greatly exceeded those of preceding years. Thus Thomism, not without difficulty, acquired its citizenship rights in a Catholic institution.

In February 1913, after the days filled with grace of Ernest Psichari's conversion, Jacques fell ill.   During two long weeks the doctor remained undecided in his diagnosis, and our anxiety grew greater and greater until the crisis on the night of February 24th–25th — the exact date of the death of my father — which appeared to me as another night of death.   But this mortal anxiety changed oddly into joy when the doctor, who had been called in early in the morning, began to laugh after having examined the patient, shook my hand and congratulated me because what he was on the point of taking for typhoid was only measles — which was just then breaking out !   And I went to bed to sleep like a top.

### Lectures on Bergson

Jacques soon resumed his courses at the College, to which he added a series of lectures on "The Philosophy of M. Bergson and Christian Philosophy," given in April and May 1913 at the Institut Catholique of Paris.

These lectures created a great sensation at the time ; Léon Bloy attended several of them. Many were scandalized at the tone of imperious certainty used by the speaker and the implacable logic of his criticisms ; others, like Psichari, were delighted to hear Jacques, breaking with all academic conventions and affirming the organic and vital union between faith and philosophy, declare to his astonished audience : "There is but one region where the soul and the intellect can live in the peace of God and grow in grace and truth : it is in the light of Thomism." He reminded Christians that baptism carried its obligation into the field of philosophy as elsewhere, and at the end of one of his lectures he cried : "In destroying Intelligence and Reason and natural Truth one destroys the foundations of Faith. That is why a philosophy which blasphemes the intellect will never be Catholic."

The agitation created each Wednesday by these lectures was continued in passionate discussions ; not the least lively were those which at Jacques' mother's house each Thursday set Péguy against Psichari. Péguy, who did not go to Jacques' lectures but received all the echoes from them, did not understand at all the flame that animated Jacques, and, putting the debate upon the grounds (his own) of the struggle against the Sorbonne and the influences struggling for dominion over minds, was indignant that Catholics should side against a philosopher who had struck the hardest blows against materialistic scientism. For Jacques it was a question of truth alone, and of the rights of intelligence.

The battle was in full fury. The stake was the integrity of faith and reason. To a young Bergsonian who said, "Maritain triumphs too easily ; it 's not fair to oppose a complete system like Thomism to a doctrine which is in the making, and still feeling its way !" Psichari replied : "But it is not a question of philosophizing ; it is a question of living or dying !"

What Jacques had in view was much less to combat Bergsonism than to finish once and for all the modernist illusions
before which so many young Catholics were then defenceless,
and especially to raise before their minds the teaching of Saint
Thomas in all its breadth, exact logic and living power.   These
lectures in 1913 were the first manifesto of the Thomistic renaissance in France.   The renewal of Thomistic studies had begun
long before, owing to Leo XIII and Cardinal Mercier.   Works
of incomparable value, written mainly by theologians, had been
devoted to the Angel of the Schools.   But now Saint Thomas
was leaving the circle of ecclesiastical controversies.   For the
first time Thomistic thought was claiming its rights in profane
life and culture, entering the lists with contemporary philosophies, entering into competition with them on their own
grounds, as young and even more alive than the doctrines of
the day.

It was at the time a great novelty, and Jacques did not worry
about opinion or the immediate results ; he thought with anxiety of the future of the spirit, and knew that the too pure
wisdom of Saint Thomas was liable to be disregarded at first.
He wished to serve it, even, if necessary, in utter solitude and in
the manner of a desperado ; he thought that some rare minds
would perhaps become interested in it, and that his work, at
first buried underground, would prepare germinations that
would spring up a long while afterward.   They sprang up
earlier than he thought : but he himself expected only contradiction — something he has never lacked.

\*

\*          \*

In an earlier chapter I tried to describe the state of mind of
French youth in 1912.   I should like to go back to the historic
circumstances in which, with these lectures in 1913, Jacques
Maritain's break with Bergsonism took place.

Not only the rediscovery of metaphysical intelligence and reason, accomplished in the light of faith and due to the teaching of Saint Thomas, opposed him to Bergsonism as a system and to the Bergsonian criticism of the intellect, but he saw cheap Bergsonism — for which Bergson himself was far from responsible — spreading among young people, especially among many young priests, and feeding theological modernism with the most crude anti-intellectual topics in which a purposeless sentimentality disguised as "intuition," a confused pragmatism and a childish passion to conform to the age were destroying in souls the sense of truth, the sense of the sanctity of truth. He was thus induced to regard the influence of the new philosophy as a mortal danger for the intellect. Thinking and seeing this, his duty was to spare nothing and no one. *Magis amica veritas*. But when one has decided to spare nothing, it also happens that one does not spare words. Such an accident was inevitable in the beginning, and it is without importance. With what he calls great naïveté, but according to a most deep-rooted tendency in his nature, Jacques made himself a knight of truth — a *Lady* no less poor than Poverty cherished by Saint Francis, and who also requires, if one wishes to serve her, that one know how to give one's self and all that belongs to one. Jacques sometimes reproaches himself with this mental attitude as presumptuous, while knowing quite well that the feelings to which it corresponded had been requested of him, given and commanded him all at once — which is God's way of doing. In the preface to the second edition of *La Philosophie Bergsonienne* he alluded to a deep and sorrowful experience when he said :

"God does not need our services, and yet He wishes us to serve Him. He commanded that there be built for Him an ark of acacia-wood covered with gold, and for this He used the art of the most skilled craftsmen. As He was having it borne on a cart drawn by oxen from Cariathiarim to Jerusalem, the

cart leaned to one side, and Oza put forth his hand to hold it
up ; he fell dead because he had touched the ark of God.
'David was angered because Jehovah had struck Oza, and on
that day he feared God.' * Blessed, when it comes, be self-
knowledge, which purifies with its taste of death an overfresh
zeal placed wholeheartedly from an inexperienced heart at the
service of truth."

### Dedicated to Friendship

After these months filled with work and excitement, we had
a splendid vacation at Binic in Brittany. Our hearts were
light, we enjoyed the beauty of the earth and sky, the gentleness of the air and the tranquillity of the beach. This vacation did a great deal of good for my mother, for Vera and
Jacques, but it almost ended fatally for me. Hardly were we
back in Versailles, at the beginning of September, when I fell
ill with a grave dysentery. After three weeks of vain effort
to improve my condition, which only grew worse, our friend
Doctor Legrain considered the case hopeless ; he withdrew and
left Jacques to his own inspiration.

Jacques' inspiration was to call in a doctor he had met two
or three times in the course of the year — Dr. Louis Pichet,
who had been introduced to him by Father Bulliot, a philosopher and amateur in physiognomy, as a devotee of Our Lady of
La Salette — which meant something for Jacques — and as
"homeopathist" — which had nothing to interest him. But
he had been quite attracted to Dr. Louis Pichet ; and now he
hoped that the mysterious homeopathy might help me since
allopathy was leaving me to die. Vera and Jacques confided
in Dr. Legrain their intention of having recourse to a homeo-
pathic physician, and received approval in the following terms :

* I Paralip., XIII, 9–12.

"In your place, my poor friends, I too would do any foolishness." So much for foolishness ! Dr. Pichet arrived with his old master, Dr. Conan.  I was not aware of anything ; I knew neither who was coming to see me nor what method would be used.  Three weeks of terrible suffering and nearly total fasting had exhausted me and made me indifferent to anything that might arise.  Dr. Conan's treatment brought about a rapid improvement and cured me completely in two weeks.

Soon we were attached to Dr. Pichet by a strong and lasting friendship.  We learned through him what homeopathy was and we often witnessed the efficacy of this therapeutic, which our friend felt himself obliged in conscience to use because of observations he had made in the course of a long medical experience.

And Dr. Pichet's conscience was really saintly in its uprightness, so much so that it forbade him the slightest material inexactitude — even the professional "lies" of a doctor to his patient which are often necessary for recovery itself (and which in reality escape being classed among lies).  But Dr. Pichet's extreme limit of concession in this respect when he was questioned by a gravely ill patient regarding his condition, was not to pronounce words that would be hard to hear but sadly to nod his head up and down — which means *yes* in any language. I saw this with my own eyes at the bedside of my sister when she was stricken with pneumonia, from which she recovered successfully through the care of her incorruptible doctor. What is surprising is that this honesty of a very pure soul disarms the patients themselves, and they usually end by being grateful to him for his sincerity, especially as he rarely fails to cure them, bringing as he does to his work much knowledge, prayer, fasting and compassion.

Dr. Pichet has a marvelous memory and a universal curiosity, which is especially attracted to rare and esoteric sciences.  He is very good in physiognomy, in music — with an obstinate preference for Rameau as against Bach — in mathematics and in prophecies.

As friend of the prophets and divine justice this good and gentle man becomes pitiless ; it is necessary for the honour of the prophets and of God that God's anger burst forth and unleash the punishment which they have been elected to proclaim to men.   Like Léon Bloy, of whom I believe he is not a fervent admirer, he is well versed in the prophecies of La Salette — most of which he is today seeing come to pass in our poor Europe, and certainly this time with more humble human pity than prophetic joy.

Thus Dr. Conan, Dr. Pichet and homeopathy cured me ; in October 1913 I was able to undergo without difficulty the strain of moving ; we left Rue de l'Orangerie for Rue Neuve, later called Rue Baillet-Reviron.   Here a slightly larger apartment permitted us to set aside a room for Father Clérissac, who though he no longer lived in Versailles but in Angers, came nevertheless quite often to Versailles.

\*

\*          \*

During the time we lived Rue de l'Orangerie my sister and I had the privilege of being helped in the work of our modest household by a woman who took and has always kept a large place in my heart : Berthe Gilbert.

She had attached herself to us with a singular intuition of what was the foundation of our lives, and I saw the faith which had slept within her since childhood come to life, increase and rapidly yield admirable fruits of Christian wisdom and intelligence.

She had a surprising gift, of which she was perfectly unaware, to express what she lived interiorly — the illuminations of faith, her confidence in God, her sufferings.   Of the latter she had a large share, for many reasons, but especially on account of her sensitiveness, and her need for greatness and beauty — which no one about her — neither her crude and taciturn husband, her children who were too young, nor her gossipy neighbours — could understand or appreciate.

Although much older than myself, Berthe came to me about everything that concerned her, and was herself ignorant of her great merits and supernatural gifts.  Between brooms and saucepans we had some singular conversations !   These instruments hardly weighed in her skilled hands, and their manipulation did not occupy her mind.   With her rather deep-set blue eyes under their black brows, and with her piercing gaze which took in everything, she had the air of a queen much above a realm which was small only by an error of fate.   But at the same time her humility was so simple, her devotion so complete, that I am still overcome in thinking of it today.

In a way her son inherited the poetry, that faithful companion of her faith, which lived in her soul.   The child of landholders, he was born with an irrepressible love of the sea, and when very young he enlisted as a ship-boy ; he has since had a fine career as a sailor.   His younger brother is with De Gaulle somewhere in Africa.

In 1913 or a little later, the whole family left Versailles to go and live on a little farm in Normandy.   There, I know, the sufferings of my poor friend were increased by an oppressive solitude ; but I also know that she has remained the same in her faith and loyalty.   And as I write these lines, I think how her heart must rejoice, despite the ruins of war, in seeing that corner of France where she lives set free from the long nightmare of German occupation.

## Jacques' First Book and the
## Beginnings of Future Work

Toward the end of 1913, in the month of October if I am not mistaken, Jacques' first book appeared : *La Philosophie Bergsonienne, Etudes critiques*.  This book was made up of the lectures of 1913, the article on *L'Evolutionnisme Bergsonien*, and the article on *Les Deux Bergsonismes*.  But all this had to be gone over carefully, and the criticism of Bergson's system and the exposition of Saint Thomas' doctrine to be restated. In this as in Jacques' preparations for his lectures I was keenly interested ; and as I was still under the influence of Bergson, I retired to the little attic on the Rue de l'Orangerie — where I went to meditate — to seek basic analogies however hidden they might be beneath the covering of systems.  We were so united in this work that Jacques has always wanted to consider this book as the first for both of us.  For both of us perhaps, but how very unequal were the two parts !  Later on, Jacques regretted the tone of the first edition ; less entangled than he in the thorns of controversy, I believe I can appreciate better than he the permanent value of the book.  The fundamental themes of Thomistic philosophy are clearly presented in their contrast with the formulations of Bergsonian philosophy, and — which is what primarily and essentially matters in the combats of our day — the principles are set forth which restore in opposition to irrationalism the nature and import of the intellect.  Jacques' preface to the second edition is one of his most important writings.

In the spring of 1914 he gave a new series of.lectures at the Institut Catholique on "The Spirit of Modern Philosophy" ; the first two were published in the *Revue de Philosophie* in June and July ; the conclusion in the *Revue Thomiste* in September–December. It was thanks to the support of Father Peillaube, dean of the faculty of philosophy, that Jacques was invited in 1913 and 1914 to give this series of lectures at the Institut Catholique of Paris, and finally that he was, in June 1914, named professor in the faculty of philosophy of this university. There opposition was strong : the rector, Monsignor Baudrillart, the friends of Abbé Piat, whom the creation of the new faculty deprived of the philosophy courses which he formerly gave under the faculty of letters, and the partisans of prudence and appeasement — all feared this new arrival who knew nothing of the art of compromise and whose gentle and timid manners concealed a complete inflexibility, and his medievalism I know not what revolutionary dynamism. In order to secure approval of the appointment it became necessary to have the intervention of Cardinal Lorenzelli, Prefect of the Congregation of Studies in Rome. The latter wrote a letter in which he insisted that the chair of history of modern philosophy be given to Jacques Maritain ; he counted upon him to see that this history was not taught as a simple matter of erudition and with an equal obligingness (or indifference) for all opinion, but as a discipline that was itself philosophical, and as an instrument of doctrinal exposition and critical discernment.

It was a happy surprise to Jacques to become a professor of higher studies after having renounced, for the sake of his independence, any such position in the State universities. With the same intransigence, he had given up the preparation of his thesis for the doctorate in letters, because he rejected the idea of having to submit his thought to the judgement of the Sorbonne, and thus recognize the intellectual authority of philosophers for whom he harboured the same feelings as Péguy, and whom he considered less as philosophers than the servants of an idealistic and scientistic theology, disruptive of reason. But as the doctor's title was necessary for him to teach as titular professor at the Institut Catholique of Paris, he received this

title in 1917 from the Roman Universities. He was delighted
to have from the Church and not from the State that doctor's
cap, the symbolism of which, so living in the time of Saint
Thomas, has become so hackneyed today.

\*

\* \*

When we came to live in the Rue Neuve a very precious
grace was granted us: the permission to have mass said in our
homes. We owed this favour to Father Thomas Pégues, the
author of a Commentary on, and an excellent translation of,
the *Summa Theologica*. Although without great originality,
the Commentary is quite useful to those beginners in scholastic
philosophy who are reading Saint Thomas for the first time.
I used it myself and retained deep gratitude to Father Pégues
who, knowing this, increased our debt toward him still further
by requesting for us the permission for a private chapel. Thus
it was that in 1914 we had the joy of seeing Father Clérissac
celebrate in our home the mass of Christmas and that of Pentecost (the last Pentecost he was to celebrate in this life), on
which occasion, in accordance with an old Dominican rite, he
blessed a great quantity of roses, and our dear Ernest Psichari
was present — for whom too this was to be the last Pentecost
here below. In his preface to *Le Mystère de l'Eglise*, Jacques
writes : "I have never attended, I will never again attend, I
believe, masses celebrated with such perfection, exactness, with
love so purely recollected, with such sovereign and almost terrible majesty as these masses said by Father Clérissac. . ."
That mass of Pentecost has remained unforgettable to us
among all others which it has been given to us to attend. These
were the last joys, too great, too beautiful, preceding by only
two months the declaration of war, and by barely three months
Psichari's death, by less than six months the death of Father
Clérissac.

Before he left again for Angers, Father Clérissac, wishing to arrange for us a truly exceptional vacation, had secured for us an invitation to England from the Benedictines of Solesmes, then living in exile on the Isle of Wight. We were never to see him again. He seemed singularly anxious for us to leave, and we decided to make the trip during the last days of July, so that we had hardly arrived on the Isle of Wight when we learned with despair that war had just been declared. At the insistence of the Father Abbot — Jacques had been exempted from military service because of the effects of an attack of pleurisy from which he nearly died in his childhood — we remained for some time near the Abbey to pray with the monks, in our indescribable anguish and stupor at what had happened.

Despite the political agitation of the preceding months and the premonition of a great forthcoming liquidation, we had never really believed in the possibility of a war, imbued as we were with the prevalent feeling that civilization could not bring itself to such barbarous manifestations. (The danger today for the minds of the young is perhaps that they believe exploits of strength to be always just and noble in themselves.)

Back in France, Jacques presented himself between 1914 and 1917 to an incredible number of draft boards before finally being pronounced "fit for service" on April 30, 1917. Called up a little later he was put into an artillery regiment stationed in Versailles, where after a first medical examination he was kept under observation for two weeks and forbidden exercise or military duty. He was dressed in an old patched uniform, and the first time he left camp the workmen who met this gunner in the woods of Satory took pity on him, exclaiming : "What a rotten government to dress a man like that !" It was his first experience in barracks. After reveille and morning coffee, the orders for him were to do nothing, so that he had to resign himself to sitting on his soldier's cot and putting down on paper the first notes for a book on Descartes. Shortly afterward, he was discharged and returned home, restored to his vocation as a philosopher.

He resumed his courses at the Institut Catholique where his most brilliant student during those years was Noële Denis (daughter of the painter Maurice Denis), who became one of our very dear friends. In 1914–15 he gave in addition a series of lectures on Germany in which he endeavoured to bring out the principal characteristics of German philosophy from Luther to our times. This was combat duty, a sort of intellectual contribution to the war against an aggressor who had begun by cutting himself off spiritually from the community of Western nations, and whose Pangermanist metaphysics had finally paved the way for a policy of domination and military conquest.

He did double duty in order to be of as great service as he could during those war years. The institutions of learning were short of professors, they had to be helped to carry on their work. In 1915–16, Jacques, while continuing his courses at the Institut Catholique, again taught at the Collège Stanislas ; in 1916–17, at the preparatory seminary in Versailles. He had that year some very remarkable students ; the one in whom he was most interested was young Michel Riquet, whose lively intelligence burned with zeal for St. Thomas. At the end of the year Michel came to Jacques to say that he had decided to enter the Society of Jesus. He swore to be always faithful to the teachings of Saint Thomas and Saint Ignatius at the same time — after all, the saints agree quite well in heaven, why should not their disciples endeavour to agree on earth ? He kept his vow, aided by the perspicacity and intellectual liberality of his novice masters. He became a religious of great merit, and for us a friend whose affection has never failed us. It was he who attended Paul Sabon in his last moments. Before the present war his superiors placed him as spiritual advisor in charge of the important "Laënnec Conference" — a religious and cultural group of Catholic doctors and medical students which numbered in Paris about a thousand members in 1939. It would have been difficult forty years earlier, despite the example and prestige of Pasteur, to assemble in Paris so much as ten physicians who were not convinced of the absolute truth of materialistic philosophy.

\*

\*　　\*

I have spoken in this volume of the beginnings of Jacques' philosophical labours. The potentialities of his future work were all there. But in order for them to take shape and be made explicit, much time, much experience and suffering were needed. The period of which I have spoken here was but a preface ; it was after the war that his work developed. Jacques has often told me that his task was to make clear the paths ; but several of these paths he worked through to the end. He sometimes regrets not having been able to proceed to a more systematic exposition of his thought, in securing for himself a tranquil life which in order better to philosophize would have ignored life — and he himself makes fun of this regret. Jacques has always been in the fight — and, with this, time for meditation has been granted him. He has had to write his books on the urgency of the moment, and of this urgency he has always been terribly aware. The sudden breaking of faith into his soul scattered all his plans for methodical work ; faith and the pricks of God prevented him from having a peaceful life in which concern for a work leisurely constructed would be the first consideration.

But that, together with this self-dispossession, on condition that we remain loyal to intellectual exactitude, as he has been, is probably the condition of an inner freedom which profits a living philosophy open to the anxieties of men's consciences. "Woe to me if I do not Thomistize !" Jacques' vocation shall have been to bring to light the vital forces of Thomism, to carry the light of this great doctrine to all the problems of our times, to widen its frontiers while holding in the strictest fashion to its principles, to reinsert it into the existential reality of the movement of culture and philosophy.

From the beginning it is in faith and theology that he has philosophized, and yet from the beginning the work he has carried on has not been theological but properly and deliberately philosophical. With time this paradox has been explained, and the characteristics peculiar to this work have taken shape. But at the price of what jolts and knocks ! and the uninterrupted labour of thirty years.

At the time Jacques published his first articles and his first book, the ardour of the intellectual combat and of the Thomistic "apostolate" covered over everything else. It was as a man of the Church and with the weapons of the Church militant that this layman confronted the public of the universities. Bossuet reproached Descartes with having too greatly feared the Church ; Jacques has not feared her, he has loved her and given himself to her with absolute trust. Yet from the beginning his work has been the work of a layman, and has more and more become confirmed as such. The more he has lived, the deeper have become his love of the Church and his consciousness of belonging to the Mystical Body of Christ. And at the same time, his freedom has grown greater, and he has better understood his vocation as a philosopher engaged in the drama of the profane world and temporal civilization.

He has become more and more convinced that the philosophy of Saint Thomas, with its incomparably powerful structure, has remained for centuries bound up in the forms of theology, without expanding for its own sake, according to its essence ; and that the time has come for it to take its proper form, its internal organization and its autonomous development as a philosophy. He has embarked upon this task, and it will be, he believes, the great task of the philosophers of the future, if the future does not betray itself, and if workers are not lacking.

At the time dealt with in this book, and for several years more, Jacques, as I have already said, concerned himself only with metaphysics and pure ideas ; he passed among men without paying a great deal of attention to them, and interested himself only in intelligible objects. To arouse the reader from his apathy he liked to irritate and disconcert him. An irony that was not always understood ran throughout his most abstruse studies, which he would not for the world make clearer, out of respect for the dignity of the queen of sciences. As for the men whose ideas he criticized, he certainly respected them personally, but they were for him scarcely more than vehicles for abstract doctrines, and it was these alone which were worthy of scrutiny by the mind. Here again it was little by little, due to art and poetry, later due to social and ethical problems, due above all to experience of the inner life, that the philosopher and his philosophy were to become humanized, to enter into the thick of human affairs and proclaim the necessity of an *integral humanism*.

# CHAPTER NINE

## The Last Years of Léon Bloy

> "Pity cannot extinguish my anger, for my anger is the daughter of infinite foreboding. I am devoured by the need for justice as though by a dragon famished since the days of the Deluge.
> "My anger is the effervescence of my pity."
>
> Léon Bloy, *Letter to Paul Adam*, September 3, 1893. (Published in the *Mendiant Ingrat.*)

### The Presence of Léon Bloy

From 1905 to 1917, during the twelve years when we knew and saw Léon Bloy, I can say, now that time has erased all that was accidental, that whether we were near him or far away he was for us, and in us, the constant witness of God.

Neither the two years we spent in Germany nor Father Clérissac's presence among us at Versailles, nor the long absences caused by illness, nor our work which soon left us little leisure — nothing could eclipse or diminish the benefits of our godfather's invisible presence in our lives. This presence acted mainly in silence ; this profound influence was exercised without confidence-making or sermons, and never resembled spiritual direction. It was something much more mysterious and much more efficacious.

It was not the greatness of the writer which thus influenced us. In this respect we went through various phases. Reading Bloy for the first time gives one in general a dazzling vision both of that faith which dwelt in the heart of this man, and of the incomparable value of faith considered in itself. Such is Léon Bloy's perpetual vocation ; it is for this that he was born — for this and to awaken in the hearts of men a sense of the Absolute, a passion for God and a love for the evangelical virtues. He experienced in himself to a rare depth the thirst for truth and justice ; faith, poverty and destitution, the love of Jesus crucified (the first among the Poor), and of the sorrowful Virgin whom he was fond of calling My Lady of Compassion. And because he really lived by these mysteries, he awakened among many others the sense of mystery — obliterated by the multiple facets of supposedly clear knowledge — the sense of the basic and very definite realities which we can understand here below only "by enigma" and in the mirror of the created, and whose limpid face is veiled to us, but of which a dim knowledge is necessary for the life of the spirit and for the beginnings within us of eternal life. His illuminations and his joy thrived in that divine night well known to the mystics, and it was as one of them that Léon Bloy spoke to us in similes and hyperboles.

Perhaps his gifts as a writer came above all from his religious experience which he lived in enthusiasm and sorrow ; in any case it magnified them, and in themselves, whatever their greatness, they were after all but secondary. Bloy realized this. "Literature, for which I do not live, and which is not my object," he wrote in *Mendiant Ingrat*, "has for a long time appeared to me as some instrument of my torture. . ." The thing for which Bloy did not live could hardly seem in his eyes anything more than a suit of armour or a cloak — but clinging to his flesh. It is true that he also wrote : "It is indispensable that truth should be clothed in glory. Splendour of style is not a luxury, it 's a necessity." However even this sets him apart. For a writer who lives for his art, "splendour," or shall we say beauty "of style," is not a "necessity" — any more than it is "a luxury" — because then it is simply a natural attribute, a gratuitous gift.

It happens that in reading Bloy for the first time, one lays to the account of great art things that pertain above all to

SHE WHO WEEPS
(Our Lady of La Salette)

Léon Bloy
At time of writing *Le Désespéré*

mystical experience. Later, on reading with eyes accustomed
to his light, one is struck by certain aspects of style peculiar to
the epoch — bombast and eloquence, stress and redundancy,
the search for some rare word or surprising detail by which the
writer wishes to force the agreement of the reader. When
they are not sustained by genius such paraphernalia become of-
fensive, as in the style of Huysmans. They are also somewhat
apparent, but are revitalized by a superior sense of beauty, in
authors like Flaubert, Barbey d'Aurevilly, Villiers de l'Isle-
Adam and Léon Bloy.

This glitter and ornamentation have become old-fashioned ;
fashion being the superficial phenomenon of a necessity which
is not superficial and which appears inevitably in art itself.

When, on reading Léon Bloy, one becomes aware of features
which are thus typical of a particular period, one feels at first
a certain disillusionment. But this impression passes, or at
least, is seen in its merely relative value, and the essential, one
might say the ontological value of Bloy's work, appears in all
its grandeur.

And we understand, in addition, that Bloy's eloquence and
bombast are not so much in his case the mark of the literary influence of Barbey d'Aurevilly or Villiers de l'Isle-Adam as they
are the amplifier which he believed necessary so that his voice
could carry his message afar — in the infinitude of souls — and
pierce the walls of indifference, contemporary mediocrity and
ignorance of God. Perhaps Pascal with a similar message escaped the eloquence of his period only because he did not
write his Apology. We are perhaps in need of a Christian
Aeschylus who, in a manner that would surpass the peculiarities
of a period, would be able to move us with the solution of the
human tragedy we owe to Jesus crucified just as deeply as the
Greek Aeschylus was able to do it with the clamour of despair
of humanity hemmed in by blind destiny. He would have at
his disposal all the amplification afforded by the theatre : bus-

kins, voluminous mantles, masks and choirs, dances and sacred
songs. . .

In order to tell what he had seen, what he felt prophetically,
what he believed, what he suffered, Léon Bloy had at his disposal only words — with which he made splendid images and
similitudes of the divine realities which he had experienced —
and which were his goal.

## At the Feet of Her Who Weeps

As we were preparing to leave for Heidelberg, Léon Bloy,
who was on a pilgrimage to La Salette, wrote us on August 21,
1906, expressing his sadness at our departure to which was
added, "to make it worse," his dejection over the welcome he
received from the chaplains who were guardians of the Sanc-
tuary.

"Raïssa, you will learn not without edification that the author of *Le Salut par les Juifs* is greatly scorned here. . ."

*Le Salut par les Juifs* had been re-edited the preceding winter
thanks to Jacques.   "The loftiest of my books," Bloy wrote on
my copy — "the only one of my books which with *La Femme
Pauvre* I would dare present to God," he often said — and
which had been "inspired long ago by that very Notre Dame
de la Salette, by that great Virgin in tears above that little foun-
tain which seems to flow from her eyes. . ."   On his arrival
he had given a copy to the chaplains ; but the poor and proud
appearance of Léon Bloy had not disposed them to treat him
like an academician.

The sadness and the bitterness which were inflicted on him
in a place where only the gentleness of brotherly charity and
holy hospitality should have reigned did not for one single
instant turn his gaze from the essential truths on which his
soul was fixed.   To us who were so young and still such weak

Christians, not yet even three months of spiritual age, he had
given on the eve of our departure this viaticum, in his own
name and in the name of his wife :

"Whatever may be the circumstances, always place the Invisible before the Visible, the Supernatural before the Natural.
By applying this rule to all your acts, we know that you will
be invested with strength and filled with profound joy."

Léon Bloy had gone to La Salette in order to meditate, before starting the book which his great friend Pierre Termier
was urging him to write, on the apparition of Our Lady in
1846, on Mélanie and Maximin, the humble witnesses of that
supernatural event, and on the words pronounced by the
Blessed Virgin when she predicted the catastrophes of our
time.

In a letter of September 20th he wrote us again :

"I was to suffer there and I knew it beforehand, just as one
knows that one must undergo a painful but beneficial treatment.   The contact with modern piety, inevitable in so small a
space, is for me, as you know, the most grievous experience, a
really pernicious sensation, capable of throwing me into despair."

On December 4th he wrote me to pray to Our Lady of La
Salette so that I would be cured.   He regarded the happenings
at La Salette as "the most extraordinary since Pentecost" ; and
he believed in the absolute value of Mélanie's revelations in her
"Secret." *   That was what he was trying to prove in *Celle qui
Pleure.*

*

*        *

* The secret words (distinct from the public message, immediately communi-
cated by the two children) which the little shepherdess Mélanie said she had
received from the Blessed Virgin, with the command not to divulge it until
after 1864, which she did in a pamphlet appearing under the imprimatur of
Mgr. Zola, bishop of Lecce, and which was for her the cause of great tribulations.

The end of that year was a dark one for the Bloys as it was
for us. "Destitution had come back" to them and Bloy fell
ill, "cruelly tormented" at the sight of "the frightfully imbe-
cilic world which has rejected, vomited out for sixty years the
miraculous warnings of La Salette . . . and continues in its
depravity, sure of saving its dear flesh and its holy money. . .
Jacques, Raïssa, Vera . . . obtain for me the courage to combat these ferocious beasts and unclean monsters."

But, as in 1879 and 1880, La Salette acted on him from a
distance. "Shadows at first, later enlightenment. I think I
shall write a beautiful book in which the good Termier will
perhaps find the light he desires. For he has been the instrument of all this. A very kindly hospitality at his
house . . ." (at Varce, near Grenoble, where the Termiers
had their family home and where the Bloys went to rest after
the trials of their pilgrimage).

Before beginning his new book, Bloy finished his study on
the Byzantine era, which was published in the *Nouvelle Revue*
and which appeared later in a separate pamphlet. He greatly
admired the works of Gustave Schlumberger on Byzantium,
and had commented upon them according to his own lights.

On October 8, 1906, he wrote to us that he was about to
start the book on La Salette, and added : "Why are you ill,
dear god-daughter ? For whom do you suffer ?" (I am ill because illness is good for me, dear godfather.)

I was indeed very ill. But how I was being prayed for !
Jacques and Vera were beside me, more tortured than I by my
suffering ; and in the distance Léon Bloy and his family.

In order for him to write *Celle qui Pleure*, documents had
been sent to Bloy without his having to search for them, "documents that are hidden and of which none ever speaks," letters
and writings of the Shepherdess of La Salette sent him by Abbé
Combe, one of Mélanie's spiritual directors in the last years of

her life in France, before her departure for Italy where she
died in 1903.

Among these documents the most remarkable is certainly
the account of the childhood of Mélanie up until the age of
fifteen, written by herself — a most beautiful and astonishing
mystical text.    Bloy published it later under the title of *La Vie
de Mélanie*, with an important preface.

While reading the correspondence of Mélanie, Bloy wrote
us on January 23, 1907 :

"I had no little joy in finding in it numerous lines which in
their ideas and views of the future might have been written by
myself, and even their form might have been mine.    As Mélanie's letters are dated, I have been able to notice, not without
emotion that several concordances of thought, of insight into
the future, even of form, are also concordances of date ; that is
to say, that in this or that of my books, certain statements or
predictions correspond to the identical words which Mélanie
wrote or uttered at the same time.    What she received by direct revelation I received by a simultaneous intuition.

"This older sister could have drawn me close in her arms
before dying in darkness and loneliness, like Marchenoir.    I
shall show the exceptionally tragic character of this story which
is like no other."

The affinity between the Shepherdess of La Salette and Bloy
is striking : both were great and melancholy, grave and full of
the absolute, with no worldliness whatsoever, no cleverness or
frivolity, both were poor and unrecognized.    And from the
things of the world and the things of God they both had the
same crucifying experience, having both been called into the
service of Our Lady of the Seven Sorrows.

The tenderness of our godfather's letters was heartbreaking :
"My beloved Jacques, Raïssa, and Vera. . . A moment ago,

at the Basilica, I thought about you at length and with delight as I read the Passion of Our Lord. Don't expect ideas or phrases from me. I am only capable of writing that I love you dearly, and would willingly give my life for you, as well as for my wife and children.

"I begot you spiritually — think of it ! . . . Remember your poor old godfather who boldly constituted himself the witness of Our Lady of Seven Sorrows, and who so needs to be helped, in every way."

For our first Easter he sent us a magnificent Easter gift — Chapter III of *Celle qui Pleure*, written in his own hand, and entitled "In Paradise."

"The meaning of Paradise, or of the idea of Paradise, is union with God in our present life, that is to say, the infinite distress of man's heart, and the union with God in a future life, in other words, Beatitude. . .

"Union with God is certainly brought about by the Saints in this present existence, and perfectly consummated immediately after their birth in the other Life, but that does not suffice them, nor does it suffice God. The most intimate union is not enough ; *identification* is necessary, and this itself will never be enough, so that Beatitude can neither be conceived of nor imagined save as an ever livelier ascension, ever more impetuous, lightning-like, not toward God but in God, in the very Essence of the Uncircumscribed. An endless theological hurricane which the Church in speaking to me, is obliged to call *Requies aeterna !*" *

In the letter which accompanied his "Paradise" Léon Bloy wrote at the end :

"Look up in your Manual of Holy Week the third nocturn of Good Friday, Psalm 87. I 've been deciphering it for twenty years in order to know what God wills of me. . ."

What does this Psalm say ?

* Léon Bloy, *Celle qui Pleure*. Mercure de France, Paris.

Jehovah, God of my salvation
I have cried in the night before Thee.
Let my prayer come before Thee
For my soul is filled with evils. . .
I am become as a man without help
Free among the dead. . .
Thou hast cast me in the lowest pit
In the dark places, in the depths.
Thy wrath is strong over me
All Thy waves Thou hast cast over me
Thou hast put away my friends from me
They have set me an abomination to themselves.
I was delivered up, and came not forth
My eyes are consumed through suffering. . .
But I, Jehovah, have cried to Thee
From the morning my prayer shall ascend to Thee
Jehovah, why castest Thou off my soul ;
Why turnest Thou away Thy face from me ?
I am poor, and ready to die from my youth up
While I suffer Thy terrors I am distracted
Thy wrath hath come upon me
Thy terrors have troubled me
They have come round about me like waters all the day
They have compassed me about all together
Friend and neighbour Thou hast put far from me
My companions are the shadows of the tomb.

Thus one understands that for Bloy "union with God in the
present life" had meant the "infinite distress" of his heart.

*

*          *

Yet there were a few bright spots.    Whatever Psalm 87 may
say, new friends who were to prove faithful, came to Bloy.    I

have already spoken of the Martineau family, Rouault and the
Termiers ; then came Ricardo Viñes, and the humble Brother
Dacien who, too poor to buy Bloy's books which he wished to
make known, copied them by hand.   They all joined Bloy's
godchildren in trying to lighten his suffering.   With what tenderness he — he who was called the ungrateful beggar — expressed to them his gratitude.

".  .  . The old beggar blesses you from the very depths of
his heart.   Many are the times he weeps with love in thinking
of you. . ." *

When there was no longer any money at all, help would
come from one or another, but always, and as if by fate, not
quickly enough to prevent God from testing the Bloy family
by crucifying days of anxiety.

"That which is altogether peculiar to my case," he wrote us,
"is that the *absolute certainty* of being helped out in time,
in some way or other, never saves me from being afraid when
danger threatens.

"My trust is never shaken, but nothing would be accomplished if God spared me anguish.

"Man would never have been saved if Jesus had not sweated
blood from fear and boredom.   *He began to be dismayed and
distressed.*   What a text !"


### *"My sad life hardly ever changes"*


Bloy finished *Celle qui Pleure* ; but the publishers showed
little enthusiasm for a book so exclusively Catholic.   On October 30, 1907, Bloy wrote us :

"I am sorrowful, habitually sore at heart.   I cannot seem to
get used to my miserable condition, to my helplessness, and the
exceptional injustice I am suffering.   The apparent impossi-

* Léon Bloy, *Lettres à ses filleuls*, May 10, 1907.

bility of getting *Celle qui Pleure* published is the last blow.
Well, but I belong to La Salette, to the Immaculate Concep-
tion stigmatized and crowned with thorns. I therefore must
suffer. I expect every tribulation."

Nevertheless, he prepared the fourth volume of his diary,
the one that appeared under the title *L'Invendable,* and where
our story can be found. He wrote us February 5, 1908 : "I
am not at all well and work is hard for me. However this one
(the preparation of *L'Invendable*) is a work after my own
heart. I am now in the second half of 1905. I had received
your first letter on June 20th, the feast of Saint Barnabas
(which was moved over from the 11th) and I saw you for the
first time on the 25th. From that time on I am meeting you
every moment." Later he wrote on a copy of *L'Invendable* :

"Suffering has not ceased, but the road becomes less bitter.
Some friends have finally appeared to accompany the traveller."

We returned to Paris. The Bloys had miserable summer
lodgings at Tréport whence our godfather wrote us on September 25, 1908 :

"You can see that my sad life hardly ever changes. Our
ever-blessed Lord probably wishes me to die, as I have lived, in
the torments of destitution. I accept, but I should like to have
time to finish my work, to give to a few souls certain books that
I have borne within me for a long time and which grow each
day in my thoughts.

"Now, I have hardly any more physical strength left. I am
becoming sleepless and losing my appetite, an obsessing sadness
stifles me and I do not see how I can go on struggling against
the daily agony of destitution with the crushing addition of
our dear children's education.

"God tempers the wind to the shorn lamb ; this I know, and I
still hope.

"Pray all you can for your old sheep of a godfather.

"Father Faber, who seems to me to be the greatest ascetic writer of the century, has come to comfort me several times here.

"Grief, he says, is a last success for those who have always been a failure. Such is my lot.

"The other day I said to Mary :

"My well beloved Sovereign, I do not know what it is to honour thee in this or that of thy mysteries according to the teachings of some of thy friends. I only want to know one thing, it is that thou art the sorrowful Mother, that thy earthly life meant only grief and that I am one of the children of thy Grief.

"I have placed myself at thy service as a slave. I have entrusted thee with my temporal and spiritual life to obtain through thee my sanctification and that of others. It is in this way only, and in behalf of this alone, that I can speak to thee.

"I am lacking in faith, hope and love. I do not know how to pray and I do not know penance. I am able to do nothing and I am nothing but a son of sorrow. I can see in myself no merit, no truly good deed which would make me pleasing to God, but one thing I am — a son of sorrow.

"Thou knowest that in other times, more than thirty years ago, obeying an impulse which certainly came from thee, I called upon myself all the sorrow possible. Because of this, I tell myself that my grief which has been great and constant can be offered unto thee. Draw from this treasure to pay my debts and those of all the beings I love. And if God allows, let me be thy witness in the torments of death. I ask this of thee in thy most sweet name of Mary."

And here is a letter which I wish to quote because of its particular gentleness, and for the bit of joy it exhibits :

"12 rue Cortot
Still here alas !
September 30, 1908

"Very dear and very sweet goddaughter of mine, beloved Raïssa,

"Why didn't I write you yesterday ? Your letter was given me the very evening of our arrival, on Monday. . .

"It seems to me that until this moment I have been living in a fog brought upon me by fatigue, insomnia, worry and constant sadness.

"We have seen our new abode, which has been nicely prepared [they were returning to Rue de la Barre, to a more spacious house than the one we had found them in when we first called on them] and renewed in our absence by a young architect among our friends who does not want to hear about our paying for it before several years.

"What a refuge ! What an oasis ! Two families could live in it.

"It is in the neighbourhood of Sacré-Cœur ; trees, fruit-trees even, flowers, a lovable poultry yard, a lovable concierge" — what terrific optimism ! — "and above all solitude, infinite separation from those horrible neighbours who caused us so much suffering.

"When you come for dinner, dearly beloved, we can keep you all night and go to communion with you the following day. What good fortune !

"Beseech Our Lady of Compassion to have pity on her old advocate, who can't go on any more, and to treat him with kindness.

"Our apartment on Rue Cortot is more revolting than ever.

"Anyway, we so much want to see you.

"I embrace you tenderly, Raïssa, Vera, Jacques."

That apartment on Rue Cortot, which luckily the Bloys were going to leave, was sinister : a kind of tumble-down studio with two small rooms. I still have before my eyes the depressing, dirty walls, the rough floors the dust of which would yield to no cleaning ; there were no neat, smooth surfaces, nothing to appease the eye.

*Celle qui Pleure* had appeared at the beginning of 1908, *L'Invendable* in June or July 1909, and *Le Sang du Pauvre* at the end of the same year. And Bloy was already writing *L'Ame de Napoléon*, and preparing the publication of a new volume of his diary — *Le Vieux de la Montagne*. These two books appeared in 1912 as also the *Vie de Mélanie* with its preface by Bloy. During the five years which followed, until his death, Léon Bloy, in spite of his increasing feebleness, in spite of the customary hardships of poverty, in spite of the illness the nightmare of the war caused him, never slowed down in his work. He wrote six more important books, the last two of which were published after his death. In 1914 appeared the second series of his *Exégèse des Lieux Communs*, and *Le Pèlerin de l'Absolu*. In 1913, *Jeanne d'Arc et l'Allemagne* ; in 1917 *Les Méditations d'un Solitaire* ; and after his death *Dans les Ténèbres* and the seventh volume of his diary — *La Porte des Humbles*.

\*

\*      \*

After our return to France in 1908, his letters naturally became much more rare. They alluded briefly to his work and to the success — meaning the customary lack of success — of his books. On July 23, 1909, he wrote to Jacques :

"Dearly beloved Jacques,
"The day after tomorrow is the feast of Saint James the Greater and of Saint Christopher. As little disposed as I am

right now to write, I want you at least to receive something in
your godfather's handwriting.   This morning I received seven
letters fairly smoking with enthusiasm in acknowledgement of
the copies of *L'Invendable* which were sent out.   Well!   I
shall answer yours only, not wishing to diminish the uncertain
number of my days.

"I have been told that estimable people in your neighbourhood have got it into their heads that your patron is James the
Less — which I cannot concede.   What would then become
of the Christophorus, that sublime Helper, liturgical companion of James the Greater *Son of Thunder,* the Christophorus
who has such a large place in my heart and to whom I entrusted
you so particularly and lovingly, so that he would carry you on
his strong shoulders through every torrent ?

"I therefore don't want to hear of any other feast for you,
and I step all over any contradiction.

"Saying which, I embrace you tenderly and go on.   Juven
has at last agreed to publish *Le Sang du Pauvre.*   This book
will appear in October or November and I am waiting for the
first proofs.   The thing was decided on the day of Our Lady
of Mount Carmel, the very day you wrote me, my kind godchildren.

"It seemed to me that same morning I received assurance on
this point.

"Our times are so vile that I don't expect the success my
friends prophesy.   But God, who put this book in me, knows
exactly the number of souls He wants it to reach and that's
enough.   Our subsistence is assured by the last verses of Chapter 6 of Saint Matthew.   This is my granary, and it is inexhaustible.

"I received three hundred copies of *Le Salut* sent by Vic-
torion.   They are safe from the dampness and even from rats,
who are more avid than men to devour books of this kind.

"The time will come, perhaps, when this book can usefully

be put back on sale. While waiting, I am glad to give some away, whenever the investment seems profitable.

"I must stop and throw myself into *L'Ame de Napoléon,* the title of my next book.

"Jacques, Raïssa, Vera, I hug you tightly in my old arms.

Léon Bloy."

### *"Le Sang du Pauvre"*

*Le Sang du Pauvre,* finished on March 25, 1909, appeared at the end of the same year ; it is one of Marchenoir's best books.

Here he is at the very heart of his experience. He has lived through poverty and destitution as he has lived by faith, hope and love of God — so near to God in his deprivation. Is not the Holy Ghost called the Father of the Poor ? — thus it is that the Church names Him in beseeching Him to come down upon us on the day of Pentecost :

*Veni Pater Pauperum*
*Veni lumen cordium. . .*

And man is so near the God of pity, "man stands so near God," writes Léon Bloy, "that the word *poor* is an expression of tenderness. . ."

This book so filled with pathos and sorrowful poetry, is rich in lightning intuitions springing from an emotion that lives in the very depths of Léon Bloy's heart.

In this work Léon Bloy scrutinizes the essential and supernatural mystery of poverty, which has its divine type in Jesus stripped of everything and in His agony.

He raises against the world — and against our present world — a cry more terrible and violent than any revolutionary clamour, because it is the cry of all those who have been abandoned, calling upon divine justice.

He condemns modern society without appeal; his book echoes the most burning social claims, but it is on another plane and one would in vain seek any effort to answer those earthly problems which weigh heavily on so many men. It is neither the book of an economist nor a sociologist, needless to say.

*"The Blood of the Poor,"* Bloy declares, *"is money.* For centuries people have lived and died for it. It expressively sums up all suffering. It is Glory, it is Power. It is Justice and Injustice. It is Torture and Delight. It is execrable and adorable, the flagrant and dripping symbol of Christ the Saviour, *in whom all things abide.* . . His Blood is that of the Poor by which men have been purchased at a great price. . . It was necessary, therefore, that money be its symbol. . . Money that people adore, the eucharistic money that men *drink* and *eat.* . . Every aspect of money is an aspect of the Son of God sweating that Blood by which all things are taken up."

This idea of the symbolism of money has little basis, I believe, in Scripture. When questioned about this, Bloy quoted one or two not very significant passages. In reality it was his own genius as a visionary familiar with shadows, similes and figurative comparisons which made him recognize in the faintest sign upon which the life of men depends and through which flows, from one to the other, what causes them to subsist, an inverted symbol of this vitalizing Blood. This intuition is one of the most profoundly revealing of Léon Bloy's spirit. It might be remarked here that Bloy always proceeds by jumping from one intuition to another, the gaps in between being filled with images, exasperated at times with their inability to

communicate perceived truth, for it was not among the gifts
of the Pilgrim of the Absolute to persuade by means of reasoning. To this intuition of the symbolism of money Bloy clung
as to a central viewpoint, and drew from it his entire exegesis
of poverty.

The blood of the poor is the money of the rich ; and the
money which the rich retains and which should bring earthly
food to all men is itself the symbol of the redeeming Blood,
which our egotism and hardness of heart prevent our brothers
from receiving in order that they may have life.

How can we be surprised that the "right to wealth," the right
to retain for one's self those goods which should be used by all,
seemed to Léon Bloy as a challenge to God ?

"The right to wealth — the effective negation of the Gospel,
an anthropological derision of the Redeemer — is inscribed in
every code. It's impossible to extract this hookworm without tearing out the entrails, yet the operation is urgent. God
will see to that. 'You have no right to enjoyment when your
brother is suffering' is the ever-louder cry of the infinite multitude of the hopeless."

Bloy knows that God is the God of all, and not only the God
of the poor. To the poet Jehan Rictus who wrote him that
"Jesus came for the poor," Bloy retorted : "Well, perhaps !
But He came for the rich too, so that they would become poor
through love, and you cannot be unaware of the fact that hun-
dreds of thousands of saints obeyed. What we should say is
that Jesus came for souls." *

Thus there are rich people who become poor through love,
and poor in spirit. "Adore wealth all you want," Léon Bloy
writes in Le Sang du Pauvre, "there is all the same a tenacious
prejudice which stubbornly militates for poverty. It is as if
the unassuming lance which pierced Jesus had pierced every
heart. This wound has not healed after twenty centuries.

* Quatre Ans de Captivité à Cochons-sur-Marne.

There are the pitiable ones without number — women, old men, little children ; there are the living and the dead.   This whole people is bleeding, this whole multitude sheds blood and water from the midst of the Cross of misery, in the Orient, in the Occident, beneath every sky, beneath every executioner, beneath every scourge, amid the storms of men and the storms of nature — since ever so long !   That is poverty, the immense poverty of the world, the total and universal poverty of Jesus Christ !   All that must count and it must be retrieved !

"There are also the priests who are not of this world, the priests who are poor or the poor priests, whichever one wishes to call them, who do not know what it is to be poor, never having seen anything but Christ crucified.   For those there are no rich and there are no poor ; there are only the blind in endless number, and a small flock of clear-eyed men of whom they are the humble shepherds.   They are together like the Hebrews of Gessen, alone in the light, in the midst of those tangible shadows of old Egypt.   When they stretch forth their arms to pray, the tips of their fingers touch the darkness."

But for Bloy there are no *good rich*.   The "good" rich man is he who practices his job of amassing wealth, who is loyal to his function of greed.   *"The bad rich are those who give"* * and who, through enough giving, become poor, 'men of desire,' as was the prophet Daniel who foreran Jesus Christ."   When the rich man is a good man, he does not cling to what he has, he gives it away, he is the servant of the desire of the poor.

"That which must some day accuse the rich so frightfully is just the Desire of the poor. . ."   This desire which knocks itself against the brass wall of avarice.

"I well know it, the evil of this world is of angelic origin, and cannot be expressed in human language.   Disobedience first, then Fratricide.   That is the whole story. . .

"The monster of Avarice alone disconcerts human rea-

* Underlined by Léon Bloy.

son . . ." avarice which, according to Saint Paul, is "Idolatry itself." "Avarice which kills the poor is just as inexplicable as Idolatry. Now Idolatry . . . consists in substituting the Visible for the Invisible, which is certainly the most monstrous, the most incomprehensible crime. . .

"God suffers all this until this evening, which could be the 'Great Evening' as the sucklings of Anarchy call it. Yet it is still day, it is only three o'clock, it is the hour of the Immolation of the Pauper. . ." And God's Indignation seeks a refuge :

"But there is no refuge for the Indignation of God. It is a wild famished maiden to whom all doors are closed, a true daughter of the desert whom no one knows. . .

"Yet she is beautiful, though not to be seduced or worn out, and she causes such terror that the earth trembles when she passes. . . Her eyes are dark abysses and her lips no longer utter a word. When she meets a priest, she becomes pale and more silent still, for the priests condemn her, finding her ill clothed, excessive, and possessing little *charity*. She knows so well that all is useless from now on ! . .

"You are too free to please me ! the world cries to her. I have laws, policemen, bailiffs and proprietors ! You shall become a trollop and pay your rent on the day it 's due.

"My day is near at hand and I shall pay very exactly, replied the Indignation of God."

\*

\*      \*

The next to the last chapter of this book on the poor is a tribute to a Jewish poet on whom Bloy bestows the title, at one time borne by Godefroy de Bouillon, of "Defender of the Holy Sepulchre."

"Yes, of the Holy Sepulchre ! And it is about a Jew, an

extraordinary Jewish poet who was never converted. But he was a Jew in the deepest sense of the word and consequently the greatest poet the Poor Man has had, which placed him very near the tomb of Jesus Christ, infinitely nearer than most Christians. . ."

A friend had given to Léon Bloy the book of Morris Rosenfeld, "poet of paupers, a pauper himself, and expressing himself in the language of paupers" — "Yiddish, a poor, ridiculed dialect" wrote Rosenfeld, "which we have appropriated as we drag ourselves about among the peoples of the earth."
Bloy quotes several poems, whose value is difficult to estimate in the French translation : it was their meaning which struck Bloy, and stirred the fullness of compassion already present in his heart, and this meaning is fearfully timely today, — which proves that suffering for the Jews is a perpetual today.

> . . . Comme ma tête était levée vers le ciel,
> Tout à coup une goutte tomba du nuage ;
> Une goutte amère tomba dans ma bouche,
> . . . C'est une larme juive, une larme de sang
> . . . Une larme de fiel, de cerveau et de sang.
> Elle sent la persécution, le malheur et le pogrom. . .
> — Nous avions un logis mais on l'a détruit,
> On a brûlé ce qui nous était le plus sacré ;
> On a fait des plus chéris et des meilleurs des
>     monceaux d'ossements.

> Les autres ont été emmenés les mains liées. . .
> Nous sommes des Juifs, des Juifs déshérités,
> Sans amis et sans joie, sans espoir de bonheur. . .
> Nous sommes des misérables semblables à des pierres,

*La terre ingrate refuse de nous accorder une place. . .*
*Quoi qu'il arrive nous sommes des Juifs*
*abandonnés.* *

And Léon Bloy adds, after having expressed his admiration for the poet :

"The Jews are the oldest of all, and when everything is in its right place, their proudest masters will feel themselves honoured to lick their wandering feet." (Which is hyperbole, after all !) "For everything is promised them, and in the meantime they are doing penance for the earth." (Which is "a flash in depth," an apperception of the truth in the absolute. Ah, what would this visionary say today of the unpunished massacre of four million Jews! †

"Rosenfeld, who was only a very ignorant workman, had probably not read St. Paul, who is little read by the Jews. . . Without knowing it he furthered the imperishable assertions

---

* As my face was lifted towards the skies
All of a sudden a drop fell from the clouds ;
A bitter drop fell into my mouth,
. . . It was a Jewish tear, a tear of blood
A tear of gall, of brain and of blood.
It tasted of persecution, misfortune, pogroms. . .
We had a home but they destroyed it ;
They burned what was most sacred to us ;
Of the most cherished and the best they have made a
    pile of bones.

Others have been led away with their hands tied. . .
We are Jews, disinherited Jews,
Without friends and without joy, without hope of happiness. . .
We are wretched, like unto stones.
The ungrateful earth refuses to grant us place. . .
Whatever happens, we are
    abandoned Jews.

† "Of the 9,300,000 Jews who lived in the various countries of Europe before this war, less than 5,000,000 remain. The Nazis have killed all the rest." Second National Conference of the Emergency Committee to save the Jewish people of Europe, *New York Post*, Aug. 3, 1944.

of the Apostle of the Nations, and never having been a poet
except for the poor, he found himself — in the most mysterious
way — the Defender of the Holy Sepulchre, a king without
crown or mantle of the poetry of those who weep, a lost sentinel
at the Tomb of the God of the poor, blessedly immolated by
his ancestors.   So by the sole power of the adorable laws, his
Judaism was passed beyond, flooded on all sides by a feeling
of universal brotherhood for the poor and for those who suffer
all over this earth. . . The tears of the Jews are the heaviest.
They bear the weight of many centuries.   Those of this poet
were generously shed over a great number of the unfortunate
who were not of his Race, and there they are now, these precious
tears on the scales of the Judge of human sorrows who is no
more a respecter of peoples than of persons."

To a woman who was "disconcerted" to read a Christian
book "ending with an apotheosis of a Jew," Bloy wrote :
"Well, of course !   How do you want it to end ?   It was
the necessary ending since the God we adore is a Jew.   What
I am writing you, dear friend, is in no way sophistic ; it is the
basis, the very basis of Christianity.

"In writing a book about the Poor, on the other hand, how
could I not have spoken of the Jews ?   What people is so
poor as the Jewish people ?   O, I know well enough, there
are the bankers and the speculators !   Legend and tradition
would have it that all Jews are usurers. . . And this legend
is a lie. . ." *

Later he wrote to another correspondent :
"And above all, O, above all, there's Chapter IX of Saint
Paul to the Romans — which you can hardly contradict.   It
is the Holy Ghost who speaks.   It says there that the gifts and
the call of God are without repentance : *Sine poenitentia enim*

* *Le Vieux de la Montagne.*   Letter to Madame X, January 2, 1910.

*sunt dona et vocatio Dei.* That is in the Absolute, and terribly positive. So the Jews are still God's People and everything is promised them. How many other texts could be cited! What does it matter to me if there be usurers, infamous speculators, or free-masons? Must I make the resolution to eat no more bread because most bakers are thieves?

"Besides, if anyone really wants to know, it's an outrageous imposture! The diabolical sophism of the *Jew* Drumont was to make people believe that the Jews are instigators, or if you wish, people who initiate, when they could never be — *by divine Decree* — but more or less subtle tools in the hands of their temporal masters — the Christians — who *through them* crucified the Redeemer. I beg you to read carefully every word of this paragraph, which is far from commonplace." (If we wish to understand the thought which Bloy expresses here in an astonishing summary, we must remember that it is through the sins of every one of us that the Redeemer was crucified.)

"God's Word is enough for me. Even if all the Jews — what an absurdity! — were rascals with the exception of one alone who would be righteous beneath the velamen, this single man would bear upon him the Promise, God's Word of honour in its fullness and its power, and nothing in it would be changed.

"In addition, let me tell you that each morning I partake of the Body of a Jew named Jesus Christ, that I spend a part of my life at the feet of a Jewess whose heart was pierced and of whom I have made myself the slave, and finally that I have put my confidence in a band of Sheenies — as you call them — one offering the Lamb, another bearing the Keys of heaven, a third commissioned to teach every nation, etc., and I know that it is only with such feelings that one can be a Christian. Anything else one might say is trite and contingent and *absolutely does not* exist.*

* *Le Pèlerin de l'Absolu.*

### The Pilgrim and the Shepherdess

In 1910, in order to prepare for writing the Vie de Mélanie, Léon Bloy made another pilgrimage to La Salette, from which this time he came back happy. "I have been favoured," he wrote to Jacques on July 12, 1910, "and the impressions I received at Corps no longer allow me to doubt my *mission*. . ."

In the month of May 1911, the Bloys definitely left Montmartre and Paris and went to settle in Bourg-la-Reine. They announced their change of address in these terms :

#### CHANGE OF ADDRESS

*M. and Madame Léon Bloy have the honour of informing you that after the fifteenth of May 1911, they will reside at Bourg-la-Reine, 3 Place Condorcet. You are begged not to encourage useless callers.*

In July they were invited by a friend to the Dordogne. Veronica's unstable health demanded these changes, but the Bloys' holidays in the country were fated to bring them only added trouble and fatigue : "We are in an oven," our godfather wrote, "and after twenty days, I am still unable to enjoy this marvelous country. . . There was a time when I did not go to the country for my holidays, and I considered myself unfortunate ! . . ."

On October 24th, Léon Bloy announced that he was coming to see us in two days ; he was going to bring Pierre van der Meer, and read us this Introduction to "The Childhood of Mélanie" which was to be published by the *Mercure*.

*Celle qui Pleure* had had "a sad fate on the Catholic market" ; but *La Vie de Mélanie* "is going remarkably well," Bloy

wrote us on March 16, 1912.   When Léon Bloy went to the
office of the *Mercure de France* where the book was published,
Rachilde — the wife of Valette, a talented writer for whom, despite all that separated them, Bloy always had an affectionate
feeling — hastily read him an article which she had just written on Mélanie "for whom she was lost in admiration. . ."
Léon Bloy wrote us ; she "whom one would have believed so
far removed from any religious feeling . . . had thrown aside
all the miserable novels it was her job to review, and had spent
the night reading this book and had immediately written for
*Paris-Journal* a really extraordinary article. . ."

The mystical document published by Léon Bloy is rare among
the rare.   I am able to speak here neither of La Salette in
general nor of Mélanie and her autobiography in a way adequate
to show their interest and importance to those who have never
turned to this order of thing.   The others perhaps will wish to
turn to Mélanie's own story and *Celle qui Pleure* ; thus they
will become acquainted with the events of La Salette which
constantly occupied Léon Bloy's thoughts during the last years
of his life, and which by their prophetic contents tower over
the misfortunes of our times.

But for those who are touched by the beauty itself of mystical
writing, I wish to quote several passages from Mélanie's story,
not without remarking that the "extraordinary" character of
the graces which are the subject of this story are in no way attached in themselves to mystical gifts or the contemplative
life.   Yet God is free with His gifts, and the pages in which
many years later Mélanie tells of her childhood (in the language of the age at which she wrote, and with that absolute
candour which always characterized her) have as their support
the saintly life and the saintly death of the Shepherdess of La
Salette.

It was in obedience to her confessor that Mélanie wrote her

story. She relates that from the age of three, practically abandoned by her mother who hated her, she was constantly guided, protected, and taught by a child who appeared to her "almost every day" ; because he called her "my sister" she called him "my little brother," and much later she recognized in him Jesus Himself as He was when a child.

"He told me he was my brother and that I was his sister, and I took his word for it. Besides, I was not used to thinking things over, I didn't have time," for since she had learned from her Brother that God, in order to save us, "had come down to take a human soul and body in order to suffer . . . I was continually plunged," she said, "in thought about this mystery of love ; I had no time to think of what was not necessary to love our good Lord." Heavenly things were familiar to her — she was sent to pick up wood in the forest of Corps : she would then see "the creation of the innumerable Angels, the revolt of a great number of them, the creation of Adam and Eve and their fall. . ." But at school she could learn nothing ; the words of this earth had no meaning for her ; it was not by means of them that she learned the divine mysteries but by almost constant interior illuminations coming from the teachings of her "little brother," and from her mystical experience of the Passion of Christ.

Her Brother advised her to shut her heart against all the sounds of the world : "Don't listen to what the world says, don't do what the world does, don't believe what the world believes." She therefore declared one day to her school teacher : "I don't want to come to school any more because there is too much noise ; I 'm afraid my heart might hear it."

When she was six years old she was given employment at a distance from her family as a shepherdess. The innocent child gathered around her not only her flock but all kinds of animals from the countryside, and like young Saint Francis of Assisi spoke to them of God.

When she was twelve the apparition of her Brother became less frequent, but "the immense light of the great presence of the All-High by no means ceased ; my soul was bound to my Beloved whom I saw resting in the depths of my heart, as if bound there by the ties of love ; the eyes of my soul were fixed on Him as if to take His orders, to follow His good pleasure. . . I hasten to add — which is really true — that the enjoyment of union with Our Lord does not come *all by itself* ; that is, it cannot dwell in our hearts without suffering — without beneficent, thirsted-for suffering. It must also be acknowledged that the fidelity of a heart in which God is present must be above any other fidelity, because the Rule of Divine Love is without mercy."

And this is how her Brother played with her :

"I always went to the fields with my whistle in my pocket. Once when my beloved, my all-good Brother came to see me, I showed Him my whistle and blew it, then I said : 'See me whistle, good brother, and guess what my whistle says.' He replied : 'It says : come, O love !' '— O, so you guessed. Now guess again for it is going to say something difficult,' and I whistled. . . 'What does it say now ?' — 'I see my road covered with thorns.' 'Ah ! you always manage to guess right !' — 'Now !' said my Brother, 'it 's my turn to make you guess ; give me the whistle. Guess, my dear sister.' He whistled : 'I hail you in the name of my brothers, O immaculate blood of the Man-God, precious coin of the ransom of sinners.' — 'O ! O !' said the untamed one, 'you have whistled a long time and I cannot guess what you say.' — 'Ah !' said my kind Brother, 'this time I will whistle a shorter time,' and He gave a short blow, but much louder, and laughed : 'Behold the bridegroom. Stand up ! Sister of my heart, what does the whistle say ?' The little she-wolf hesitated before answering : 'My Brother, perhaps you said : Here is Jesus and you haven't done anything

good.' — 'O ! (and then laughing with all His heart) You are
only half right, you have not guessed all : it's still my turn to
whistle.' And so the game continued until he disappeared."

Mélanie takes her autobiography up to the age of fifteen.
Frightened by a priest's praise of what she had written, she
refused to continue her tale. She was fifteen — having been
born November 7, 1831 — when Our Lady appeared to her
on the mountain of La Salette, and this apparition was not for
the little Shepherdess an "extraordinary" event.

### From "L'Ame de Napoléon" to "Le Seuil de l'Apocalypse"

L'Ame de Napoléon appeared in October, 1912. Again Bloy
hoped for the success "through which, God willing, our lives
would be easier." On October 12th, the eve of the book's
publication, he wrote us :
"Let's hope for a great deal, my dearly beloved. Everything leads me to believe that I am at a happy turning point
in my miserable life. And I also feel within me an extraordinary evolution, as if God were approaching." Yes, God was
approaching, but not success in this world.
"I humanly confess," he wrote me on January 11, 1913, "that
the lack of success, certain from now on, of the book on which
I had counted so much, is a terrible disappointment to me.
"I had dreamed of acquiring by means of this book a little
of that authority which is so necessary to me in teaching my
contemporaries about God and His Word. And it seems to
me that such appears to be my mission. And this very teaching is being denied me. So I no longer know what to do, and
I suffer."
To like this book of Bloy's one doubtless must like Napoleon
and the glory of conquerors. The heroic legend of the Em-

peror had fascinated Bloy from his childhood, and moreover it stood for the mystical exegetist of History as an image of gigantic proportions. Here as always Bloy's intention is to lead us to the threshold of a divine and impenetrable mystery when we expect to find only an illusorily clear story of human deeds. In this respect the best pages of *L'Ame de Napoléon* seem to me to be the Introduction, where after having enumerated a certain number of "huge mistakes" which it seems Napoleon might so easily have avoided, he writes :

"I ceased suffering from these things the day I was able to understand, or at least have an inkling of, the purely symbolical destiny of this extraordinary being.

"In reality every man is symbolic, and it is in proportion to his symbol that he is living. It is true that this proportion is unknown, as unknown and unknowable as the network of infinite combinations in the universal Solidarity. He who, by a prodigious infusion of knowledge, would know the exact significance of any individual whatsoever, would have before his eyes, like a planisphere, the complete divine Order.

"What the Church calls the Communion of Saints is an article of Faith and can be nothing else. . . The Lord's Prayer teaches that we must ask for *our* daily bread and not for *my* bread. This for the whole earth and for all ages. This means an identity between the bread of Caesar and the bread of the slave ; a universal identity of impetration ; a mysterious equilibrium between weakness and strength on the Scales where all is weighed. There is no human being who can with certainty say what he is. No one knows what he has come to do in this world, or to what his acts, feelings and thoughts correspond ; or who, among all men, are nearest to him, neither does he know his real *name*, his imperishable Name in the registry of Light. Emperor or longshoreman no one knows his burden or his crown.

"History is like an immense liturgical Text in which the smallest letters and periods are worth as much as verses or entire chapters, yet the importance of one and the other are not to be determined and are deeply hidden. So if I believe that Napoleon was a very small *iota* shining with glory, I am forced at the same time to tell myself that the battle of Friedland, for instance, could have been won by a little girl of three, or a hundred-year-old tramp praying to God that His Will be done on earth as it is in heaven. . .

"This fact remains, for Napoleon and for the multitude of his inferiors, that we are all together similes of the Invisible and that we can neither move a finger nor massacre two million men without signifying something which will only become clear in the beatific Vision."

After having read *L'Ame de Napoléon*, Eugène Borrel, a friend of Bloy's, wrote him :

"From the point of view of Faith, it's obvious you could write the same supernatural story of any other soul, even that of a bailiff."

"No doubt, my dear Borrel," replied Léon Bloy, "but where do I find the soul of a bailiff ?"

When *Napoléon* came out, a small Marseillaise review, *Les Marches de Provence*, published a special number entirely devoted to Léon Bloy, containing several remarkable articles. In this tribute one finds the names of Jeanne Boussac-Termier, the Abbé Cornuau, Barthélemy, Pierre van der Meer, Jacques. . . . Jeanne Bloy's also appears, with some touching pages on her husband. Léon Bloy reproduced these articles in *Le Pèlerin de l'Absolu*.

*

*　　　*

Bloy's life continued in a labour which successive disappointments were not able to hinder, visited only by happenings invisible to the human eye.

"What an Easter week for us !" he wrote to Jacques on March 27, 1913, in a letter announcing a visit. "This morning, *Thursday*, we had a shock over which I weep at this moment and which will make us suffer for a long time. We could not go to mass or communion on such a day ! to me, one of the most precious of the year.

"*Why weepest thou ? Because they have taken away my Lord, and I know not where they have laid Him.*"

He was working on the sixth volume of his diary, *Le Pèlerin de l'Absolu* ; a new edition of *Sueur de Sang* ; the second series of the *Exégèse des Lieux Communs*, and correcting the proofs of a new edition of *Le Désespéré* which was to appear in the *Mercure de France*.

And up until the war the habitual routine of work and suffering succeeded one another both for the Bloys and ourselves. On July 7, 1914, Léon Bloy wrote us :

"We are leaving Thursday for Saint-Piat. Madeleine and I will come to ask you to lunch, arriving in Versailles at about 11.30.

"Jeanne and Véronique, who is still ailing, will not be able to stop.

"We have not been able to do better.

"May God bless us all. I am overwhelmed with sorrow and misery, and I am thinking of the last resting-place beneath the cypresses.

"I embrace you

Léon Bloy

"On Friday I will be sixty-eight."

*<br>*　　*

He was sixty-eight ; he had written his main great books :
*La Femme Pauvre, Le Désespéré, Le Salut par les Juifs, Celle
qui Pleure, Le Sang du Pauvre,* and had published six volumes
of his diary.   All this described much sorrowful going about
in this valley of tears, in a quest which sought to reach the
depths of souls.

Léon Bloy was tired ; and his mind, irresistibly revolving
about and tortured by the terrible future of the nations, knew
no rest.   When war was declared he was not surprised, but
he was heartbroken.   It was not despair which broke his heart
— Léon Bloy never despaired.   It was rather the premonition
of the great misfortunes which were going to strike the earth,
and of which the war of 1914 "was only the beginning."   In
expectation of those catastrophes which would strike France
he had once asked himself :

" — Léon Bloy, what do you hope for ?   I am hoping for
what it is reasonable to hope, that is, that God will resurrect
France which is the kingdom of His Mother, but after a frightful death which she can no longer avoid." *

Was he speaking for today ?   Or does today only mirror a
more tragic tomorrow ? — prophetic warnings which have a
way of coming true variously at different levels in history. . .

But Bloy first lived in full the tragedy of his own time, and
even died from it.   He suffered from a constant "tightening
of the heart."   He rapidly lost his strength.   He grew thin
and stooped.   How pitiful it was to see him wasted away by
sorrow !   His head was still magnificent, and his large blue eyes
were just as keen in anger, just as bright in tears.   But from
the outbreak of war he lived "as if in a painful dream."

"This morning, in our poor church, I was thinking of those
who died yesterday and today, of all the dying, of all the mourn-
ers, of all that hangs over us ; and, at the same time, I could see

* *Le Vieux de la Montagne,* November 24, 1907.

my whole cruel life over again.  There came back to me with
agonizing sharpness things that I had seen or heard thirty-five
years ago, when I was living as a contemplative. . ."

"The endless nightmare of this diabolical war weighs on me
terribly.  Since its beginning I have been gripped by anguish.
Around me . . . I see people going about their business as if
nothing were happening, entertaining themselves as much as
they can, while each day thousands of men are being massacred.
There's a total indifference among all those whom the war does
not threaten.  Supernatural blindness."

Perhaps because of a premonition of the war, Léon Bloy had
begun on July 14, 1914, to write his *Jeanne d'Arc et l'Allemagne*.
Upon the declaration of war, he composed the important Introduction.  Then for three months his work was interrupted ;
he took it up again in November and it was finished on February 8, 1915.  It was a work of piety and sweetness toward the
Saint, the perpetual auxiliatrix of her country, a book of consolation and hope offered to France in her misfortune.  Then
he started to prepare the seventh volume of his Diary, from
1913 to 1915 — *Au Seuil de l'Apocalypse* — which was published during his lifetime.  The eighth and last, published
posthumously — *La Porte des Humbles* (1915–1917) — in
combination with the preceding volume constitutes the real
war diary of Léon Bloy.

However much he kept repeating over the long years that
the "practical atheism" and "disobedience" of the Christian
world would draw inevitable punishment on France, the spectacle of that noble country trampled and bruised *by inferiors*
was strictly intolerable to him.  This conflict between the injustice which he saw spreading and the invisible justice which
he had proclaimed, was a cross of anguish for his mind.  In
vain he sought for souls, in vain for human greatness.  He
called for the impossible.  Had he not hoped for the Pope to

cast an interdict upon Germany ? The neutrality of the Holy
See overwhelmed him with sorrow, and at moments he over-
stepped bounds in speaking of it. But what were bounds for
Léon Bloy ? Above all it was the indifference of hearts which
made him shudder. People did not turn toward God ; Germany would be defeated, but he foresaw horrors piling up for
the morrow of victory. The war was to him an epitome of the
nightmares of suffering among which his whole life had been
passed.

Preface of *Au Seuil de l'Apocalypse* : "In the nineteenth and
twentieth centuries a nation was found to undertake something that had never been seen since the beginning of History :
THE EXTINCTION OF SOULS. This was called *German Culture*.

"To enslave and abase souls was no longer enough for the
Prince of Darkness. He wanted to extinguish them and he
succeeded. Prussianized Germany ceased to belong to the
human race. It became a monstrous, ferocious brute threaten-
ing the entire world.

"In a book written long before present events, devoted to
my reminiscences of 1870, I tried to sound a warning. I was
considered excessive, intemperate and profoundly unjust. The
numbed French soul did not perceive the approach of the
monster.

"The awakening was what it was bound to be : infinite
horror and almost death. It's been over a year of frightful
struggle, not only in France, but everywhere, to save the poor
lamp of humanity.

"God grant that this book, written by an old recluse, may
have the power to comfort, even though it be at the hour of
death, a few friends of God, a few rare and suffering defenders
of Christian Grandeur and Beauty which are threatened with
annihilation !"

The last words of the book : "I await the Cossacks and the Holy Ghost."

The Cossacks have come. Today they are sweeping down on the Germany which Hitler took pains to conform to the most frightful visions of Léon Bloy.

*Au Seuil de l'Apocalypse* appeared in 1916.

### "La Porte des Humbles"

On December 30, 1915, Bloy wrote with a premonition only too true : "I am on the point of moving ; for the last time, I imagine, before the cemetery."

In the month of January, the whole family settled in the house where Péguy had lived, Rue André Theuriet, at Bourg-la-Reine. Pierre van der Meer, Jacques and Georges Auric went to help Bloy unpack his books.

Scarcely two months before, Viñes had brought to the Bloys' home that young musical prodigy — he must have been seventeen at the time — one of the great hopes of that famous group of the "Six" to which Poulenc and Darius Milhaud belonged, which had Satie at its head and Jean Cocteau as its theorist. Auric was quickly adopted by the Bloys, and his name appears often in *La Porte des Humbles*. He accompanied on the piano Madeleine, who played the violin ; and silently — as silently as Rouault was when at the Bloys' — he listened with profound respect and without revealing his thoughts to the words of the great man of meditation, words that were rare and uttered in a subdued voice.

What still further increased Auric's reserve — in addition to that timidity, gravity and modesty which might well be expected of a budding genius — was that "human respect" which is anything but a virtue, and which made him hide his opinions and his friendships as others might hide their faults.

Soon we too were attached to him by a keen sympathy, and after the war he often came to Versailles with Pierre van der Meer.   We spent hours listening to him, as without the least fatigue he worked out entire scores on the piano.   Thus one day he played for us the whole of *Boris Godunov*, singing this opera from one end to the other.   We were all mad about Moussorgsky, a blessed madness from which one does not recover.   We sang his melodies — the *Enfantines* and the others.   Those hours were beautiful, and they are unforgettable.   Around the piano the singing and laughter had the crystal resonance of a joy that nothing could trouble.   It is difficult to remember the precise date of all these things.   To-day it seems to me as if they took place outside time.   The personal work of the young composer was close to our hearts, and later all the first auditions of his compositions were to be great events for us.   What emotion at the first night of his ballet *Les Fâcheux* !   It was a brilliant "overture" for modern music in general, and for Auric a very great success.   But how far away all that was from 1916 !

* 
* *

Fatigued perhaps by the moving, Bloy felt very ill.   On the 9th of February he received Extreme Unction.   *Heal, we beseech Thee, by the grace of the Holy Spirit, the ills of this Thy sick one ; forgive him his sins ; and drive out of him every pain of body and mind. . .*

Death drew away from Bloy ; but it touched several of his dearest friends, who were taken from him by the war : Philippe Raoux, André Dupont, Jean Boussac. . . Nevertheless, under the veil of mourning, he obstinately continued to work.   *Au Seuil de l'Apocalypse* appeared in January.   Bloy wrote on Jacques' copy :

"When you stand on this threshold, my dear spiritual child, look behind you before entering. In the distance you will see your old godfather dragging himself along on legs that are no longer young and who has almost no more strength to carry his own heart. You will wait for him with tears, and your pity will perhaps keep you from thinking of the coming terrors."

And on mine :

"It was My Lady of Compassion who inspired this book which will perhaps be my last. The 'Door of the Humble,' which is the door of the Apocalypse itself, is so narrow and so fearfully padlocked that I do not know how I will ever be able to get through it. Ask of Her who weeps to turn me into one of those tiny lizards of the colour of hope which can slip through the crevices of the wall of doves mentioned in the Canticle."

More and more numerous became the friends who gathered around Bloy and his family. What sweetness prevailed in this home! All was so real and simple ; poverty was foiled by the ingenuity and good humour of Jeanne Bloy. On April 11th, the feast of Saint Leo, with what love Léon Bloy was surrounded! Among the constant visitors were Pierre Termier, Jeanne Boussac his oldest daughter, the Van der Meers, and naturally ourselves, along with Rouault, Viñes, Auric, the Martineau family, La Laurencie — and later Henry de Groux and his daughter Elisabeth, the Dutch painter Otto Van Rees whose cubism Bloy looked upon with apprehension, and who has made a beautiful portrait of Jacques — and others whom I forget. All were fervent and devoted, filled with veneration for the old man who remained his old self in his inflexible intransigence and his passion for the Absolute, the expression of which now seemed at times to follow along the slope of acquired habit, but which still was nourished by intuitions of genius.

But what could friendship do in the face of God's call? All

our affection was powerless to put a stop to Bloy's growing
feebleness.   He felt his health was irremediably lost.

In August and September we had the joy of spending several
weeks at our godfather's — a joy which was dimmed by melancholy when, suddenly seeing his emaciated body, our hearts
were painfully gripped with sad premonitions.   But such peace
reigned in this house that the memory we have always kept of
this visit is infinitely sweet.

Every morning, early, unless his strength completely failed
him, Bloy went to church with Jacques.   "I can still see him
in the gray light of early morning — at that hour when the
heart, 'not yet sullied with the base enchantments of light,
reaches out toward the quiet tabernacles,' walking with his
heavy tired step to the first mass . . ." Jacques wrote in recalling these precious hours.*

Then all day long Léon Bloy wrote or prayed or read the lives
of the saints.   Often, when he was pleased with his work, he
came down to read us the pages he had just written, still throb-
bing with the inspiration from which they had sprung and
which caused his low voice, so clear and penetrating, to tremble
a little.   Sometimes he wept in reading them, and we wept
with him.   He was then writing *Les Méditations d'un Solitaire
en 1916*, and I remember how overcome we were when he read
to us the first meditation, *Je suis Seul*, as soon as he had finished
writing it — for we felt him so deeply convinced of the proxim-
ity of his death.

"I am *alone*.   Yet I have a wife and two daughters who
cherish me and whom I cherish.   I have godsons and god-
daughters who seem to have been chosen for me by the Holy
Ghost.   I have fast and tried friends, far more numerous than
people ordinarily have.

* *Quelques Pages sur Léon Bloy.*

"But, just the same, I am alone of my kind. I am alone in the anteroom of God. When it will be my turn to appear before Him, where will they be — all those whom I have loved and who have loved me ? I know well that those who know how to pray will pray for me with all their hearts, but they will be so far away from me then, and I shall be so frightfully alone before my Judge.

"The nearer one draws to God the more one is alone. It is the infinity of solitude.

"At that moment all the holy Words, read so many times in my dark cellar, will be revealed to me and the Precept to hate father, mother, children, brothers and sisters and even one's own soul, if one wishes to go to Jesus, will weigh upon me like a mountain of incandescent granite.

"Where will they be, the humble little churches with gentle walls in which I prayed with so much love sometimes for the living and the dead ? And where will be those dear tears which were my hope as a sinner, when I was worn out with loving and suffering ? And what will have become of my poor books in which I searched for the history of the merciful Trinity ?

"On whom, on what shall I lean ? Will the prayers of my loved ones whom I gave to the Church have the time and the strength to reach me ? Nothing can assure me that the Angel entrusted with my care will not himself be trembling with compassion and shivering like a pauper shabbily clothed and forgotten at the door in the very great cold. I shall be unutterably alone and I know in advance that I shall not even have a second to throw myself into the gulf of light or the gulf of darkness. . ."

Often friends announced themselves ; they came for lunch, or in the afternoon, or for dinner. Bloy welcomed them with tender affection. They stayed in the garden which grew wild and offered us the shade of a few big trees.

In the evening, when we were alone, Bloy played chess with Jacques or Jeanne Bloy, or just dominoes with his daughters and godchildren. And always, before parting for the night, we knelt on the floor and recited the rosary together. What "an unforgettable picture of faith and humility" was set before us by our old godfather ! His recollection was so great, so great were his love and simplicity, that just to look at him distracted me in my prayers.

"We must pray. All else is vain and stupid," Léon Bloy told us all. "We must pray in order to endure the horror of this world, we must pray in order to be pure, we must pray for the strength *to wait*. There's no despair, no bitter sadness for the man who prays a great deal. Let me tell you. If you only knew what a right I have to do so ! . . . Faith, Hope, Charity and Sorrow which is their substratum are diamonds, and diamonds are rare. . . They cost a great deal. . . Their cost is Prayer, itself a priceless jewel which it is necessary to win. , ,"

\*

\*          \*

The summer of 1916 brought to Léon Bloy the consolation of Henry de Groux' return to their old friendship. The inexplicable estrangement of De Groux had wounded Bloy very deeply. At the time of this break Elisabeth de Groux, his goddaughter, was scarcely two years old. When she reached her eighteenth year she resolved to seek out her godfather and bring about a reconciliation between him and her father. She succeeded perfectly. Jacques who had been sent as an emissary made De Groux confess and acknowledge the absurdity of the grudges he bore against such a faithful friend, the greatest admirer of his tragic art.

When finally De Groux came to the Bloys', in October 1916,

we were there with Pierre Termier and Jeanne Boussac. Léon
Bloy went to meet him and welcomed him with these simple
words :
"You 've grown a little stout since yesterday." And they
immediately resumed where they had left off, ignoring the
long years of misunderstanding.

Léon Bloy suffered greatly from the hard winter of 1916–
1917. On January 12th he had a passing attack of paralysis.
For several hours he was deprived of speech and the use of his
right arm. The next morning his heroic wife half carried him
to church where he wanted to go for consolation. We came
for lunch : Bloy was cheerful, and seemed entirely recovered ;
he ate with appetite.

New friends could be met at the Bloys' at this time : André
Baron who later became a priest, and whom Bloy especially
loved and esteemed. The former's brother and sister of whom
Bloy speaks with affection in his diary. A very young man
— who was to marry Madeleine Bloy — Edouard Souberbielle ;
and "the Japanese Lady," his mother. Abbé Petit, the friend
of young musicians ; the painter Charles Bisson ; Léopold Le-
vaux and his wife, enthusiastic admirers from Belgium ; they
later became our friends, and one of their sons was to be my
godson. Felix Raugel ; and Abbé Roblot, a priest after Bloy's
heart. . . But in spite of so many sincere and devoted friends,
in spite of Pierre Termier's generosity and Jacques' efforts,
poverty made itself harshly felt on certain days. Poverty and
illness. . . In his diary Bloy noted "frightful days" as well
as happier ones. On March 15th : — "very gay dinner" with
Pierre van der Meer, Auric, De Groux, etc.

A new summer began ; the visitors were more numerous.
The *Méditations d'un Solitaire* appeared. Bloy dedicated
copies :

"May 22nd.

"To Jacques. — His old godfather, *a wild ass accustomed to solitude.*

"To Raïssa. — What is a solitary man in the Absolute ? He is a lover of God.

"To Vera. — So that she may isolate herself like her old godfather in a small cell filled with joy where one can suffer for those who do not know how to suffer."

* * *

We spent the summer at Bures with the Van der Meers ; and from there we went often to Bourg-la-Reine. And Bloy noted in his diary :

"July 18th.

"At 9 o'clock, sudden and very agreeable appearance of my god-daughter Vera, coming as an advance-guard. The whole colony from Bures is going to descend on us.

"Indeed, everybody came and also, at the end of lunch, Souberbielle.

"The whole day was a good one even for myself, as I felt a little less tired than usual. Souberbielle and Madeleine played the sonata of Franck together, then I read my chapter 'Le Mépris,' which was much applauded."

"Le Mépris" was one of the meditations from the new book which Bloy began on July 10th, and which appeared after his death under the title *Dans les Ténèbres.*

The month of August was crushing for Bloy, who felt sicker than ever, and destitution showed once again its horrible face. In general, friends were not informed until all other remedies had been exhausted.

Bloy continued to work, but as if "by force ; as if under a lash, in spite of grief, discouragement and continual fatigue."

On October 5th he noted in his diary :

"Overcome with an unbearable sadness I asked that we recite the rosary together, which gave me a little comfort."

Still a few notations during the course of the month, in which Bloy mentioned his growing fatigue and the appearance of fever. Saturday, October 20, 1917, finishes the diary of Léon Bloy.

### The Death of Léon Bloy

His last book — *Dans les Ténèbres* — was finished.  In one of the meditations which compose it, he noted these words of Mary heard in the depths of his soul which was worn out with suffering and sympathizing :

"You and I, dear child, are the People of God.  We are in the promised Land and I Myself am this blessed land. . . Remember ! . . My Son has said that those who weep are blessed and it is because I have wept all the tears and suffered all the agonies of generations, that all generations shall call Me blessed.  The marvels of Egypt are nothing, neither are the marvels of the Desert, in comparison with the dazzling light which I bring you for all eternity."  I suppose that Egypt here means the world; and the Desert, contemplation in the shadow of the Cross.

\*

\*    \*

And now Léon Bloy had only a few days to live.  Toward the end of October he had an attack of uremia.  On October 31st, while I was at his bedside he confessed to me that he was in great suffering.  "You are suffering for your godchildren," I replied with a great desire to help him in some way.  But he went on : "The baseness of my nature is expiated by . . ." His voice was scarcely audible and I did not hear the last words.

"I wish I could do something for you," he said to me lovingly
a moment afterwards.   And I replied, my heart breaking with
pity : "You have done everything for me, since you made me
know God."   I added : "I wish I could take your suffering
upon me."   "Don't say that !" he said with a certain vivacity,
and looking at me gravely : "You don't know what you are asking for."   At that moment his wife drew near, murmuring :
*Ave o Crux spes unica.*   As weak as he was, he corrected dis-
tinctly her slight mistake : *O Crux ave spes unica. . .*

During those days of cruel suffering he still took, whenever
he spoke, extreme care in regard to exactness of language and
purity of expression.   But he spoke very little, his rare words
emerged from a deep silence, not inert but intensely vigilant,
an august silence which filled us with respect and fear, in which
we felt that alone, truly alone, as he had written, he was facing
his God and looking upon his life, passing over in his heart for
the last time the mysterious promises he had been given, accepting the supreme purifications in the night of faith.

He received communion for the last time, in the form of the
viaticum, the first of November, in the presence of his wife, his
daughters, Pierre Termier and us three.   The bells were ringing for the mass of All Souls, and the universal Church was
reading over the whole world the gospel of the Beatitudes :
"Blessed are the poor in spirit. . . Blessed are they that
mourn . . . blessed are they that hunger and thirst after justice. . . Blessed are they that have suffered persecution for
justice's sake. . . And blessed are ye when they shall . . .
speak all evil against you . . . because of Me. . ." *

What a liturgy for Léon Bloy !   And what an echo of his
sorrowful life !   As he always did after receiving communion,
he recited the Magnificat, and his whole family said it with him.

He seemed to be suffering acutely — but remained in a great
peace.   A few days before his death, at the end of a painful

* Matthew v, 3–11.

night, he had said to his wife : "I alone know the strength that God has given me for the combat." * It was with this strength he faced his death agony.

There was not a shade of fear in him ; only deep wonder in the face of death which came without the bloody martyrdom he had expected and besought with his whole heart for so many years.

We saw this peace and this wonder on his face in the very last hours of his life. The martyrdom of blood would have been in his soul the illumined symbol of the constant martyrdom he had suffered during long and hard years in which his life and labours had no other aim than to give witness to Truth and Faith and the exigencies of God.

It was thus that he imitated his Lady of Compassion, the *Queen of Martyrs,* whose martyrdom consisted in agony of heart, and whose corporal death was but a gentle *dormition.*

*

*   *

Saturday, the 3rd of November 1917, the day of his death, Léon Bloy got up once more in the morning. He told his wife that he no longer suffered. "But he had to lie down almost immediately. The day was peaceful. Little by little he fell into slumber, and toward evening, at the hour of the Angelus, without a last gasp or death-throe, he passed through the Door of the Humble." †

---

* Related by Jeanne Bloy in the conclusion of the *Porte des Humbles.*
† Jeanne Bloy, Conclusion of *La Porte des Humbles.*